OLE MISS
BUSINESS

THE FIRST

100

YEARS

1917 - 2017

# DEAN KEN CYREE
## CENTENNIAL CELEBRATION SPEECH

*On September 8, 2017, in the courtyard between Conner Hall and Holman Hall on the Ole Miss Campus,*
*Dean Ken Cyree delivered the following speech to a crowd of faculty, students, and alumni.*

Established as the School of Commerce in October 1917, the business school became a separate school of the university during the academic year 1919-1920.

The first faculty of the school included a dean, a professor of economics, a professor of business law, a professor of accountancy and secretarial work, and four other professors.

The School of Commerce produced its first graduate, Mr. Henry Anderson Butler, in 1920, and its second, Mr. Durwood William Aiken, in 1923.

The first woman graduate, Ms. Mary Frances Clark, was in 1930. She served as treasurer of her class and married her classmate, Mr. Claude M. "Tad" Smith, in whose honor the former basketball arena was named. The average salary in the U.S. was $1,970, and the average cost of a new car was $640. Gas was ten cents per gallon.

In 1933, the number of graduates was 24, and by 1943 it was 64.

In 1941, the Master of Business Administration (MBA) was established, and Ph.D. programs in business and economics were established shortly thereafter. An average U.S. home cost $4,075. Of course, the U.S. entered World War II after the attack on Pearl Harbor.

The school received its initial accreditation in 1944 from AACSB.

In 1949, the first graduate of the insurance program, Mr. Bill Bryson, graduated. Bill serves on our Risk Management and Insurance Board to this day.

In 1961, graduates grew to a total of 210. Enrollment grew to nearly 1,100. I would love to tell you it was a great curricular innovation that caused this huge jump in enrollment, but more likely it was that Conner Hall got air conditioning that summer. Also in 1961, Alan Shepard became the first American in space,

and "Tossin' and Turnin'" by Bobby Lewis was number one on the music charts.

In 1962, accountancy was added to the curriculum. Also in 1962, Decca Records rejected the Beatles, stating, "We don't like their sound, and guitar music is on the way out."

In 1968, the name of the School of Business and Government changed to the School of Business Administration. The average U.S. income was $7,850 per year, and the number-one single was "Hey Jude" by that band formed in Liverpool, England, that Decca Records took a pass on six years earlier.

In 1977, the School of Business Administration became the largest business school in the state, with enrollment of 2,307. Music icon Elvis Presley passed away at the age of 42 in Memphis.

In 1981, a Business Advisory Council was organized. Ronald Reagan became President; *Raiders of the Lost Ark* appeared in theaters, and the most popular TV show was *Dallas*, even though we had already learned who shot J.R. Ewing.

Mobile Communications Corporation of America gave an endowment of $1 million to the school in December 1986.

In 1987, Robert Hearin and Leon Hess gave $2 million to the school.

By 1990, there was a full-time teaching staff with 83 percent holding doctoral degrees from a wide range of prestigious institutions.

In 1993, the PBS production *Firing Line* was taped at the university and was hosted by the business school. "I Will Always Love You" by Whitney Houston was the number-one single; average income per year was $31,230, and a gallon of gas was $1.16 per gallon.

Holman Hall was completed in 1999, and Conner Hall was completed in 2000.

In 2000, enrollment of the school of business was more than

2,500, which accounted for one fourth of the total enrollment of the university. Tiger Woods won the U.S. Open in golf, and the Y2K fears we all had proved to be unfounded, or at least were adeptly handled.

In 2004, the Ole Miss MBA students took top honors in the Babcock Elevator Business Plan National Competition at Wake Forest University.

In the nine years from 1996-2004 there was an increase in enrollment by 62 percent, while the enrollment in non-business majors across campus only increased by 34 percent.

In 2005, the Ole Miss MBA Program and the Trent Lott Leadership Institute co-hosted the first annual Speaker's Edge competition, the high-impact public speaking competition for MBA students.

Also in 2005, the Gillespie Business Plan Competition was launched. In the same year, Mark Zuckerberg offered to sell Facebook to Myspace for $75 million, but the offer was rejected by MySpace CEO Chris De-Wolfe.

In 2006-2007, the online PMBA program was offered for each semester and summer sessions and consisted of four online classes.

In 2009-2010, the online MBA Program was ranked 13 out of 133 competing, accredited, online MBA nationwide programs, and Bruce and Karen Moore donated $1 million to the faculty support commitment. Additionally, the New Orleans Saints won the Super Bowl.

In the fall of 2012, 66 business freshman started living on the floor of the new Ridge dormitories. The first Student Career Guide was published at no charge to business school students.

In 2014-2015, the online PMBA program was ranked 16 by *U.S. News and World Report*. The campus MBA program was ranked 76 in the nation from *Businessweek*. Also in 2015, Ole Miss beat Alabama 43-37, winning for the second year in a row.

Today, the business school has more than 3,800 students, 63 FTE faculty, and 18 staff. Last year, we graduated almost 800 students. The school enjoys some of the highest rankings in history with the on-campus MBA at number 68 and 36 among public universities.

Facts and figures like these I have quoted will be in our 100-year celebration book about the business school that will be ready in November, unveiled in our book signing at Square Books. Stella Connell has a cover over there and also has some *BusinessFirst* magazines you might want to take with you.

These facts and figures also point to two themes throughout the history of the school of business. First is the story of tremendous growth and impact. Second is the story of changing lives. Underlying most of the statistics are the people who made them happen. Thousands of lives have been changed; thousands of opportunities created, and thousands of people making a difference. I am proud of what we have done, and we could not do it without the support of Ole Miss alumni, faculty, staff, students, the administration, and our friends. I look forward to the next 100 years and know we are poised to do great things with the dedication and commitment of this group of people in the School of Business and the giant who came before us.

Thank you all for coming. May God bless the next century for the School of Business, Ole Miss, the state of Mississippi, and the United States of America.

# CONTENTS

# BONUS SECTIONS & SIDEBARS

# HALL OF FAME ALUMNI PROFILES

*Ole Miss Business: The First 100 Years (1917-2017)* © copyright, 2017, The School of Business Administration, the University of Mississippi

For information contact Nautilus Publishing, 426 South Lamar Blvd., Suite 16, Oxford, MS 38655.

ISBN: 978-1-936-946-75-4

The Nautilus Publishing Company
426 South Lamar Blvd., Suite 16
Oxford, Mississippi 38655
Tel: 662-513-0159
www.nautiluspublishing.com

**The University of Mississippi School of Business Administration**
**Dean:** Ken Cyree
**Senior Associate Dean:** Del Hawley
**Assistant Dean for Undergraduate Programs:** Danielle Ammeter
**Communications:** Stella Connell

First Edition

**Editors:** Stella Connell and Neil White
**Writers:** Neil White, Sinclair Rishel, Wil Oakes
Front cover design by Le'Herman Payton
Front cover photography courtesy of Campbell McCool, Ole Miss Communications, the National Cotton Council of America, the Ole Miss Alumni Association, and the Ole Miss annual staff.

The School of Business Administration would like to thank the following individuals for their generous support of this commemorative book: Jennifer Ford, Lauren Rogers, and Greg Johnson at the J.D. Williams library archives; Clay Cavett, Martha Dollarhide, Jim Urbanek, and Suzy Norwood at the Ole Miss Alumni Association. Chad Hathcock, Becky Kesler, Haley Myatt, Teresa Ronsey, and Kathy Mikell, Karen Bryant, and Carroll Moore.

Library of Congress Cataloging-in-Publication Data has been applied for.

10  9  8  7  6  5  4  3  2  1

Our **mission** is to improve business and society by inspiring students, business and community leaders through advancing business knowledge and capabilities.

Our **vision** is to cultivate innovative and effective leaders through transformational educational opportunities that foster business knowledge acquisition, a strong work ethic, and collaboration skills to improve Mississippi, the region, and the world.

Printed in Canada

# 100 YEARS OF OLE MISS BUSINESS

## FROM THE EDITORS

The Ole Miss School of Business Administration is celebrating 100 years — and what a rich century is has been. Graduates of the school have changed not only the business world, but also the history of our country.

When James Warsaw Bell was named dean of the new School of Commerce in 1917, he could never have imagined that graduates from the Ole Miss school of business would go on to be ambassadors, university presidents, technology innovators, financial leaders, sports legends, commodities pioneers, visionary politicians, and forward-looking generals in the armed forces (just to name a few).

Even the deans of the school have had a huge impact on Ole Miss, the state of Mississippi, and the nation. The school's first dean, James Bell, led young men into battle in Italy during World War I (and he also almost single-handedly kept Ole Miss football in operation during the early 1900s). The second and third deans, Horace Brown and McDonald Horne, were both instrumental in setting policy for cotton brokers in the United States. The next dean, Clive Dunham, led the business school through the Meredith riots while simultaneously guiding some of Ole Miss's most distinguished alumni through their undergraduate years. Ben McNew, the school's fifth dean, ushered through the business school's first black graduates, as well as one of the most beloved sports figures of all time, Archie Manning. Lynn Spruill, the first dean of the 1980s, introduced himself to the Ole Miss community by singing "The Only Home I Know" from *Shenandoah* in front of an audience of 900 at the Summer Theatre Showcase (he also befriended John Palmer, who eventually gave the first $1 million gift to a university in Mississippi). Rex Cottle followed Spruill as dean and not only officially received John Palmer's gift, but also received a $2 million gift the following year from a Mississippi businessman and the owner of the New York Jets. The eighth dean, Randy Boxx, ushered the school into its state-of-the-art home, Holman Hall. Mike Harvey followed Dean Boxx and directed the school through one of its most challenging and contentious eras. By the time the school's tenth dean, Brian Reithel, was appointed in 2003, he had already made his mark on the university by co-chairing the Campaign for Excellence, which raised $525 million dollars for Ole Miss. Of course, Dean Reithel helped lay the foundation upon which our 21st century progress was built.

This book, *Ole Miss Business: The First 100 Years*, is not your typical history book. You won't find a mundane recitation of historic facts on these pages. The book features fascinating human interest stories about our graduates, faculty, and administrators. But it also features a compelling 100-year narrative that includes great acts of sacrifice alongside tawdry scandals, triumphs against seemingly impossible odds, as well as political maneuvering, heartfelt friendships, and knock-down-drag-out fights.

It has certainly been a long and fascinating journey.

We hope you enjoy reading about it as much as we have enjoyed compiling it.

The Editors

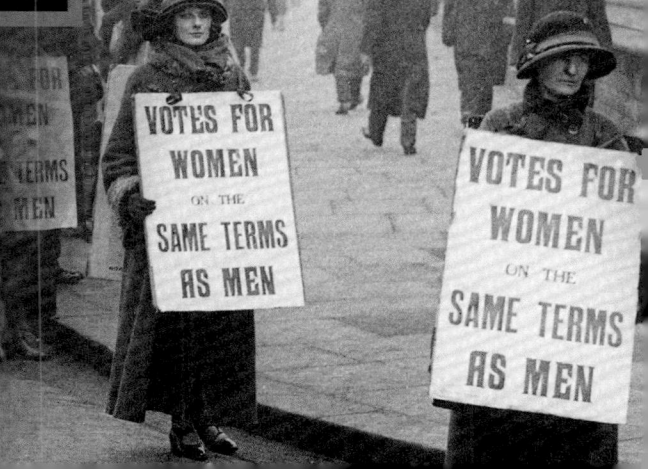

# OLE MISS
# BUSINESS

## THE EARLY DAYS

### DEAN
### JAMES WARSAW BELL

### 1917 - 1941

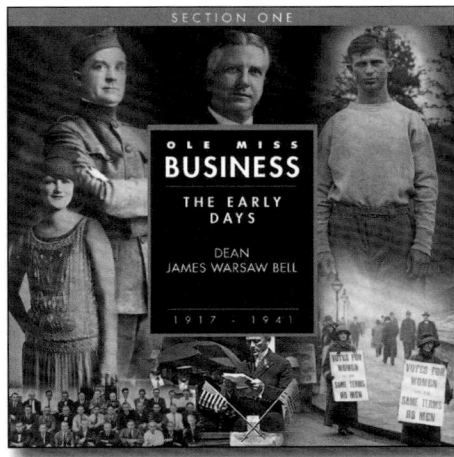

Clockwise from top left: James Warsaw Bell in World War I (1919), Chancellor Joseph Neely Powers, C.M. "Tad" Smith, Suffragettes, Governor Theodore Bilbo at Mississippi's centennial celebration (1917), the first members of the Commercial Club, and the first woman to enroll in the School of Commerce, Ella Pugh Roberts (1924)

# JAMES WARSAW BELL
## DEAN 1917-1941

"The moral fiber — the hardihood and integrity of Ole Miss — were gathered in Dean Bell as pure waters are gathered into a silver cup. May they never be spilled."

Walter Stewart, *Commercial Appeal,* April 12, 1948

No individual had more of an impact on the Ole Miss business school than its first dean, James Warsaw Bell. He led the "School of Commerce" from its inception in 1917 until 1941.

His influence in the classroom, on the athletics field, and in the realm of Mississippi politics is still felt today.

Jim Bell was once described by a Memphis journalist as "possessing the power to be bitingly sarcastic when the tenseness of opposition presented itself, but also possessing of a sense of humor which was the balance in his loveable personality. A curt remark made in a militant outburst one moment would be completely counterbalanced by a humorous remark in the next exchange."

Governor Theodore Bilbo spoke during Mississippi's centennial celebration in Mississippi City in 1917 — the same year the School of Commerce was founded at Ole Miss.

Dean Bell considered himself an "old school" teacher who expanded his lectures far past the limits of a dull recitation of routine facts. He injected down-to-earth logic and expounded on knowledge far beyond a printed textbook.

A friend once noted, "James Bell was proud of his outward 'gruffness,' which he boasted made him the most 'cussed' man at Ole Miss."

"You may not learn much about money and banking in here," Bell would tell his students, "but you're gonna learn a lot about ole Bell's philosophy."

### Early Life & Education

J.W. Bell was born on Owl Creek in Pontotoc County on January 4, 1869. He was raised in Middle Tennessee, but soon returned to his beloved Pontotoc County.

Bell came to the university as a freshman during the second semester of the 1890-1891 term. He interrupted his studies to serve as principal of Jackson High School from 1894-1897.

Bell, as a senior, played on the 1898 Ole Miss football squad, coached by T.G. Scarbrough. The team went a dismal 1-1, but Bell (who played left guard) was taken with collegiate athletics.

In addition to the football squad, Bell was a member of the

Hermaean Literary Society.

The 1898 Ole Miss annual listed all members of the class of 1898 in an "Oddities" section (that listed nicknames, favorite drinks, traits, et al).

Bell's oddities included:

**Nickname:** Uncle Jim
**Usual Drink:** Buck beer
**Common Saying:** Dog gone
**Recreation:** Whistling
**Future:** Country schoolmaster

The annual staffers' prediction for Uncle Jim wasn't so much a prophecy. Prior to coming to Ole Miss, Bell had been a teacher in rural schools since 1887. Apparently he was so proficient at the post, he was hired (before completing his college degree) as principal of Jackson High School where he served as principal for three years.

By the time Bell graduated from Ole Miss, his career as an educator had already been firmly cemented.

"Uncle Jim" was distinctive among his fellow classmates in other ways, too. At the age of twenty-nine, he was old enough to actually be the uncle of most students. And he was the only man in the class of 1898 to sport a gunslinger mustache.

The 1898 Ole Miss football squad. James Warsaw Bell is kneeling (back row) with the gunslinger mustache. Bell played left guard. The team went a dismal 1-1, but Bell was taken with collegiate athletics.

### Back to the Schoolhouse: 1898 - 1902

After Bell received his bachelor of philosophy degree from the university in 1898, he was hired as superintendent of Water Valley Schools. While there, he met Miss Sophia Boyd. They were married one year later on November 15, 1899. Bell served as su-perintendent of the school system until 1902.

He was lured away by the position of principal at Jefferson County High School in Fayette, Mississippi. He stayed for one year. Then a position opened at his alma mater.

### The Higher Education Years: 1903-1907

Bell joined the faculty at Ole Miss on September 1, 1903, as an associate professor of pedagogy. However, the following year, he left to take a position as professor of mathematics at Mississippi Industrial Institute and College (later renamed Mississippi State College for Women and subsequently renamed Mississippi University for Women). Bell stayed in Columbus for three years. During the summer months of 1906, he studied at the University of Michigan.

In 1907, Bell — newly shaven — rejoined the faculty at Ole Miss and taught mathematics. Again, during the summer months from 1907-1910, he studied at the University of Chicago and Columbia University.

Chancellor Kincannon was installed on September 19, 1907. Chancellor Kincannon and James Warsaw Bell would endure many difficult years together.

Kincannon's tenure did result in the construction of many buildings on campus — a new power plant, four men's dormitories, and a new library. In spite of the new buildings, Kincannon couldn't increase enrollment.

Bills went unpaid. Lawsuits were filed against the university, as well as the chancellor personally, to collect debts. And one semester, the faculty and staff went unpaid . . . or were paid late.

Most of the faculty and staff pitched in during these tough

times to help prop up the university, including Bell. Bell first served on the Faculty Athletic Committee in 1908-1909. He was a fanatical football fan. In fact, for several years between 1907 and 1911, Bell paid for the football program out of his own pocket.

This generosity would come back to haunt him.

**Dean of Education and a Scandal . . . Or Two**

In 1910, Bell accepted the position of dean in the Department of Education. Considering his experience in secondary education, coupled with three-year experience in Columbus at the women's teaching college, he seemed perfectly suited for the job.

In addition to serving as dean of the School of Education, Bell lived on campus. He even raised hogs to help feed the students.

In 1912, newspapers ran a story that Chancellor Kincannon, Bell, and the university's business manager had been accused of "profiting by taking slop from the dormitories, fattening the hogs therewith, and selling the hogs to the university."

A joint legislative investigative committee convened to look into the charges. In short order, the group discovered the charges were baseless; however, public perception had been cast.

James Warsaw Bell wrote a scathing, rather hysterical letter to newspaper editors. The *Jackson Daily News* printed the letter on October 8, 1913. They introduced the letter by stating that "all who know Jim Bell at once branded the charges as ridiculous. There is not an abler educator or more thorough gentleman in Mississippi."

Bell wrote, "During the fall, winter, and spring, we fed our hogs with slop from Gordon Hall, the boys' boarding house. From time to time during the year, we had a hog killed, dressed it, and stored it in the pantry at Gordon Hall, until we had placed there twelve hundred and sixty pounds of dressed pork for which we did not charge the boys a solitary thing."

He ended the tirade with "I wouldn't mind so much if 'they' accused me of stealing hogs, but to accuse me of stealing 'swill' is a little too much."

As soon as the "swill" scandal subsided, Kincannon and Bell had to contend with an investigation of the university's athletic program by the Southern Intercollegiate Athletic Association (SIAA).

In 1911, a group of alumni and two professors, James Bell and Judge William Hemingway, signed a $288 promissory note to pay the fees and other expenses for five students (who just happened to be fine football players).

The note specified that the debt would be paid by the receipts from a Thanksgiving Day football game between Ole Miss and Mississippi A&M.

The arrangement was in violation of the Southern Intercollegiate Athletic Association rules. The SIAA suspended Ole Miss, and two coaches were dismissed. (There was also an accusation of ineligible players participating in games during 1912-1913.) The team also forfeited games played in 1912-1914.

The suspension sparked interest in Ole Miss withdrawing from the SIAA. It ultimately led to the formation of the SEC.

The scandals and financial problems left Kincannon vulnerable. In 1913, he resigned.

Jim Bell (left) in 1904 as an instructor at Mississippi Industrial Institute and College. Bell (right) in 1907, newly shaven, when he returned to Ole Miss.

## The First Joseph Neely Powers Era

When Chancellor Joseph Neely Powers took over in 1914, he brought renewed energy to the campus, along with a promise of financial transparency.

In 1915, Bell — who had endured two scandals and a year without pay, and who had become disillusioned with administration — resigned as dean of the Department of Education to focus strictly on the classroom. He taught political science.

Chancellor Powers understood the need for a school of commerce at Ole Miss. He also knew James Bell was the man to build such a school.

Then, in 1916, Columbia University in New York City offered Bell a position as lecturer in economics.

When Bell told Chancellor Powers about the opportunity in New York, Powers offered Bell an opportunity.

## A Slow Start

Chancellor Powers, afraid he might lose the popular professor permanently to Columbia, suggested that Bell might build a new school at Ole Miss — and serve as the inaugural dean for a school of commerce.

The concept intrigued Bell, but he knew the new school would have to be approved by the Board of Trustees. He conditionally accepted Powers' offer, but planned to honor his contract with Columbia University.

In 1917, the Board of Trustees authorized the establishment of a School of Commerce and Business Administration at Ole Miss. The 1917 Ole Miss Bulletin listed Bell as "Professor Economics and Political Science (on leave of absence at Columbia University, 1917)." During his absence, Arthur Boone Crosier, who taught accounting and filing, served as acting dean.

Plans were underway for the school to be fully operational, under the direction of Dean James Warsaw Bell, but the United States entered the Great War. So many students withdrew to enlist that commencement exercises were not held in 1917.

Dean Bell enlisted himself — at age forty-nine. Bell received orders to report to New York for overseas Y.M.C.A work. On July 15, he reported for duty.

Bell led young men who served with the Sixth Italian Army on the Ariago Plateau. He also served with the 20th Corps during the great invasion into Austrian territory in the fall of 1918. He served until January 1919. Upon discharge, Bell was honored with the Italian Cross of War.

During Bell's absence, Crosier again served as acting dean.

## The Early Days

In reality, the business school didn't get traction until 1919. It became a separate school under Dean Bell's leadership during the 1919-1920 academic year. Bell, the faculty, and students hit the ground running.

The School of Commerce was housed on the third floor of the Lyceum (its home until 1961). Dean Bell occupied office

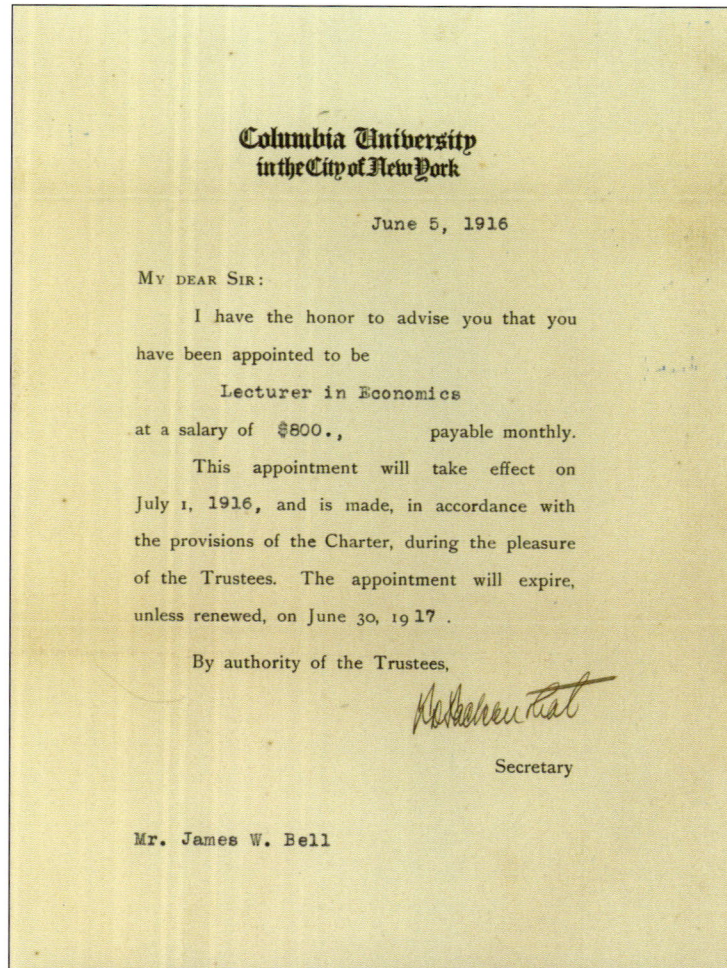

**Columbia University**
**in the City of New York**

June 5, 1916

MY DEAR SIR:

I have the honor to advise you that you have been appointed to be

Lecturer in Economics

at a salary of $800., payable monthly.

This appointment will take effect on July 1, 1916, and is made, in accordance with the provisions of the Charter, during the pleasure of the Trustees. The appointment will expire, unless renewed, on June 30, 1917.

By authority of the Trustees,

Secretary

Mr. James W. Bell

A letter offering James W. Bell a position at Columbia University.

number 306.

In 1920, the school offered the following courses:
- American Government and Politics
- Government and Industry
- Elements of Economics
- Money and Banking
- Shorthand
- Typewriting
- Accounting (Retail and Wholesale) (*Students who took Wholesale paid an additional $1.50 fee for use of the Burrough's banking machine.*)
- Office Training for Stenographers
- Modern Filing
- Salesmanship
- Selling by Correspondence
- Business Communication
- Commercial Law
- Reporting Shorthand
- Business Psychology (*Note: Professor Winn David Hedleston, who taught Business Psychology, had no degrees in the field.*)

The school produced its first graduate, Mr. Henry Anderson Butler, in 1920.

There was another first for Dean Bell in May 1920. He produced a twelve-page bulletin entitled *Government and the Voter*. In the introduction, Bell wrote:

*This bulletin is issued to serve the interests of the women of the state. The great need of our country now is for a greater number of intelligent voters. Intelligent voting can come only through careful study of the nature of government and the questions constantly arising for solution.*

*Our women have always risen to the necessities of the occasion. We believe such will be the case when this new and important responsibility devolves upon them.*

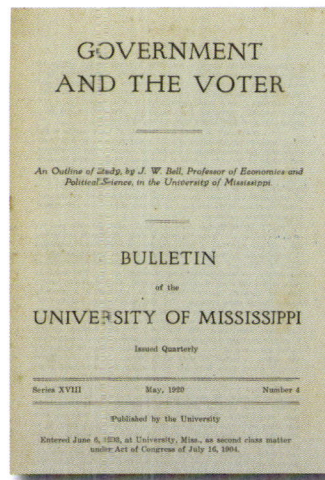

The bulletin was published and mailed five months before the final ratification of the 19th Amendment — and a full five years before women in Mississippi were allowed to cast ballots.

## Yet Another Scandal

In 1921, the acting dean of the School of Education, Roswell D. Rogers, accused Chancellor Powers of "gross immorality." According to the *Arkansas Democrat*, Rogers accused Powers of "going with a red-haired woman alone into a room of a certain second-class rooming house in the city of Jackson, Mississippi, then and there for immoral purpose."

At the hearings, which were open to the public and chaired by Governor Lee Russell (an Oxford native), Mrs. Powers sat next to her husband.

During the cross examination of the accuser, it was revealed that Professor Rogers had received a letter from Chancellor Powers indicating than another professor would be appointed to the permanent dean position.

The "red-haired woman" testified late into the night on a Saturday. She said she arranged for a liaison with one of her boarders and witnessed Chancellor Powers disrobe with this woman. After being on the stand for two hours and enduring brutal cross-examination, she asked the governor for a recess, left the courtroom, and fainted. The Sunday paper headlines read: "Red-Haired Woman Testifies Against Powers: Faints."

The following day, the woman signed an affidavit repudiating her testimony. It read, "I want to make a confession. I was forced to tell what I told on the witness stand. The whole thing is a lie."

According to the *Jackson Daily News*, the red-haired woman caught an Illinois Central train and left the state permanently.

Chancellor Powers took the stand and attributed the entire

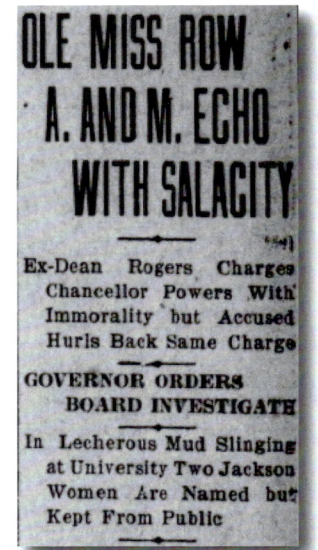

OLE MISS ROW A. AND M. ECHO WITH SALACITY

Ex-Dean Rogers Charges Chancellor Powers With Immorality but Accused Hurls Back Same Charge

GOVERNOR ORDERS BOARD INVESTIGATE

In Lecherous Mud Slinging at University Two Jackson Women Are Named but Kept From Public

Headline from the June 11, 1921, *Jackson Daily News*

mess to Professor Rogers being passed over for the deanship.

A number of character witnesses spoke on behalf of Chancellor Powers. Then, James Warsaw Bell testified. He knew both the accuser and the accused well. Bell testified that Professor Rogers had previously been charged with sexual misconduct in Texas and that he had recently registered in a hotel in Memphis with a woman under the pseudonyms "Mr. and Mrs. Bookout."

At the end of the day, the legislative committee exonerated Chancellor Powers of all charges.

Fred Sullins, editor of the *Jackson Daily News*, wrote that Professor Rogers had "used his own mistress" in an attempt to falsely accuse Chancellor Powers of sexual misconduct.

It was the third scandal Chancellor Powers and Dean Bell endured together.

But Mississippi politics would soon put their interests at odds.

### A New Governor and Chancellor

Henry Whitfield defeated Theodore Bilbo in the 1923 governor's race. Whitfield and Powers had been adversaries for years. In deliberate preparation to dismiss Powers from the chancellorship, Whitfield demanded to know how Powers planned to make the university fiscally solvent. Chancellor Powers responded in a letter dated April 1924, that a possible remedy would be to "abolish the School of Commerce and Business Administration, saving approximately $4,300.00 a year."

Governor Whitfield had no intention of abolishing the school, but he had plans to put an end to Powers' chancellorship. During the June 1924 Board of Trustees meeting, a motion to rehire

Chancellor Powers (above) hired James Bell in 1917 to start the School of Commerce. He also offered to Governor Whitfield to abolish the school in 1924 in order to save his own job.

Chancellor Alfred Hume was appointed chancellor in 1924, the same day Chancellor Powers was ousted.

Powers ended in a 4-4 tie. Whitfield, who as governor was the chair of the board, cast the tie-breaking vote to dismiss Powers from his position.

On the same day, a motion to hire Alfred Hume as chancellor ended in a 4-4 tie. Whitfield cast the deciding vote to appoint Hume as the new chancellor of the university.

### Rapid Growth in the Roaring 20s

Despite the distractions of Mississippi's political shenanigans, the business school flourished and grew in popularity with the students. It produced its second graduate, Mr. Durwood William Aiken, in 1923. By 1924, the Ole Miss annual listed the School of Commerce students in their own section, in addition to liberal arts, engineering, medicine, law, and pharmacy.

Also in 1924, the first woman — Ella Pugh Roberts — was listed among those enrolled in the business school. She was also voted "Most Popular Girl" by the student body.

In 1924, nine new classes were added:
- Politics of the State
  *(taught by Dean Bell)*
- Labor Problems
- Transportation
- Marketing
- Auditing
- State and Federal Income Accounting
- Composition
- Business Math/Algebra
- History of Western Europe

In 1925, more than 116 students were members of the Commerce Club.

### 1927 Election and Governor Theodore Bilbo

The 1927 governor's race was one of the most

The Commercial Club photo from the 1925 Ole Miss annual. That year, the club listed 116 members.

contentious on record. Theodore Bilbo and three other candidates were vying for the position.

A number of Ole Miss administrators and faculty voiced opposition to Bilbo. Among the most vocal was William Hemingway, a law professor and former mayor of Jackson, who ridiculed Bilbo's redneck platform in his lectures.

News leaked that if Bilbo were elected, he would relocate the university from Oxford to Jackson. Bilbo referred to his visionary school as The Greater University.

The state was split. The editor of the *Jackson Daily News* wrote in support of the move to Jackson, "Oxford is, always has been, and always will be, a stupid country town."

Martin V.B. Miller, an Ole Miss alumnus and member of the Board of Trustees, accused the Jackson supporters of being "selfish and greedy."

In a speech to persuade legislators to keep the university in Ox-

ford, Chancellor Hume said, "You may uproot the university from the hallowed ground on which it has stood for eighty years. You may take it from these surroundings that have become so dear to the thousands who have gone from its doors. But, gentlemen, don't call it Ole Miss."

In the end, Hume asked Dean James Warsaw Bell to go to Jackson as his representative to fight for the university on two fronts: first, to prevent the university's relocation; and second, to garner the appropriations necessary to keep the university in operation.

For nearly three months in early 1928, Dean Bell talked to, persuaded, and lobbied legislators, journalists, businessmen, and former students to keep Ole Miss in Oxford.

Bell conspired with a legislator and member of the Holly Springs bar association, Fred M. Belk, to draft a resolution to prevent the relocation of the university.

After great effort on behalf of Bell and other Ole Miss alumni

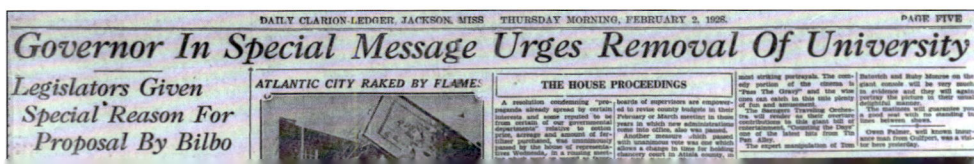

DAILY CLARION-LEDGER, JACKSON, MISS  THURSDAY MORNING, FEBRUARY 2, 1928.   PAGE FIVE

**Governor In Special Message Urges Removal Of University**

Legislators Given Special Reason For Proposal By Bilbo

in the legislature, the resolution passed 109 to 9 (of note, representative John C. Stennis, a grad of Mississippi A&M, voted against the resolution).

Bilbo's dreams were, at least temporarily, dashed.

## The 1928 Appropriation

Having secured Ole Miss's future in Oxford, Dean Bell went to work lobbying to secure funds for the coming years. Legislative funding was always a battle; however, Bell was about to encounter an unexpected ally.

After Bilbo lost the battle to move his "Greater University" to Jackson, most expected him to pull support from Ole Miss. Several weeks after his defeat, in an address to the joint session of the legislature, Bilbo did, as expected, berate opponents who voted to block the relocation. At the end of his speech, however, he surprised almost everyone by inviting lawmakers to join him in building a great university in Oxford. Then, he asked them to fund the university to the tune of $5 million.

The legislators guffawed at Bilbo's request. But, by comparison, it made the request of Chancellor Hume and Dean Bell seem reasonable. The Ole Miss appropriation approved by the legislature — $1.6 million — was the largest in history.

Bell returned to Oxford exhausted but satisfied with his work.

It would be the beginning of a long career of behind-the-scenes work Dean Bell would conduct on behalf of the university and the Board of Trustees.

By the time Dean Bell returned in 1928, the school had seventeen full-time professors and had added advanced courses like CPA Problems and Practices, Merchandising, Foreign Trade, Comparative Government, and Business Cycles.

Because Dean Bell served on the Athletics Committee, star football players chose to study in the School of Commerce. In 1928, the first notable Ole Miss athlete graduated from the school. C.M. "Tad" Smith was an exceptional football and baseball player. In football circles, Smith was regarded as the greatest punt returner in the south. He hated fair catches. He tried to return each punt on a dead run. He also refused to wear a helmet. Instead, Smith taped his ears to prevent them from slowing him down.

In the summer of 1928, the School of Commerce almost lost its founder.

## Buckner's Trestle

On June 10, 1928, the No. 34 train, known as "The Bilbo," made its way from Water Valley to Oxford. Just south of town, the train crossed Buckner's Trestle, a 100-foot long, 50-foot high wooden railway bridge. When the train hit the bridge its timbers gave way and collapsed due to heavy rains.

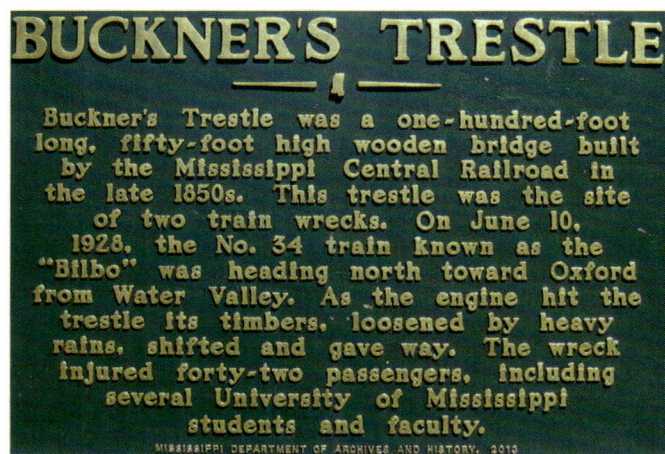

**BUCKNER'S TRESTLE**

Buckner's Trestle was a one-hundred-foot long, fifty-foot high wooden bridge built by the Mississippi Central Railroad in the late 1850s. This trestle was the site of two train wrecks. On June 10, 1928, the No. 34 train known as the "Bilbo" was heading north toward Oxford from Water Valley. As the engine hit the trestle its timbers, loosened by heavy rains, shifted and gave way. The wreck injured forty-two passengers, including several University of Mississippi students and faculty.

MISSISSIPPI DEPARTMENT OF ARCHIVES AND HISTORY. 2013

Forty-two people were injured, including Dean Bell and his wife, Sophie, who had been visiting Sophie's parents in Water Valley. Dean Bell was thrown from the train and broke his back.

In spite of the injury, Dean Bell continued to manage the school in the finest fashion (though he did have to give up a few classes the year following the accident).

The university's business manager, Murry Cuthbert Falkner (father of William Faulkner), refused to pay Bell his full salary. The battle to collect the salary endured for years.

On March 26, 1929, one year after the wreck, Chancellor Hume wrote, "This division [the School of Commerce] of the university has shown steady growth and now ranks second in size among the major divisions of the university."

In 1929, Thadeus "Pi" Vann graduated from the School of Commerce. Vann, who was captain of the football team, took lessons from his fellow School of Commerce colleague Tad Smith. Vann said, "Tad just taped his ears against his head and let her rip. Showed me how to do it, too, and I played several games without a helmet."

Vann went on to coach the Southern Mississippi football team and was inducted into the College Football Hall of Fame in 1987.

In 1930, Mary Frances Clark of Biloxi was the first woman graduate of the business school. Clark served as treasurer of her class and married her classmate, Mr. C.M. "Tad" Smith.

## Bilbo's Purge

Although Bilbo wanted to fund higher education in Mississippi, he was concerned about academic problems at Ole Miss, and he was also determined to replace individuals who had "deficiencies."

Over the next two years, "Bilbo's Purge" saw three university presidents, fifty-three faculty members, and one hundred and twenty-five staff members removed. Murry Falkner was demoted from his position as business manager; William Hemingway and Robert Farley were removed from the law school.

By 1930, Bilbo had appointed enough Board of Trustee members to have Chancellor Hume removed. He was replaced the same day with former chancellor Joseph Neely Powers.

The Southern Association of Colleges reacted to the purge by swiftly suspending Ole Miss from the organization. The school would ultimately lose accreditation.

Ole Miss students were so infuriated by the suspension that they raised a flaming likeness of Bilbo (dressed in pajamas) up a flagpole. In typical Bilbo response, the governor said, "The joke is on the students because I don't wear pajamas."

# OLE MISS STUDENTS BURN GOV. BILBO IN EFFIGY ON CAMPUS

UNIVERSITY, Dec. 6—Gov. Theodore G. Bilbo of Mississippi was burned in effigy tonight on the campus of the State University by a crowd of students estimated to number several hundred. The act was directly attributable to suspension of the institution this week by the Southern Association of Colleges

effigy on the school campus. Gov. Lee Russell was the object of mock cremation when all fraternities were barred from the campus through his efforts as chief executive.

Kelly Hammond, administration legislator, who was named night-watchman by the Bilbo-controlled board of trustees, was

# FIRST FEMALE GRADUATE: 1930 MARY FRANCES CLARK

Mary Frances "Bunch" Clark was the first woman to graduate from the School of Commerce in 1930.

Bunch grew up in Biloxi. Bunch's mother, Clair Clark, often played bridge with Jefferson Davis's wife on the coast. William Clark, Bunch's father, was a business man who sold materials to shipbuilders along the coast. Bunch wanted to follow in her father's footsteps and enrolled in the business school for this purpose.

She met C.M. "Tad" Smith when they were both students. They eloped as students (Mrs. Hefley, dean of women, who controlled the conduct of female students at Ole Miss, wouldn't allow girls to marry while in school).

Following their wedding, Tad and Bunch lived on the third floor of the "Y" building.

When World War II broke-out, Tad enlisted in the Navy. He was sent to Panama. While Tad was away, Bunch went to work for Pure Oil Company in Oxford — a distributorship of gas and oil for automobiles.

Biloxi native Mary Frances "Bunch" Clark, circa 1930. She was the School of Commerce's first female grad.

After returning from the war, Tad asked Bunch to quit working for Pure Oil because he did not like her working with other men. She eventually went back into the work force as a secretary at University High School in Oxford.

Despite his insistence that Bunch limit her professional career, Tad respected her intellect and instincts. Bunch encouraged Tad to establish Ole Miss's Loyalty Foundation. She also encouraged him to embrace air travel for the football team to play "away" games that would be a hardship for the players to travel by road.

Mary Frances "Bunch" Clark Smith died on September 15, 1984, of congestive heart failure. It was the Saturday of the 1984 Ole Miss-LSU game.

# TALLEY RIDDELL, SR.

## 1931 • BSC IN BUSINESS ADMINISTRATION • QUITMAN, MS

Tally Riddell (class of 1931) served in many public capacities, including: the office of state senator from Lauderdale County (1940-44); state counsel for comptroller of banks in Jackson (1942-45); alderman, city of Quitman (1949-53); and chairman of the State Educational Finance Commission from 1954-56, which organization had the responsibility for reorganizing the secondary schools of the state of Mississippi.

He was a law school classmate (at George Washington University) of J.P. Coleman. When Coleman was elected governor, he appointed Riddell as a member of the Board of Trustees of Institutions of Higher Learning of the state of Mississippi. He served from 1956-68.

As a result, when the moderate Coleman was replaced with the more radical Ross Barnett, Riddell was faced with remarkably difficult decisions.

Riddell stood in favor of "compliance over contempt of court charges" in the IHL vote over whether to admit James Meredith. And, according to reports, the sharp division between the governor and Riddell became so heated Riddell had to be taken to the hospital for a heart condition.

Tally Riddell (right) greets fellow Ole Miss Alumni Association President James McClure.

Riddell later admitted that he had feigned a heart condition because Governor Barnett had become so combative, so profane that Riddell drew back his fist and was prepared to sock the governor.

Riddell suddenly realized he was seconds away from assaulting the governor of Mississippi.

Riddell was also president of the Mississippi Economic Council from 1965-66 and served as a member of its Board of Directors for more than ten years. He was president of the Clarke County Bar Association;

president of the Mississippi State Bar Association (1972-73); a member of the Mississippi Bar Foundation; member of the American Bar Association, the American Judicature Society, and the Federal Bar Association; a fellow in the American College of Trial Lawyers; a member of the Mississippi Defense Lawyers Association, the Mississippi Judicial Nominating Committee, and the American Academy of Hospital Attorneys.

For more than twenty-eight years, he served as division counsel for Southern Railway System for the state of Mississippi and was president of the Mississippi Railroad Association and a member of the National Association of Railroad Trial Counsel.

Riddell was president of the Ole Miss Alumni Association (1977-78) and was inducted into the Ole Miss Hall of Fame in 1983. Prior to that time he served on the Board of Directors and Executive Committee numerous times.

Riddell was a member of the First Baptist Church of Quitman where he taught the Men's Senior Bible Class. Also, he was a veteran of World War II, a member of the American Legion, a Mason, and a Shriner.

Riddell died on January 15, 2008.

> In 1962, during the Meredith crisis, Ole Miss alum and IHL board member Tally Riddell realized he was seconds away from assaulting the governor of Mississippi

## The 1930s
## Three Chancellors, Stagnation, and Politics

After the stock market crash of 1929 and the onset of the Great Depression, growth in the School of Commerce came to a virtual standstill.

Chancellor Powers, in spite of being newly appointed by Bilbo, found conditions at the university less than perfect. In 1931, money was so tight several professors in the School of Commerce were paid partial salaries.

Dean Bell also lost substantial savings in failed banks. He served as the chairman of the depositors' committee in at least one litigation against Guaranty Bank and Trust Company.

In the 1931 election, the voters selected Martin Sennett Conner as governor of the state. Conner went to work to regain accreditation, as well as to replace those faculty and administrators who had been removed by Bilbo.

Hume was reappointed as chancellor. Both Farley and Hemingway were rehired at the law school. And Ole Miss was well on its way to reaccreditation. However, money was still tight.

Chancellor Hume, determined to get finances in order, contemplated firing two of Dean Bell's professors.

On June 4, 1932, Bell wrote a long letter to Hume pleading for the jobs of six men (including his own).

"I do know that these men are willing to take whatever reductions in salary may be necessary to make for the university as a whole. We make this sacrifice willingly, provided that other parts of the university will show the same spirit. We feel that we can safely leave that phase of the matter entirely in your hands without any fear that partiality will be shown."

Two weeks later Hume wrote a form letter to Bell congratulating him on being hired at a salary of $3000 (a $900 reduction from his previous salary). Hume added a handwritten postscript: "I have written both Howerton and Stone that they are out."

One of Governor Conner's most controversial (and effective) initiatives was the institution of a two percent state sales tax. The issue was so contentious that the Conner had to place guards at the governor's mansion to keep his family safe from protesters.

The sales tax initiative ultimately passed. It was the first state sales tax levied in the United States.

## A "Spy" of Sorts

Board of Trustees president H.L. "Heck" Currie depended on Dean Bell to be not only his eyes and ears on campus, but also a voice of reason. Bell had proven himself to be persuasive, trustworthy, and reasonable. Politicians, governors, chancellors, and members of the Board of Trustees looked to him for guidance and counsel. Two Board of Trustees members, H.L. "Heck" Currie and Martin Van Buren Miller, took a particular interest in Jim Bell.

On at least one occasion (particularly on the evening of September 24, 1932), Bell found himself so enthusiastic about Ole Miss athletics that he agreed to seek out a $750,000 loan to build a concrete football stadium.

Later that night, he thought better of it and wrote a letter to the Board of Trustees asking they remove his name from the resolution.

(L to R): Martin Van Buren Miller (Class of '09), Governor Hugh White (Class of '99), and J.H. "Heck" Currie (Class of '08). Miller and Currie both served as president of the board of trustees. Both men also depended on the knowledge, influence, and intellect of Dean Bell.

"I am willing to do anything possible for the University of Mississippi," he wrote, "but I cannot permit my name to be used in making what I deem to be an utterly unreasonable request."

## The Beginning of a Research Component

In 1933, Dean Bell, Grady Guyton, and R.L. Sackett conducted a survey of the effectiveness of the sales tax one year after it passed. In the foreword to a 1933 edition of *The Bulletin of the University of Mississippi* entitled *Mississippi's General Sales Tax: How it Works*, Bell and his colleagues eloquently explained the fine balance that must be met by governments when imposing a sale tax.

"The taxing power is one of the most delicate instruments used by government. Badly used, the body politic suffers. Wisely used, the people are contented. Governments, like individuals, find themselves in dire need. It happens at times that experiments must be made with schemes for raising funds. Mississippi found itself confronted with such a situation in January 1932. The government elected to use the general sales tax method to rescue itself from its financial embarrassment. Did it make a wise choice? It is the purpose of this survey to attempt to find the answer to that question.

> J.W. Bell
> Grady Guyton
> R.L. Sackett"

The publication would be the model for conducting research on behalf of Mississippi businesses and government agencies (*see*

*Bureau of Business Research*, Section II).

In spite of the financial success of the sales tax, resentment over the imposition on retailers lingered. In 1934, Robert Torrey (a legislator who supported the sales tax) applied for a math instructor position at the university. The citizens of Oxford mounted a campaign against him.

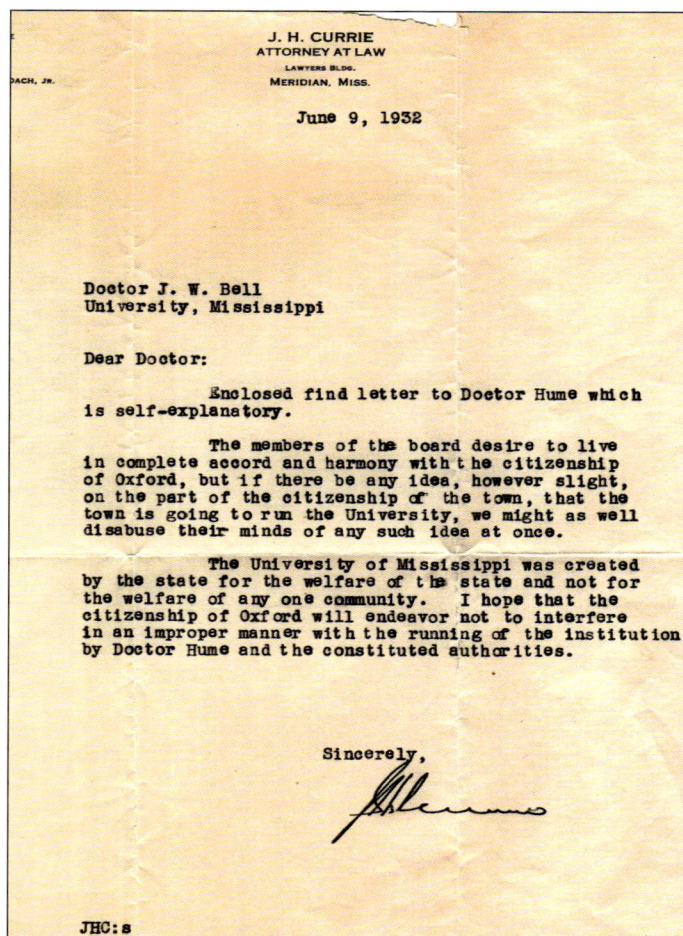

J.H. "Heck" Currie, president of the Board of Trustees, was infuriated by Oxford residents interfering with university business. In a scathing letter to Dean Bell dated June 9, 1932, Currie chastised the townspeople for meddling in affairs handled by the Board of Trustees.

## A New Business Manager

The two gentlemen, Currie and Bell, also worked together to solve the problem of an unseasoned, recently hired business manager, Lee Gainey, who was interjecting his opinions on Coach Walker's football program, as well as trying to take away a concessions revenue stream that funded the football program.

Currie asked Bell to use his influence to get compromises from Hume and Gainey (who wanted to take the store from athletics).

"You can count on my doing everything in my power," Bell wrote in a letter dated December 7, 1934, "to solve the condition in which we find ourselves with out the University's being brought into unfavorable public notice."

Bell wrote in a private letter to his friend Chuck Trotter, "It has seemed to me for some time that Dr. Hume had the largest

*Continued on page 26*

# LUCIAN S. MINOR

Lucian S. Minor, long-time Memphis CPA and business advisor, was born January 24, 1916, in Brooksville, Mississippi. After graduating from Ole Miss in 1937, Minor was recruited by General Mills, Inc. to join the company's internal audit staff in Minneapolis, where he worked until beginning his service in the U.S. Navy in 1942.

Minor was stationed with Douglas Aircraft Co. in Los Angeles as a cost inspector and passed the CPA exam during his enlistment.

Minor was discharged in 1946, at which time he opened his own accounting firm in Memphis. During the next twenty years, his firm, Minor and Moore, grew to be the largest accounting firm in Memphis.

In 1969, he merged his firm with the international accounting firm of Ernst & Ernst and became partner in charge of the Memphis office until his retirement in 1978.

As a young man, he enjoyed entertaining friends to hunt quail and dove at his family's Circle M. Ranch at Paulette (Macon), Mississippi, and later at his farm, "the Old Rainey Place," at Blue Mountain, Mississippi. He was a member of Menasha Hunting and Fishing Club in Arkansas for over fifty years, and of the Memphis Hunt and Polo Club. One of his favorite pastimes was playing a round of golf with his friends at Memphis Country Club or Gulf Stream Golf Club in Delray Beach, Florida.

Minor served as a mentor to young professionals all of his life. He was a loyal supporter of Ole Miss. He was inducted into the Ole Miss Alumni Association's Hall of Fame in 2005. In April 2013, Minor Hall was dedicated in his honor.

Minor died April 7, 2014, at the age of ninety-eight.

Lucian Minor and his wife, Mary, in 2013, at the dedication of Minor Hall.

> Minor built the largest accounting firm in Memphis. In 1969, his firm merged with the international accounting firm of Ernst & Ernst.

# FRANK MANNING KINARD

1938 • BSC IN BUSINESS ADMINISTRATION • PELAHATCHIE, MS

Frank M. "Bruiser" Kinard was an outstanding football player on the freshman team at Ole Miss. As a sophomore, Kinard made an immediate impact on varsity coach Ed Walker (who later coached at Princeton). Walker said, "He is the best lineman ever to play the game." Kinard was not only durable (he once played 562 consecutive minutes), but he was fast (he was once clocked in full uniform in the 100-yard dash at 10.4 seconds).

In his sophomore season (1935), Kinard and the Ole Miss Rebels posted a 9-2 record and lost the Orange Bowl to Catholic University 20-19. Ole Miss had mediocre teams the next two seasons, but Kinard earned consensus All-America honors both years.

He graduated from Ole Miss as the first Rebel to earn All-Southeastern Conference recognition, the first Ole Miss All-America, and the first Rebel to play in the prestigious College All-Star game in Chicago.

Kinard was taken in the second round of the NFL's player-draft by the Brooklyn Dodgers, a pro football team named after their major league baseball counterparts.

Kinard's smothering style of defense and rugged defensive blocking would earn him All-Pro accolades after each season of his nine-year career.

During the 1939 season, Kinard and his fellow Dodgers were unsuspecting participants in the first NFL telecast. The Dodgers' game at Ebbetts Field versus the Philadelphia Eagles on October 22 was televised by the National Broadcasting Company (NBC). With television in its infancy, the Dodgers' 23-14 victory was beamed (via one stationary camera) to approximately 500 televisions that existed in New York at the time.

Kinard (right) with fellow School of Business alum Archie Manning.

Kinard retired as a player before the 1948 season and returned to his alma mater as a line coach, and in 1971 became director of athletics.

In 1971, Kinard was inducted into the Pro Football Hall of Fame (1971). When Kinard was asked how he wanted his Pro Football Hall of Fame ring to read, he said, "Better make it Bruiser; if it said Frank, no one would know it was mine."

Kinard is a charter member of the College Football Hall of Fame (1959.) Once nearly universally regarded as "the South's finest lineman," he is still considered by many to have retained that honor.

In addition to the many "firsts" Bruiser Kinard achieved in his lifetime, he was also part of the NFL's first televised game.

# HOW "BRUISER" INFLUENCED MODERN PUBLIC RELATIONS

15-year-old Harold Burson as depicted in the 1937 Ole Miss annual.

In 1936, a fifteen-year-old Memphis teenager named Harold Burson boarded a Greyhound bus for Oxford. The following is an excerpt from Burson's forthcoming memoir, *The Business of Persuasion*.

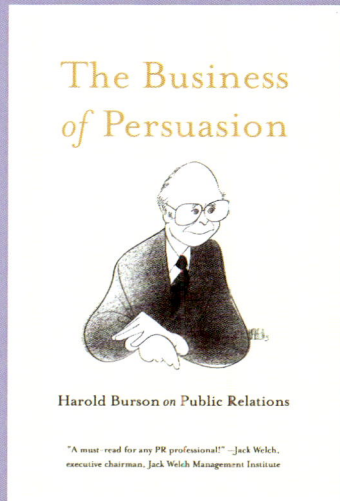

"Shortly after arriving on campus, I met a remarkable third-year student, Billy Gates, the *Jackson Daily News* stringer whose major interest in life was the Ole Miss Rebel football team. From the outset, he was my mentor and one of my closest college friends. Because the Ole Miss athletic department did not then have a publicity director, Gates assumed that role without pay. When we met, his one overriding goal was churning out copy about a left tackle named Kinard. Gates's goal was to make Kinard the first Ole Miss All-American football player. At that time the two-platoon system calling for different teams for offensive and defensive play did not yet exist. During his career at Ole Miss, Kinard played sixty minutes of every game, a feat he had also accomplished in high school. Billy Gates was Kinard's Boswell; he kept track of every block and every tackle during Kinard's varsity years at Ole Miss. He also organized and implemented a publicity campaign directed to the nation's top sports writers who voted in All-America team selections. Every week he mailed them a kit of articles with photos and statistics updating them on Kinard's feats on the gridiron. While Gates hoped sports editors would publish his articles, he settled for their merely reading about Bruiser week after week for the entire football season. It worked. In 1936, Bruiser Kinard became the first Ole Miss player voted All-American.

Watching Billy Gates propel Bruiser Kinard into All-American status was my first exposure to an honest-to-goodness publicity campaign. By example, he was an effective teacher with a work ethic few could emulate."

Burson, an Ole Miss economics major (class of 1940), is generally regarded as the "father of public relations." Burson developed his early skill set watching those men and women around him at Ole Miss. Burson is the co-founder of Burson-Marsteller, one of the largest public relations firms in the world. Burson played a leading role in transforming the practice of PR from a cottage industry to a global enterprise over the course of the 20th century. He has been called "the century's most influential PR figure" by *PRWeek* — a reflection of his role as a counselor for generations of CEOs, government officials, and public sector leaders.

Burson joined forces in 1953 with Bill Marsteller to establish Burson-Marsteller, which today operates in sixty-plus wholly owned offices on six continents.

He has received numerous awards from PR organizations including Hall of Fame designations by the Public Relations Society of America, *PRWeek*, *PR News*, and the Institute of Public Relations. He was awarded an honorary degree by Boston University in 1988, and a chair in PR was established in his name in 1995. He was also active in numerous public service organizations, principally the John F. Kennedy Center for the Performing Arts. He has been a Presidential appointee to the Commission on the Fine Arts, a member of the board of trustees for the Museum of the American Revolution, and a public relations advisor to President Reagan.

Harold Burson was married to Bette Foster Burson for sixty-three years. He has two sons and five grandchildren and lives in New York City. At the age of ninety-six, he continues to go to his office five days a week.

**Harold Burson in his New York offices circa 1960.**

## James Warsaw Bell

**Personal History** Born in the best place I know of to be born—Pontotoc County, on Owl Creek. Lived there as long as I could and then moved around over the state, marrying in Yalobusha County. Have no choice as to where I may die. Recently made Dean Emeritus of the School of Commerce and Business Administration.

**Like** A good many things and some people—things best.

**Hate** Nothing nor nobody.

**Enjoy** Bragging on my wife, children and grandchildren, especially the latter.

**Choose** Cook's Goldblume.

**Remember** The narrow escapes I had in not marrying "those other" girls.

**Confess** I want to do something where I'll not have to turn red in the face to make folks know I mean "no" when I say it.

---

capacity for taking bad advice of any one with whom I have come in contact lately."

The following day Currie sent a Western Union telegraph to the chancellor and Bell that read, "Are children or men going to direct affairs at University."

That same day, Bell met with Chancellor Hume and convinced him to allow the decision about concessions to be made by the board.

The board, of course, concluded and that all revenues be directed toward the Athletic Association.

**A Tribute to a Friend**
**The Naming of a Stadium**

On November 5, 1937, William Hemingway died. His dear friend Jim Bell wrote the obituary.

"His most valuable service to the University outside of his work as a professor in the law school was as Chairman of the Athletic Committee. He was an enthusiastic advocate of all athletic sports and did all in his power to elevate competitive sports both in quantity and quality. His wished to win but did not want to do so by any kind of short cut, it is a source of keen regret to his friends that he did not live to see the concrete stadium completed.

It would be a fitting tribute to his memory to name the stadium for him."

**A New Hire**

A.B. Crosier had been the only accounting professor in the School of Commerce from 1917-1935. In 1935, Sam Simmons was hired to assist with the teaching load, but he left after one year. In 1936, Preston Whitcomb Kimball replaced Simmons, but he also left after one year on the faculty.

Determined to find a skilled, dedicated accounting professor, Dean Bell contacted a young professor at the University of South Dakota named Clive Dunham. In a letter dated February 17, 1937, Bell promised Dr. Dunham the title of Associate Professor and Acting Head of the Department.

James Warsaw Bell featured in the "Meet Your Professor" profile from *The Mississippian* (circa 1941)

# J. LUCIEN "LUKE" SMITH, JR.

## 1937 • BSC IN BUSINESS ADMINISTRATION

After graduating from Ole Miss, J. Lucien "Luke" Smith joined a Coca-Cola bottling company in Dallas, Texas, in 1940. He was placed in charge of Coca-Cola's bottler sales organization in 1949; became a vice president in 1961; and was elected president of Coca-Cola USA, the domestic soft drink division, in 1971.

During the 1970s, under the direction of Chairman J. Paul Austin and President J. Lucien Smith, Coca-Cola was introduced in Russia, as well as in China. To enter the Chinese market, the company sponsored five scholarships for Chinese students at the Harvard Business School and supported China's soccer and table tennis teams. The beverage also became available in Egypt in 1979, after an absence there of twelve years. Austin and Smith strongly believed in free trade and opposed boycotts. They felt that business, in terms of international relations, should be used to improve national economies and could be a strong deterrent to war. Under the direction of the two men, Coca-Cola also started technological and educational programs in developing nations in which it conducted business, introducing clean water technology and sponsoring sports programs in countries too poor to provide these benefits for themselves.

Austin's emphasis was on foreign expansion. Smith was responsible for everyday operation of the company.

In 1977, Coca-Cola USA was struggling domestically. Smith was charged with renegotiating an ancient bottling contract, which did not allow for increased labor costs, advertising, overhead, or ingredients. With inflation raging, Austin asked Smith to renegotiate with the bottlers.

In the book *For God, Country, and Coca-Cola*, Mark Pendergrast wrote: "If anyone could pull off a seemingly impossible task, it was Smith, a traditional, warm southerner whom the bottlers loved and trusted." Though it wasn't easy, Smith was able to accomplish what both parties needed in order to grow the business.

Smith died on July 19, 1980, at the age of sixty-one. He had a heart attack aboard his houseboat at Lake Lanier, about thirty miles north of Atlanta.

In his honor, the J. Lucien Smith, Jr. Memorial Scholarship was endowed at the University of Mississippi in 1992. The scholarship for $1,000 per semester is available for any incoming freshman from the greater Atlanta, Georgia, area.

**Under the direction of Ole Miss School of Commerce grad Luke Smith, Coca-Cola expanded into Russia, China, and the Middle East.**

When Dunham arrived at the university he was impressed with Dean Bell and the chancellor. He was also impressed with the university culture.

Dunham's initial thoughts about Ole Miss were recorded in Dale Flesher's *Accountancy at Ole Miss: A Sesquicentennial Salute.*

"The character of the university was reflected by a dozen or more old men. They pretty much dominated policy. They had survived political interference and the depression with poise and patience. They taught the best of the old but welcomed the new provided it had high intellectual content. I heard someone refer to them as 'the true aristocrats.' In the vernacular, they had class. So had the university as a whole."

Dunham was the first professor of accountancy in the state of Mississippi to hold both a doctorate and a CPA certificate.

In 1938, a young man named Jimmy Fried from Vicksburg, Mississippi, enrolled in the School of Commerce. Nine years later, he would become the first MBA graduate of the school (see interview, pages 22-23). In 1941, the Master of Business Administration (MBA) was established ( Ph.D. programs in business and economics were established shortly thereafter).

**Retirement as Dean**

During Dean Bell's tenure, he experienced five changes in chancellorships and nine changes in governorships. He survived them all; however, he did experience moments of doubt, anxiety about his future, and a sense of being under-appreciated. In a revealing,

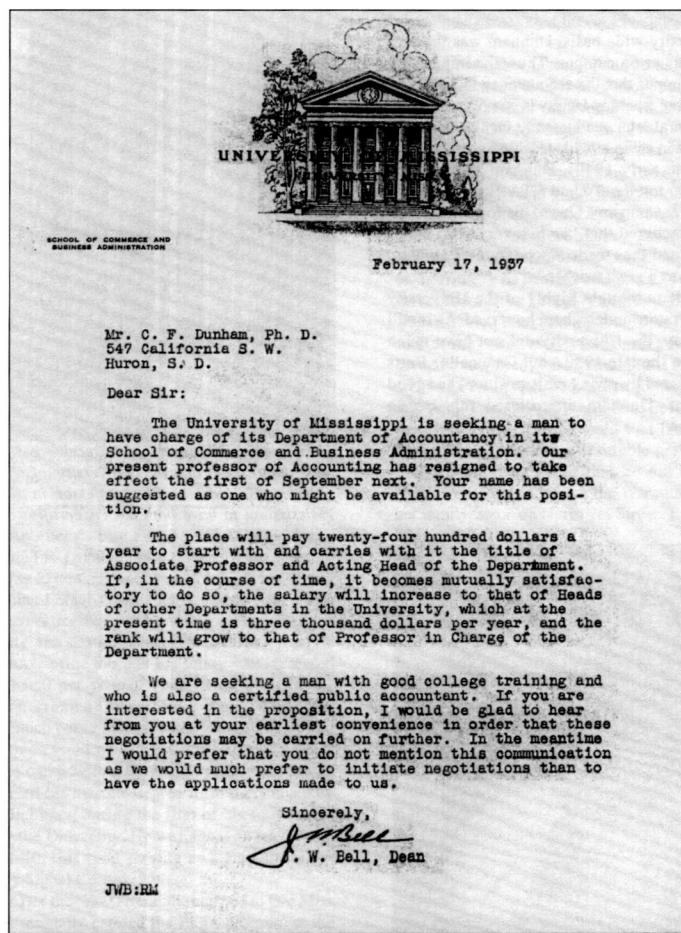

UNIVERSITY OF MISSISSIPPI

SCHOOL OF COMMERCE AND
BUSINESS ADMINISTRATION

February 17, 1937

Mr. C. F. Dunham, Ph. D.
547 California S. W.
Huron, S. D.

Dear Sir:

The University of Mississippi is seeking a man to have charge of its Department of Accountancy in its School of Commerce and Business Administration. Our present professor of Accounting has resigned to take effect the first of September next. Your name has been suggested as one who might be available for this position.

The place will pay twenty-four hundred dollars a year to start with and carries with it the title of Associate Professor and Acting Head of the Department. If, in the course of time, it becomes mutually satisfactory to do so, the salary will increase to that of Heads of other Departments in the University, which at the present time is three thousand dollars per year, and the rank will grow to that of Professor in Charge of the Department.

We are seeking a man with good college training and who is also a certified public accountant. If you are interested in the proposition, I would be glad to hear from you at your earliest convenience in order that these negotiations may be carried on further. In the meantime I would prefer that you do not mention this communication as we would much prefer to initiate negotiations than to have the applications made to us.

Sincerely,

J. W. Bell, Dean

JWB:RM

reflective, and personal letter to his friend Chuck Trotter, Bell wrote —

"I thank you for what you say with respect to my remaining at the University. I do not know what to say about it.

"I was — in that as I have been in every other act of mine connected with the University — doing and saying what I thought would be for the best interest of the University. I have always and do yet place the University first. You know better than lots of other folks the long hard fight I have made for the University. You also know better than most people that it was done without any expectation of reward of any kind and in those expectations you know I have not been disappointed.

"I am willing to stand or fall on the basis of my record here at the University. You know something of what I did for the University in securing each of the two large appropriations made for the material advancement of the institution. In 1928, when the Legislature had under consideration: first, the question of the removal of the University; second, the question of making a considerable appropriation for its material betterment, I spent the major part of three months in Jackson as the representative of the Chancellor and of the people of Oxford. As to whether or not I am due any credit for what happened, I leave it to others to say.

"I think you also know that the School of Commerce and Business at the University of Mississippi is the product of my efforts. I am its first and only Dean today. It began in 1917 with nothing, during the period of the war, with everything disrupted. From the beginning, however, the progress of the school has been continuing. You also know that what has been done with the School of Commerce and Business has been done with no help and little encouragement from the authorities of the University. I have now a small faculty of as efficient and loyal helpers as can be found in any other similar institution in the land. I state this as a fact and not as an opinion. I state it further (I should say, I suppose as a matter of opinion) that the School of Commerce and Business is discriminated against in favor of other parts of the University. Take the student hour cost in the school of Commerce and Business and the salaries paid to those who render this service and compare it with that of other parts of the institution and you will see what I am getting at. But for the parsimonious economy exercised toward the School of Commerce and Business, it would be impossible for the School of Medicine to exist. The fees paid by the students in the School of Commerce and Business into the General Treasury almost takes care of the payroll of the School of Commerce and Business. With an enrollment of more than two hundred in the School of Commerce and Business, the school does not cost the General Fund as much as Five Thousand Dollars a year (Less that $25.00 per student) from the General Fund of the institution. It is my understanding that the apportionment made to the University by the Board of Trustees from funds appropriated by the State Legislature amounted to something like $100.00 per capita. But there is no necessity of my going into all this with you. What I am trying to get across to you is that if my record as Dean of School of Commerce and Business and as a teacher and worker for the institution does not justify my continuance as a member of the faculty, I do not wish to remain. At the same time I want to say that in my opinion no fair-minded man can say that my record here is not a good one. It may be immodest in me to say so. I say it nevertheless. I believe Bennie Butts is a fair minded man with good judgement, therefore, I look to the future with comfort. If, however, you should run up on anything that makes you doubt what the future may hold in store for me, I wish you would let me know. I know the time is coming and that it is not many years in the future when my active connection with the University must be broken. It does not make any difference how long it may be until that time comes, nor does it make any difference what may be the cause of my relation with the University being severed, I know it is going to break my heart. No man can work as long and as hard, as disinterestedly and as loyally for an institution as I have for the University of Mississippi and not love it with an abiding love.

"I am sorry that you said that you did not see that red-headed granddaughter of mine. She is a beauty and the universal comment is that she is the split image of her grandfather.

"The whole Bell family joins me in love to the entire Trotter family."

Sincerely your friend,
J.W. Bell"

Dean Bell dedicated his life to Ole Miss, the School of Commerce, and UM Athletics. In his later years, he struggled with uncertainty about his future."

James Warsaw Bell retired as dean in 1941. But he was far from being finished with Ole Miss, the direction of its athletic programs, or the politics that would rock Mississippi post-World War II.

# INTERVIEW WITH JAMES FRIED, CPA
## THE SCHOOL OF COMMERCE'S FIRST MBA GRADUATE

*Fried is a past president of the Louisiana Society of CPAs, past president of the New Orleans chapter of the National Association of Cost Accountants, and the first MBA graduate from Ole Miss.*

THIS INTERVIEW TOOK PLACE JUNE 26, 2017

**Tell us about your family.**

My father was an electrical engineer, and he had an electrical company in Vicksburg that wired houses and businesses and buildings. I worked for him in the afternoons when I was at school and in the summer times. In the afternoons when I was in school, I took care of the office in the afternoon and in the summertime, I actually worked as an electrician.

**Did you attend Ole Miss as an undergraduate?**

I went to Ole Miss in 1938. I really had in mind that I would take law at Ole Miss, but I was taking accounting in high school and I liked it, so I decided to use the business school as pre-law. But as I got further into the business school, I decided I really liked accounting and decided to become a CPA. I did that, and I graduated in four years. Then the war broke out. I was moved around for nearly three years and didn't arrive overseas until mid-January 1945.

I reported to my company commander, and he said to me "Lieutenant, your platoon" — a platoon in the infantry was about forty men — "your platoon is right over there."

I looked over there, and I didn't see but one man. I walked over to him.

"Sergeant, I'm looking for my platoon."

"Lieutenant," he said, "I'm it. Everyone in this platoon except me has been killed or wounded in the Battle of the Bulge."

I was eventually involved in about four or five battles in northern France, and then I was wounded. A bullet broke my jawbone. In fact, it went in my cheek. It hit my jaw bone and broke it and came out the back of my neck. It missed my spine by about a quarter of an inch.

**When did you get back to Ole Miss?**

In 1946. The master of business administration program had only been established right before I went into the service. And I finished all my subjects, but I didn't finish my thesis. At that time they required a thesis for the MBA. So I went back to school that summer, reviewed my accounting courses, and wrote my thesis.

And then I had an early examination, and I did happen to pass that, and they awarded an MBA in I guess July or August of 1946. And that was the first MBA they had given.

**Do you remember who your examiners were?**

I know Dr. Brown was there, and the dean of the graduate school was one of my examiners, and the professor of accounting was on the examining board. It was an oral examination.

**Do you remember what you wrote your thesis on?**

Oh yes, I do. I wrote my thesis on husband and wife partnerships. At that time, there were no joint income tax returns. My thesis was on husband and wife partnerships and when they were accepted and when they were not accepted as partnerships. But the basis of my thesis was really that in Louisiana, where they had community property, the husband and wife could always split the income because in Louisiana, half your income belongs to your spouse. I wrote about the unfair nature of that law. And of course, later it was not important because they allowed husbands and wife to file joint returns and that did

Jimmy Fried in the 1942 Ole Miss Yearbook

the same thing. But at the time that I wrote it, it was a big problem.

**Who were your mentors at Ole Miss?**

My accounting professor, Clive Dunham, was my favorite teacher. Dr. Brown was wonderful too, but Dunham was the most patient person I'd ever seen. He was born with the left arm half the length of a normal arm so he couldn't use his left arm.

He would get before the class — I'll never forget this — and someone would ask him a question, and he would very patiently answer that question. And two minutes later, someone else would ask the same question, and he'd answer with the same patience.

He was very thorough and he was a terrific teacher. Dr. Brown was too. I learned a lot from both of them.

**What did Dr. Brown teach?**

Dr. Brown taught economics, and I graded for him in my senior year and as a graduate student. So the first time there was a test, he called me to his office and said, "Here are the papers, go grade them." That's all the instruction that I got. So I went and I graded the papers. Well mine was included, and I didn't grade it.

I went back to him and I said, "Dr. Brown, here are all the papers and the grades."

And he looked down at them and said, "Well, you didn't grade yours."

"No," I said, "I thought perhaps you would like to grade mine, that you wouldn't want me to."

"Absolutely not," he said, "You go back and grade that paper."

**What did you give yourself?**

I made an A! I don't think I cheated.

**Did you know Dean Bell?**

I knew him well. Dean Bell was older and nearly deaf by the time I got there. He was the dean, but he taught economics too. There were three or four football players in that class. During the lecture, one of the football players would raise his hand and, without making any sound with his mouth, would ask a question. Dean Bell would take his hand and punch that doggone hearing aid he had that was right over his chest.

Then he'd look back at the football player. "Now, what did you

Jimmy Fried in 2017

say?"

The football players had a good time.

**Tell us about your career.**

I think I probably had as good a career as anybody I know. After I got my master's degree, I said, "I want to go into public accounting, so I'd better go to a pretty nice size city." And to myself, I said, "Well the three largest cities in Mississippi are Memphis, Mobile, and New Orleans."

So I picked one of those. I came to New Orleans. I started with Ernst and Ernst. Then I went out on my own with a partner. We grew into about a fifty-man firm. And it was really a nice group. Fifteen years later, Arthur Young wanted to start a group, and through contacts, they contacted us, and the firm of Colton and Fried became a part of Arthur Young and Company. And I became a partner in Arthur Young. I retired from Arthur Young in 1980. In 1982, Arthur Young and Ernst and Ernst merged. I became a retired partner in Ernst and Young, and I think I can say I'm one of their oldest retired partners at this time.

*At the time of this interview, Mr. Fried was ninety-seven.*

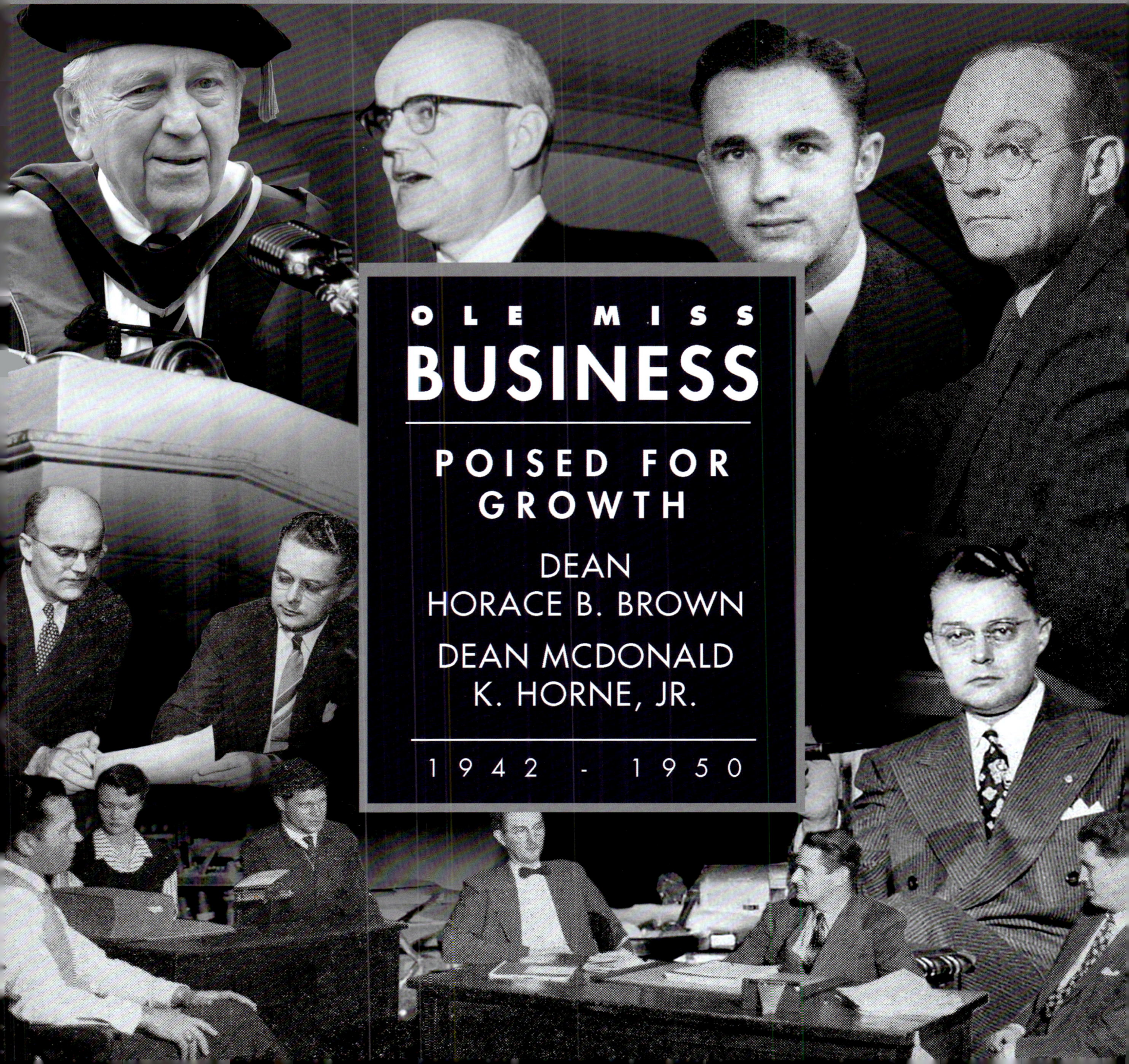

# OLE MISS BUSINESS

## POISED FOR GROWTH

### DEAN HORACE B. BROWN

### DEAN MCDONALD K. HORNE, JR.

#### 1942 - 1950

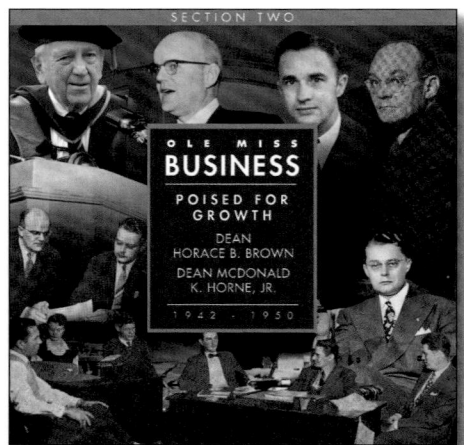

Clockwise from top left: John Brademas, Dean McDonald Horne, George Street, journalism chair Dr. Gerald Forbes, Dean Horace Brown, researchers from the Bureau of Business Research, Deans Horne and Brown.

# HORACE BRIGHTBERRY BROWN
## DEAN 1941-1948

"I audited Dean Brown's class just to learn his teaching techniques."

Dr. McDonald K. Horne, Jr., *Dean, School of Commerce, 1949*

In 1942, after twenty-five years under the tutelage of Dean Bell, the School of Business and Commerce appointed its second dean — Dr. Horace Brightberry Brown.

Brown was a native of Holly Springs and a 1931 graduate of Ole Miss. After he graduated, Brown married his wife, Dorothy, and accepted a position teaching economics at in the business school. He went on to earn his master of business administration degree in 1932 and his Ph.D. in 1941, both from Northwestern University, and all while continuing to teach at the University of Mississippi. He immediately set out to improve the business school's academic standing.

Dean Bell had initiated the application process for accreditation by the American Association of Collegiate Schools of Business (AACSB) in 1940. A visitation committee toured the school at that time to inspect the general facilities, and they delivered a favorable report. But the AACSB wanted to observe the school longer before they granted membership and accreditation.

Over the next three years, Dean Bell and Dr. Brown worked together to bring the School of Business and Commerce up to the rigorous standards held by the AACSB. One stipulation cited in the correspondence with AACSB included expansion of the student honor societies present in the school.

A chapter of Delta Sigma Pi — a business and commerce honor society — had been established at the university in 1927.

Horace Brown in his senior year, from the 1931 Ole Miss annual.

In 1943, a chapter of Beta Gamma Sigma was added. This highly selective sub-society, which was a division of Delta Sigma Pi, was open only to the top ten percent of senior men and the top three percent of junior men in the school. The mission statement of Delta Sigma Pi reads as follows:

*"Delta Sigma Pi is a professional fraternity organized to foster the study of business in universities; to encourage scholarship, social activity and the association of students for their mutual advancement by research and practice; to promote closer affiliation between the commercial world and students of commerce, and to further a higher standard of commercial ethics and culture and the civic and commercial welfare of the community."*

The business school also focused on improving the facilities available to students during the accreditation application process. As of 1942, the School of Business and Commerce had a separate division in the university library with 1,400 square feet designated as the Commerce Reading Room. It contained current publications in economics and commerce available for student use. There was also a space in the Lyceum that included an accounting and statistics lab, a typing lab, and a business machine room.

The Bureau of Business Research was established in 1942. The Bureau studied significant developments in the business world and maintained close contact with the on-the-ground realities of business in Mississippi. A primary focus of the Bureau was on cotton economics, and they worked closely with the National

Cotton Council, based in Memphis, Tennessee.

Two of the earliest publications of the Bureau of Business Research were "Five Brief Studies for Mississippi Businessmen" and "Cotton Counts Its Customers."

In 1943, the School of Business and Commerce earned a full accreditation by the American Association of Collegiate Schools of Business, an honor which the business school still maintains today. The school was the first in the state to earn membership in AACSB.

In short order, Dr. Brown followed this achievement with two more accreditations, one from the National Conference of State University Schools of Business; the second from the National Business and Education Council. Both accreditations were earned in 1943.

The mission statement of the school as quoted in the University of Mississippi Bulletin for 1942 and 1943 placed great weight on the importance of developing critical thinking skills, deep understanding of economic factors, and adaptability in their students.

The bulletin read —

*"Business men must comprehend the meaning of innumerable market influences, of changes in the banking and monetary system, of public finance, of new departures in legislation and legal interpretation, of international complications, of labor problems, and of even more fundamental questions of economics and philosophy which influence the course of a dynamic age."*

This emphasis on a full mastery of all the complex facets of the business world is a philosophy that served the business school well.

**Brown ushered in three accreditations for the School of Commerce in 1942-1943. Prior to that date, the school had no accreditations.**

Dean Horace Brightberry Brown in his office, room 212 of the Lyceum, with his huge collection of pipes.

The student curriculum in the 1940s was designed to build a broad foundation of general knowledge that would support a more in-depth focus of study in the later years of the degree. During the first two years of a business student's education, he or she would focus on a set of general education courses and pre-requisites – English, business math, history, principles of accounting, typing, etc. The last two years would be focused primarily on the chosen field of study. In 1942, a student could choose from one of eleven courses of study:

- accountancy and auditing
- banking, finance, and insurance
- commercial education
- food and textile management
- industrial management
- marketing and merchandising
- personnel management
- pre-law
- public administration
- secretarial training
- statistics.

Dean Brown's tenure at the business school was shaped primarily by America's entry into World War II.

According the David Sansing's *The University of Mississippi: A Sesquicentennial History,* on the day the Japanese attacked Pearl Harbor, Ole Miss students and faculty assembled in Fulton Chapel to listen to President Franklin D. Roosevelt's radio broadcast calling the nation to arms. Within six months, thousands of students, as well as Chancellor Butts, had joined the nation's military forces.

In 1942, the school established a War Division and an Army Administration School, of which Brown was made head.

Faculty and students left the university to go to war in such astounding numbers that Brown had to press his wife, Dorothy,

During the war, Dean Brown rode his bike to campus from their family home on Van Buren Avenue.

into service as a Russian geography teacher, despite the fact that she knew very little about the topic.

Dr. McDonald K. Horne, who would later serve as dean of the business school and who served at the time as a professor of economics and the director of the Bureau of Business Research, was among those given a military leave of absence. He served as a lieutenant commander in WWII before returning to the school in 1947.

Classes were added with such subjects as "Economics of War," "Labor Problems" (described as "a consideration of the major problems confronting the wage earner in a modern economic society, with emphasis on the position of labor in a war economy"), and "Marketing" ("an analysis of modern methods as they are related to consumers and producers living under the conditions of war. Effects of rationing. Attention is given to both wartime and peacetime problems").

Brown's son, Dr. H. Jack Brown, recalls that his father rode a bicycle to work from their Van Buren Avenue home to save gasoline (which was being rationed during the war). Dean Brown converted their back yard into a chicken farm to provide Oxford with eggs. Brown was also appointed the head of the post-war planning committee in 1945.

Despite the chaos of the war, the school continued its work both within the university and in the state. In 1945, the Bureau of Public Administration joined the Bureau of Business Research. Together, they conducted research into problems faced by state and local government and cooperated with similar organizations sponsored by other Southern universities to form

> Faculty left to go to war in such astounding numbers that Dean Brown pressed his wife into teaching Russian geography (about which she knew very little).

# JOHN BRADEMAS

1946 • BUSINESS MAJOR • MISHAWAKA, INDIANA

Brademas in his NYU office.

John Brademas was born on March 2, 1927, in Mishawaka, Indiana. His father, a Greek immigrant, ran a restaurant and quoted Socrates to him: "Things of value come only after hard work." His mother was an elementary-school teacher. In high school, he was quarterback of the football team, as well as valedictorian.

He enrolled at the University of Mississippi in 1946, where he joined a Navy officer training program. After his freshman year, he won a scholarship and transferred to Harvard.

After graduating from Harvard with high honors in 1949, he attended Oxford University as a Rhodes Scholar and in 1954 earned a social studies doctorate

He served in Congress as a representative from Indiana from 1959 to 1981. Brademas became known as "Mr. Education" and "Mr. Arts." He sponsored bills that nearly doubled federal aid for elementary and secondary education in the mid-1960s and that created the National Endowment for the Arts and Humanities.

He lost a re-election bid in 1980 and was appointed president of New York University. Between 1981 and 1992, Brademas transformed the nation's largest private university from a commuter school into one of the world's premier residential research and teaching institutions.

His *New York Times* obituary read, "Looking collegiate in tweeds and sweaters, displaying boundless energy, Mr. Brademas plunged into meetings with deans, trustees, students and faculty members to learn N.Y.U.'s strengths and weaknesses. He courted investment bankers, foundation executives, real estate moguls and private philanthropists, and reached out to N.Y.U. alumni across the country and around the world. By the end of his tenure he had raised $800 million for N.Y.U. and nearly doubled its endowment to $540 million."

Brademas died in New York City on July 11, 2016, at the age of 89.

> By the end of Brademas' tenure, he had raised $800 million for NYU and nearly doubled its endowment to $540 million.

Brademas in full academic regalia.

The Department of Research in Business and Public Administration was organized in 1946-1947. The department was formed by combining the Bureau of Business Research (established in 1942) and the Bureau of Public Administration (established in 1945)

a regional research program. This group fulfilled three purposes: to provide students of the school with training in research methods, to render services upon request to municipalities and public agencies, and to conduct major administrative studies.

The Bureau of Business Research's stated mission was to —

*"by its studies of significant developments in the business world…assist the School of Commerce and Business Administration in maintaining close and realistic contact with the subject matter of the courses taught. At the same time the Bureau assists in making the research and thinking of a trained business faculty available to all the citizens of the State."*

In 1946, the School of Business and Commerce granted their first Master of Business Administration degree. Although the degree had been offered for many years, on August 23, 1946, Jacob M. Fried, Jr. became the first master's graduate of the business school.

Dr. Gerald Forbes was the first chair of the Journalism Department in the School of Commerce.

By 1947, the business school enrollment was the second-largest in the university, just behind liberal arts. The focus of courses moved away from wartime economics and into subjects more pertinent to a post-war economy. For instance, in the 1942-43 edition of the University of Mississippi Bulletin, the description of the class, Introduction to Economics, read, "A survey of the elementary principles of economics. Scope and method of economics, with special attention to price analysis. Price control and war measures are considered. Study of governmental war agencies and their economic effects."

Other class descriptions of the time included similar war-time foci. Later class catalogs included such courses as Post War Economics, described as "Problems of economic reconstruction, demobilization, employment, taxation, price structure, development of new industries, and international trade and other

*Continued on page 46*

# GEORGE STREET

George Street came to Ole Miss as an undergraduate in 1945, and he never left. After earning a B.B.A. degree in finance, he earned a juris doctor degree in 1949.

Street began his career as supervisor of housing and institutional advisor for veterans. He oversaw services for thousands of veterans enrolled in the G.I. Bill. He also implemented Veteran's Village that later became married student housing.

After serving as assistant dean of men, Street created the prototype for future Ole Miss admissions counselors. He represented Ole Miss at hundreds of high schools and junior colleges throughout the south.

Street then started the first-ever placement bureau, as well as the first student financial aid office on campus.

He was named director of development in 1966.

Street was well-known in state and national organizations, including the National Association of College and University Attorneys (he was the Mississippi chairman). He was president of the Southern College Placement Officers Association and a member of the National College Placement Council.

In 1973, he was the first person appointed to the position of director of university relations.

Many students remember Street visiting their homes to personally award the prestigious Carrier scholarships.

One young student — who told Street that he wanted to work at the university — remembered this advice: "If you want to work at this university, you're going to have to earn a post-graduate degree."

That student was Robert Khayat.

Street died on February 6, 1996, at the age of 76.

Bottom Left: Street reviewing plans; Top: Street as an undergrad; Above: Street's Hall of Fame portrait; Below: the George Street House

# THE BUREAU OF BUSINESS RESEARCH

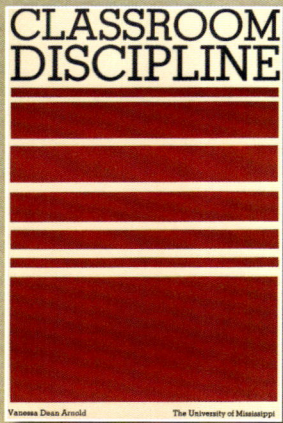

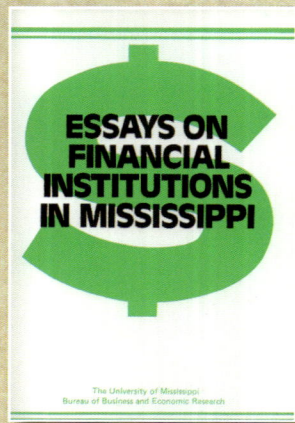

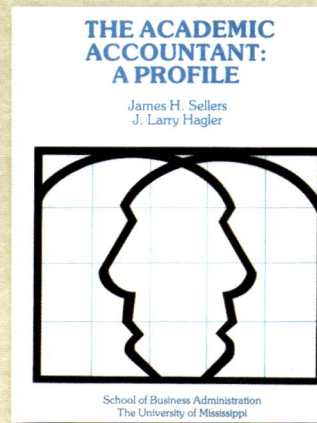

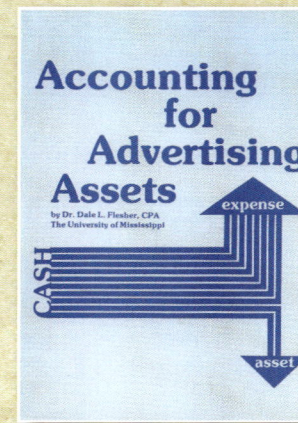

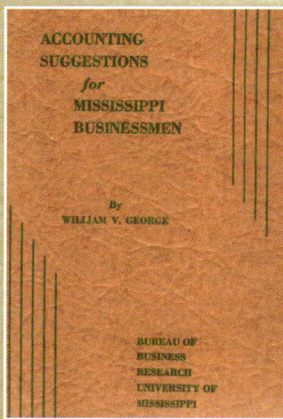

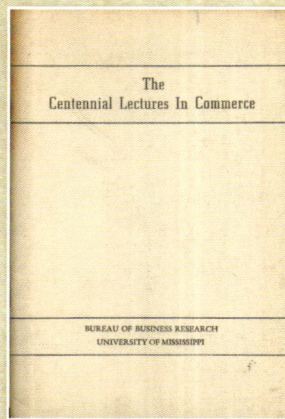

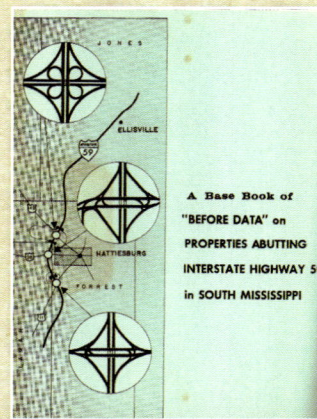

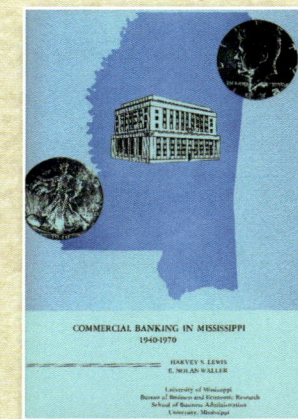

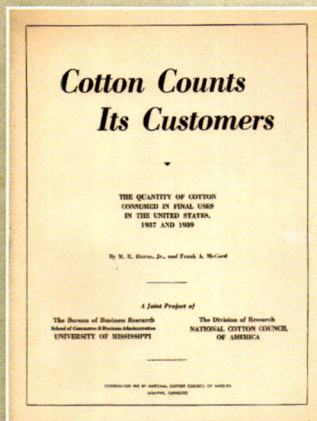

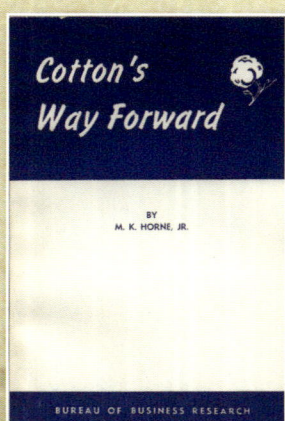

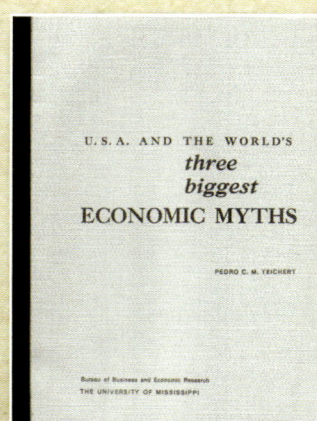

**FORMALIZED PLANNING** *for* Institutions of Higher Learning

Jerry W. Johnson
W. Randy Boxx

The University of Mississippi
Bureau of Business and Economic Research
School of Business Administration

**HIGHWAY-USER TAX PLANS for MISSISSIPPI**

A Supplement to

MONEY FOR MILES IN MISSISSIPPI

**Training Needs As Perceived By Managerial Personnel**

Bureau of Business and Economic Research
The University of Mississippi

ESSAYS IN BUSINESS AND ECONOMICS

A LOOK AT *Natchez:* ITS ECONOMIC RESOURCES

BY EARL L. BAILEY
Bureau of Business Research • University of Mississippi

**MISSISSIPPI** | *in* **maps**

INDUSTRY  RESOURCES  AGRICULTURE

Edward H. Hobbs
Ernest K. Waller
Fred C. DeLong

BUREAU OF BUSINESS RESEARCH • UNIVERSITY OF MISSISSIPPI

**Tung Oil in Mississippi**
By
RANDOLPH G. KINABREW

BUREAU OF BUSINESS RESEARCH
UNIVERSITY OF MISSISSIPPI

AN ECONOMIC ANALYSIS OF A MISSISSIPPI COMMUNITY

**Meridian**

BY EARL L. BAILEY

Bureau of Business Research
University of Mississippi

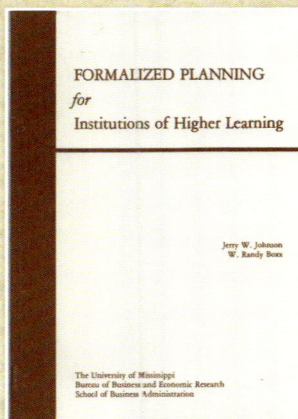

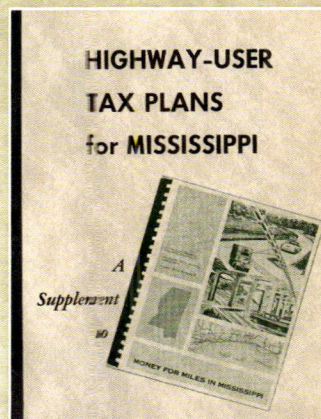

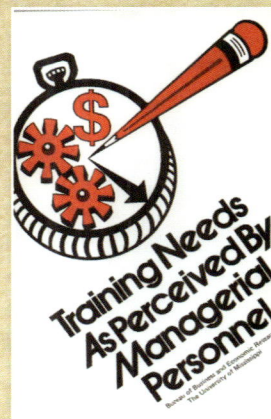

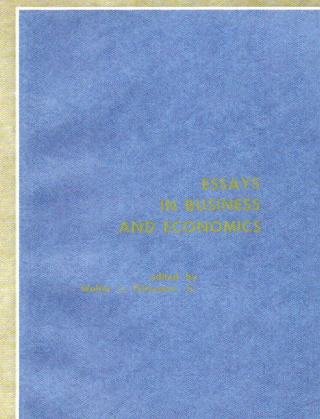

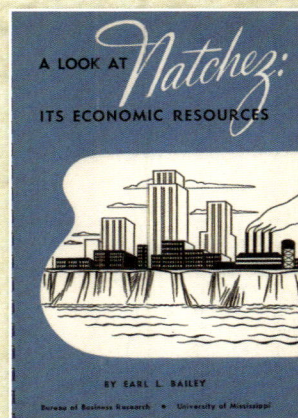

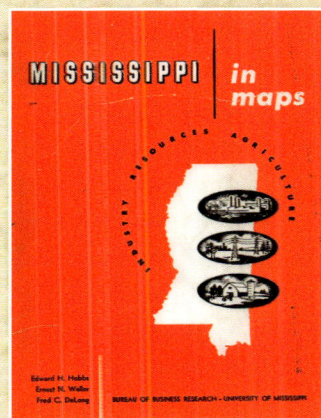

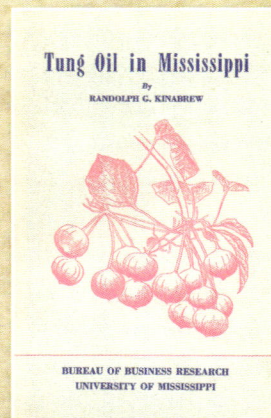

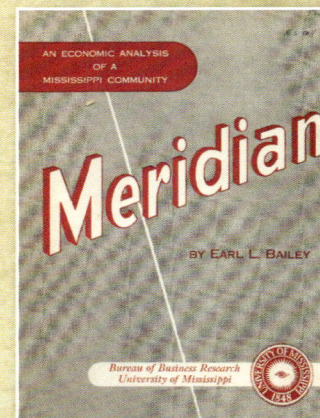

Since its humble beginnings in 1942 under the direction of Dean Horace Brown, the Bureau of Business Research has produced more than 375 publications to assist government agencies, private sector industries, and business men and women in Mississippi. The first director of the bureau was McDonald Horne.

Some of the topics covered by the researchers included —

- USA and the World's Greatest Economic Myths
- The Effect of Price of Water Consumption
- Fortran Applications in Management Education
- The Mississippi Tourist Market
- Store Layout Suggestions
- Crime Prevention for Small Business

- Mississippi's Labor Force
- Training Needs as Perceived by Managerial Personnel
- Locate that Apparel Plant in Mississippi
- Cotton's Way Forward
- Suggestions for Inventory Control
- College Students' Attitudes Toward the IRS

# DEAN EMERITUS BELL STILL DEEPLY INVOLVED IN UNIVERSITY AFFAIRS

After Bell's retirement from his deanship, he continued to teach economics at the School of Commerce and Business Administration. He was also actively involved in athletics. From 1944-1945 he once again served as chair of the Athletics Committee.

Bell also seemed to enjoy ridiculing bureaucratic requirements of the state. In a IHL Professional and Personal Record he completed in 1945, Bell wrote in a section open for *self-appraisal of teaching skills*, "Self Praise is Half Scandal. Hope to hold out two or three more years longer, 'then goodbye, thank you!'" His final notes: "I know I talk too much. Some of the old boys thank me when they see me. It makes me feel good. My former students range from 'hang-man's-noose' to United States Senate."

**A "Point of Contact" for State Officials**

Bell continued to be the eyes and ears of state officials from Jackson (though his answers were often laced with sarcasm).

On June 19, 1943, an officer for the state tax commission who was attempting to collect from a bootlegger, wrote Bell and asked him to "estimate" how much whiskey the bootlegger had sold. Bell responded, "So, how much whiskey he may have sold during the several years that he as been operating, I do not know, but I am thoroughly convinced that he has sold all he could get his hands on."

211 Years of Service

THE FAITHFUL—Dr. Alfred Hume, Dr. David H. Bishop, Dr. Christopher Longest, Dean James W. Bell and Dr. William Lee Kennon, pictured as listed, who collectively have served the University as teachers and administrators a total of 211 years.

From the 1949 Alumni Review with Hume, Bishop, Longest, and Kennon. Dean Emeritus Bell is seated second from right.

In a letter dated February 14, 1946 (during a period of post-war Communist paranoia), Martin V.B. Miller wrote to Bell, "I've known for years that everybody who don't agree with certain people's views are communists."

The letter detailed a request from Walter Sillers to investigate the dean of the School of Education for sympathizing with those who favored federal aid. Sillers wrote, "Federal aid would more or less, sooner or later, place the schools of the country under the influence of federal domination." Sillers continued to spiral into a frenzy. "I gathered from these reports that this party favored the federal aid, and favored the passage of the bill pending in Congress. I also gathered from these newspaper reports, and from a conversation I had with a prominent citizen of Greenville, that this gentlemen's views on the course of instruction, the method thereof, and the discipline of the conduct of the pupils, is quite liberal and tending to embrace what is known as 'Progressive Education' as advocated by Professors Rugge and Dewey; and that this is the same educational program espoused by Teachers College of New York University, which has the reputation of being the hot-bed of communism and other foreign ideologies, which are in conflict with our constitutional form of government."

Miller wrote, "When I see Sillers, I can tell him that I had you make an investigation. I don't reckon you are communist in his eyes."

## Fighting for a New Building

In another exchange with Miller on May 17, 1946, Bell wrote, "There is another matter in which I'm vitally concerned and that is in respect to the proposed building to house the School of Commerce and Business Administration. You know that is my child, and I am very fond of him. I hope you will feel that you are personally representing me when that matter comes before either the Board or the Building Commission, and see that we are not put off with any small sum on the theory that anything will do. $350,000 is the minimum that could be economically spent at the present time, and in my opinion in from five to ten years the capacity of the building would have to be doubled. In that period of time the School of Commerce and Business Administration will have an enrollment of not less than 1,000 students."

## Tad Smith, John Vaught, and the Delta Bowl

When C.M. "Tad" Smith returned from World War II in 1945, Dean Emeritus Bell met him in Memphis. Bell, who was a member of the athletics committee, offered Smith the job of athletics director at Ole Miss.

A year later, John Vaught arrived at Ole Miss. He served as offensive line coach for the Rebels under then head coach Harold "Red" Drew.

Following the 1946 season, Drew, a long-time assistant coach at Alabama, returned to Tuscaloosa to replace the ailing Frank Thomas as head coach.

Smith asked Vaught to take over as head coach. Vaught was reluctant, but eventually agreed. Not expecting to perform well in 1947, the Rebels signed a contract (before the season began) to play in the Delta Bowl in Memphis. But 1947 turned out to be a turning point in Ole Miss football. The Rebels won the SEC and were offered a spot in the Sugar Bowl. Rumor had it that the Orange Bowl was about to extend an invitation.

Bell said, "We are bound by honor to play in Memphis and we will play in Memphis. Taking another bid would besmirch the name of Ole Miss, and our good name is worth more than anything I know of. We might make more money somewhere else, but it would only be money — and not quite clean."

Jim Bell, after supporting the team for more than fifty years, saw the Rebel football team reach new heights. He endured the bitter cold of the Delta Bowl and watched the Rebels win.

The following Spring, he attended a baseball game and saw Ole Miss beat Florida 8-1. That night, he walked home and died in his sleep.

•••

During Jim Bell's tenure as dean there were five changes in the chancellorship and eight changes in the governor's office. Faculty members were hired and fired, but for fifty years, Jim Bell "stayed right where he is, fixed and immovable, because he is an asset quite too valuable to be displaced. No political schemer in the field of education would dare attempt to have his chair declared vacant." (from an editorial in *The Mississippian*)

related subjects will be treated."

Dr. Horne returned from military leave in 1947 and took up a position as the chairman of the Department of Economics.

As students and staff returned home from wartime duties, new degrees were added, including a Master of Business Administration for Business Teachers, later to become a Master of Business Education, in 1947, and a Bachelor of Science in Journalism in 1948. Courses of study were added for insurance, food service management, and textile management (though the latter two of these would last only until 1950). The business education course of study was divided in 1948 into a secretarial and accounting concentration and a general business and accounting concentration. The curricula in the accounting and law and in the business and law courses were combined, and office management was added as a course of study the same year.

In 1949, Dean Brown was offered a position as dean of the business school at the University of Oklahoma.

His son recalled, "The University of Oklahoma offered my father the princely sum of $10,000 a year. I believe his salary at Ole Miss was $6,000. So we moved to Norman."

The growth of the School of Commerce under Dean Brown was remarkable. From an enrollment of 349 in 1941-42, enrollment grew to 1,012 in 1948-49. In addition, in 1941-42 there were six different courses of study. In 1948-49 there were seventeen.

A 1949 edition of the *Ole Miss Alumni Review* featured Dean Brown and Dean Horne complimenting one another.

"In my opinion," Dean Brown said, "the University is most fortunate in having McDonald Horne take over the deanship of the school. Dean Horne is one of the most capable men in the United States in the field of collegiate business education. He is a national authority on cotton economics, and experienced and

ALUMNI INVOLVED IN CHANGES—Dr. McDonald K. Horne, Jr., '30, (left), succeeds Dr. Horace B. Brown, Jr., '31, as dean of the university's School of Commerce and Business Administration on Aug. 15. Dr. Brown has accepted a similar position at the University of Oklahoma.

**From the 1949 Alumni Review**

highly successful classroom instructor, and able administrator, and a gentleman of the highest order. Being a native Mississippian, he is well aware of the economic problems and business needs of the state. I am positive that our School of Commerce and Business Administration will continue to move forward under his able leadership."

On the eve of taking over the dean's office, Horne said, "This is a double loss to me, first, because Horace Brown is one of my best and oldest friends, and second, because our alma mater is losing one of the very best school of business deans in the United States. I cannot express my sense of obligation to Dean Brown for all of the wise guidance and unselfish cooperation that he has given me through the years. He has proven himself to be one of the best teachers and one of the best administrators I have ever known."

Horne continued, "Ole Miss is eternally indebted to him for his great contribution to the progress which the School of Commerce and Business Administration has made. Those of us who remain to carry on this progress will miss the wise leadership which Horace Brown has shown."

Horne would take over the deanship from Brown, but his tenure would be short lived.

• • •

Brown moved to Oklahoma and then went on to become a visiting professor at Harvard, national vice president of Beta Gamma Sigma, and president of the American Association of Collegiate Schools of Business.

He died on December 17, 1988, and is buried in Holly Springs, Mississippi.

# MCDONALD K. HORNE, JR.
## DEAN 1949-1950

"It was this very high regard that I had for him that caused me to bring him back
in 1941 as director of the Bureau of Business Research."

Horace Brightberry Brown., *Dean School of Commerce*

After Dr. Brown departed for Norman, Oklahoma, in 1949, Dr. McDonald K. Horne, Jr. was appointed dean of the School of Business and Commerce.

Horne was born in Winona, Mississippi, in 1909 and graduated from the University of Mississippi in 1930. He and Horace Brown were friends in college) Horne went on to earn a master's degree and a doctorate in 1932 and 1940, respectively. Both degrees were from the University of North Carolina. For a time, Horne was the managing editor of the *Tupelo Journal*. Then in 1935, at the request of Chancellor Butts, Horne returned to Oxford to operate the Ole Miss News Bureau and serve as a professor of economics.

Mac Horne speaking to the Cotton Council.

When he first returned, Horne audited some of Brown's courses "just to learn his teaching technique."

During his career, Horne bounced back and forth between the University of Mississippi and the National Cotton Council. He left Ole Miss in 1939 to become an economist and writer in the newly-formed NCC's Domestic Promotion Division. This appointment was the beginning of a lifelong affiliation with the NCC. When he was hired in 1939, Dr. Horne was likely seen as the third most important figure in the Cotton Council. But over the years, Mac Horne became widely acknowledged as the voice of the entire U.S. cotton industry.

However, he held his first position with the Cotton Council for just two years before he returned to Ole Miss and took up a position as the director of the Bureau of Business Research. There he remained until 1942, when he was placed on a military leave of absence.

Dr. Horne served as a lieutenant commander in WWII. After the war ended, he returned home. He was honorably discharged from the Navy in June 1945 and returned to the University of Mississippi, taking up his position as chairman of the department of economics in 1947.

As it happened, Horne was dean of the business school for only the 1949-1950 school year. His tenure saw twenty-eight Master of Business Administration students graduate, a testament to the emphasis Dr. Horne placed throughout his career on the importance of advanced degrees. Some minor changes to the courses of study were offered, and a Master of Arts in Business degree was made available.

The country was moving out of a wartime mindset and was quickly settling into the Cold War. The Berlin Blockade and the Second Red Scare both began during his time at the school.

In 1950, Horne received an offer from the National Cotton Council of America to serve as their chief economist. The Cotton Council, based out of Memphis, incorporated the seventeen cotton-producing states and worked to "establish policies reflecting the common interests and promoting mutual benefits for its broad membership and ancillary industries."

Horne accepted the Cotton Council's offer and relocated to Memphis on July 1, 1950, where he lived out the rest of his life.

Horne's acceptance of the Cotton Council's offer left the business school without a dean.

Chancellor J.D. Williams appointed the chair of the accounting department, Clive Dunham, to the position of dean. The appointment would prove to be one of the best moves in the history of the business school.

Mac Horne with Cotton Council colleagues.

Horne was a strong supporter of market research. His belief that only hard research would be effective in advancing the cotton industry became an unofficial doctrine of the Cotton Council. A history of the Cotton Council reports that "he knew that if the Council was to handle adequately its industry assignment in research and promotion and save the markets, it had to have the guiding hand of market research, the best economic data, and the best technical and promotional brains available."

He did extensive work with the Pace Committee, which in July 1947 released its study of cotton's competitive position by end-uses. The information Horne and his colleagues provided was called "invaluable" in the Cotton Council's 1987 history and was widely used in the council and in the cotton industry. In the 1970s, he headed up a landmark economic study to assess the future stability of income from cotton-producing farms.

By 1960, Horne was a member of the Economics Research Advisory Committee to the Secretary of Agriculture. He produced many publications, including *Price and the Future of U.S. Cotton* and an article entitled "Cotton" in *The Annals of the American Academy of Political and Social Science*. He was also a member of the Presbyterian church and the Rotary Club. Horne served as the Cotton Council's chief economist until July 1, 1969.

He left his department operating at peak efficiency and was succeeded by Dabney Wellford. In 1971, arrangements were made to retain Horne on a part-time basis for special assignments. In 1973, he retired from the Cotton Council altogether.

### Horne's Post-Ole Miss Work

Horne's work with the Cotton Council was groundbreaking, leading the U.S. cotton industry to work toward both competitive cotton prices and grower-financed cotton research.

Gaylon Booker, a former president of the Cotton Council, said of Horne, "He was a man who placed a high value on accuracy. He placed a high value on integrity. He placed a high value on — and was good at — clarity in writing and in oral communication. He was a very convincing man. When he spoke, he commanded the attention of the audience."

Horne demanded perfection from his team members, and they went to great lengths to achieve it.

## Dean Carroll Replaces Dean Carroll at N. Carolina

DEAN THOMAS H. CARROLL, *California*, left the College of Business Administration at the University of Syracuse to replace Dean D. D. Carroll, of the School of Commerce at the University of North Carolina, who has retired. Brother Tom Carroll had been dean at the University of Syracuse for four years and, in 1946, when he assumed his deanship there he was only 31 years old, making him one of the youngest deans in the country.

Brother Carroll is a native of San Francisco and he received his B.S. Degree and Master's Degree in business administration from the University of California. From there he went to Harvard where he received the degree of Doctor of Commercial Science. In the capacity of research assistant, he remained at Harvard, later becoming a member of the faculty and then, finally, assistant dean before he entered the navy in World War II.

While in service, he attained the rank of lieutenant commander and was in charge of the officer candidate section, Bureau of Naval Personnel in Washington, D.C. Brother Carroll has also been very active in educational circles and has served on the executive committee of the American Association of Collegiate Schools of Business.

## Clive Dunham New Dean at U. of Mississippi

DR. CLIVE F. DUNHAM, *South Dakota*, who became Dean of the School of Commerce and Business Administration on July 1, has been on the University of Mississippi faculty for the past thirteen years, serving for one year as an associate professor and then as professor and head of the Department of Accountancy.

**CLIVE F. DUNHAM, South Dakota**

Brother Dunham was at one time an assistant in the Bureau of Research at the University of Illinois and a teaching assistant in accountancy. He was graduated from Illinois in 1929 with a B.S. in accountancy, receiving his master's degree in the same field from that school in 1932 and his doctorate in economics, also from Illinois, in 1935. He became a Certified Public Accountant in 1935.

Following his graduation, he was professor of economics at Huron College, and was later assistant professor of business administration at the University of South Dakota.

## THE CENTRAL OFFICE REGISTER

THE FOLLOWING MEMBERS of Delta Sigma Pi have visited the Central Office since the last issue of THE DELTASIG. If there is no city shown after the name it indicates they reside in Chicago.

LAWRENCE P. AVRIL, *Kent State*, Bloomington, Indiana; CHARLES L. LeCROY, JR., *Georgia-Pi*, Bloomington, Indiana; JAMES A. GATES, *De Paul*; JAMES S. KAREL, *Illinois*, Riverside, Illinois; PETER G. SIGALOS, *Illinois*; ROBSON D. McINTYRE, *Kentucky*, Lexington, Kentucky; ROBERT O. LEWIS, *Northwestern-Beta*; NORMAN A. PRUSINSKI, *Illinois*; FRED M. VANCE, *Illinois*; ROBERT J. ZIMA, *Illinois*; ROBERT LANDEKIL, JR., *Michigan State*; GLENN A. KLINELL, *Northwestern-Beta*; ROBERT J. PERDUE, *Northwestern-Beta*; ROBERT H. KING, *Rider*, Olean, New York; ROBERT J. BLACK, *Northwestern-Beta*, Oak Park, Illinois; JOHN A. BRDECKA, *Northwestern-Zeta*, Evanston, Illinois; DUANE H. McELMURRY, *Northwestern-Zeta*, Superior, Wisconsin; VIRGIL N. SHURTS, *Miami U.*, Oxford, Ohio; ROBERT I. PANUNCIALMAN, *De Paul*; JOHN WANDA, JR., *De Paul*; RAYMOND J. BOCHENSKI, *De Paul*; DENNIS J. MOLLAHAN, *De Paul*; WALTER J. KOEHLER, JR., *De Paul*; ROGER T. LARSON, *Nebraska*, Omaha, Nebraska; LEONARD S. SHOMELL, *Alabama*; ALLEN L. FOWLER, *Pennsylvania*, St. Davids, Pennsylvania; FRANCES D. CARR, *Michigan*, Ann Arbor, Michigan; CARL W. KUHN, *De Paul*, Glen Ellyn, Illinois; HAROLD S. CRAWLEY, JR., *De Paul*; ROLLAND R. FLOCH, *Northwestern-Zeta*, La Grange, Illinois; CLARENCE T. NAGEL, *Northwestern-Beta*.

RUDOLPH JANZEN, *Minnesota*, Minneapolis, Minnesota; DAVID A. NELSON, *Northwestern-Zeta*, Evanston, Illinois; RAY J. GLAZOWSKI, *Northwestern-Zeta*; ROBERT G. BUSSE, *Rutgers-Beta Omicron*, Kalamazoo, Michigan; THEODORE LAKE, JR., *De Paul*; DAVID L. POWELL, *Pennsylvania*, Philadelphia, Pennsylvania; ROBERT A. SAUERBERG, *Northwestern-Zeta*; GEORGE T. ANTON, *Northwestern-Zeta*, Evanston, Illinois; R. P. LINDMILLER, *Ohio State*, Cleveland, Ohio; JOHN R. ITTERSOGEN, *New Mexico*; JOSEPH C. KRIVAN, *Temple*, Detroit, Michigan; ROGER HYNES, *De Paul*; KENNETH B. WHITE, *Boston*, Dallas, Texas; RANDOLPH K. VINSON, *Northwestern-Beta*; HARRY D. SERANTONI, *De Paul*; HENRY S. BROWN, *Northwestern-Zeta*; WILLIAM R. MUIRHEAD, *Rutgers-Beta Omicron*, Newark, New Jersey; PAUL J. BOND, JR., *Northwestern-Beta*, Des Plaines, Illinois.

HENRY A. ZWARYCZ, *De Paul*; CLIFFORD H. RASMUSSEN, *Northwestern-Beta*, Webster Groves, Missouri; WAYNE P. HANSEN, *De Paul*, Skokie, Illinois; JOSEPH N. THOMAS, *Indiana*, Gary, Indiana; MICHAEL B. SCHNEIDER, *De Paul*; CLARENCE C. LUBINSKI, *Illinois*; WALTER P. WEITH, *Illinois*; WILLIAM J. GRZENA, *Northwestern-Beta*; HUGH K. McKEE, JR., *Mississippi*, Picayune, Mississippi; MAURICE S. MURRAY, *St. Louis*, Richmond Heights, Missouri; LEONARD C. JONES, *Nebraska*, Western Springs, Illinois; CLIFFORD A. SELL, *Illinois*; PATRICK J. GILL, *De Paul*; ROBERT K. OWEN, *Northwestern-Zeta*, Park Forest, Illinois; VERNON O. SCHROEDER, *Louisiana Tech*, Alexandria, Louisiana; CHARLES J. GAISOR, *Denver*; ROBERT O. HUGHES, *Pennsylvania*, Drexel Hill, Pennsylvania; WILLIAM R. GALIS, *De Paul*; ALEXANDER R. CHISHOLM, *Northwestern-Beta*, Crete, Illinois; WILBERT W. PATE, *Northwestern-Beta*, Arlington Heights, Illinois.

DALE H. ASKEY, *Nebraska*, Lincoln, Nebraska; RICHARD H. MAHONEY, *Michigan State*, Oak Park, Illinois; CALVIN M. C. BRANDES, *Georgia-Kappa*, San Francisco, California; WILLIAM R. MERRICK, *Baylor*, Dallas, Texas; HENRY C. LUCAS, *Nebraska*, Omaha, Nebraska; CLYDE KITCHENS, *Georgia-Kappa*, Atlanta, Georgia; J. HARRY F[...], *Johns Hopkins*, Baltimore, Maryland; [...] METCALF, *Northwestern-Beta*; H. [...] LIPPINCOTT, Pennsylvania, Philadelphia; [...]WYN L. GILMORE, *South Dakota*, Ft. [...] Iowa; JAMES A. KERR, *Northwestern*, [...] Tulsa, Oklahoma; RUDOLPH H. WEBER, *Northwestern-Beta*; DOUGLAS J. W. CLARK, *Rutgers-Beta Omicron*, Long Valley, New Jersey; [...]LIAM T. MONCIER, *Tennessee*, Bristol, [...]see; MAYBEN P. NEWBY, *Illinois*, Kansas[...] Missouri; and GLENN W. CHAMBERS, *[...]Kappa*, Monroe, Michigan.

## Horne Becomes Chief Economist of Cotton Council

McDONALD K. HORNE, JR., *Mississippi*, has resigned his office as dean of the School of Commerce and Business Administra-

**McDONALD K. HORNE, JR., Mississippi**

tion at the University of Mississippi, to become the chief economist for the National Cotton Council. His office will be located in Memphis, and he will serve as an advisor of economic policies for the nation's cotton industry, which is devoted to the growing, marketing and processing of cotton.

Brother Horne was born in Winona, Mississippi, in 1909, received his early schooling there and in 1930 he graduated from the University of Mississippi with an A.B. Degree. He secured his Master's Degree in 1932 from North Carolina and his Doctor's Degree in 1940. His first position was that of managing editor of the *Tupelo Journal* in 1934. In 1935 he joined the staff of the University of Mississippi, where he later directed the Bureau of Business Research and headed the Department of Economics and Business Administration before becoming dean of the School of Commerce and Business Administration.

In the last ten years, Brother Horne has served as advisor to many governmental committees and headed several commissions particularly in relation to the cotton industry and labor relations. He also served in the navy during the last war and held the rank of lieutenant commander.

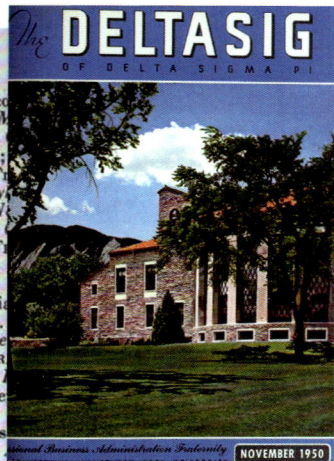

A 1950 edition of *Delta Sig* featured Mac Horne's departure to the Cotton Council, as well as the appointment of Clive Dunham as Dean of the School of Commerce.

# AN ESSAY BY BILL BRYSON
## FIRST GRADUATE OF THE INSURANCE PROGRAM
### HOW THE RMI PROGRAM GOT ITS START

When I graduated from Ole Miss in 1949, only two other students in my class were insurance majors. I did not know either of them, and we did not cross paths in the insurance business in the years following graduation. There was very little interest in the major as an avenue for employment at that time, but there is a great deal now — especially at Ole Miss. As I understand it, there is a waiting list now to enter the program.

To the best of my knowledge, a college insurance program in Mississippi was started by an insurance professor named Dr. Luck at Mississippi State during the 1950s. Dr. Luck raised money to support his program with the major contributor being the Farm Bureau. I gave a small amount because I thought the program was a good idea.

During that time, most of the Mississippi insurance industry was located in the Old Plaza Building in Jackson. The coffee shop there was a good place to find out what was happening in the industry. One conversation that caught the interest of the Ole Miss people was a remark by a student named Richard Aiken. He commented that he had learned more by studying for the agent's examination than he had during his insurance course of study at Ole Miss.

We discussed the problem with some people in the Ole Miss administration, and we were told there was very little they could do as long as so few students were enrolled in the insurance program, which begs the question: Which comes first? A good program or more students in the major? And to make things more difficult, insurance companies showed very little interest in supporting the program at Ole Miss.

In the meantime, Mississippi State fired Dr. Luck. It appeared their interest was in an "Insurance Day" rather than the insurance major Dr. Luck was developing. Dr. Luck went to Delta State and started a program there that lasted about a year. He then retired someplace out west. I attended his retirement party.

The change at Mississippi State raised our hopes, so with the help of the university, we organized the Ole Miss Insurance Excellence Program. The organizers were Lamar Maxwell, Tom Joiner, and Rufus Jones from the university, and myself. Rufus was our version of Clay Cavett (the university's current associate director of alumni affairs).

We worked hard at raising interest and money, and things began to progress fairly well. To strengthen the program, we needed more students, and things were not improving in that area. We received support from many people. I especially remember Perrin Caldwell, Tommy Brown, Jack Stevens, Keith Bills, and Dick Aiken.

One thing we had done right, however, was to restrict the use of funds we had raised for the program. The money was with the University of Mississippi Foundation and invested by them, but it was restricted to our use for an insurance program. With this money, interest from the business school, and the fact that Mississippi State no longer had an insurance program, the Ole Miss business school agreed to employ a recognized insurance professor.

Dr. Joe Murray from Arkansas State was hired. This was in the 1990s, when my daughter was attending Ole Miss and majoring in insurance, so I remained well-informed. Things were going OK, but we still were lacking many students.

Then, on one of the annual trips around the state, an Ole Miss alumnus gave the dean a difficult time over the fact that Mississippi State had an annual "Insurance Day" but Ole Miss did not. At the dean's request, Dr. Murray contacted us, and we organized one in the middle of football season. Dr. Murray even reserved a block of rooms at the Holiday Inn in Oxford. It is my understanding that a fairly new assistant manager at the motel was fired for reserving the rooms at regular rates on a Friday night before a big football game.

With several of us working on it, we managed to put together good speakers and programs for the next few years. We had local insurance professionals available, and several of us had contacts in high places. It also helped that most everyone wanted to visit Ole Miss. I was able to convince the president of the Professional Insurance Agents Association to come to the meeting before the Georgia game since he was a Georgia fan. We were also fortunate to secure the services of a speaker named Joel Wood, who worked for the Professional Insurance Agents Association. Joel is an Ole Miss alumnus and has relatives in Jackson. He still is a welcome addition at our meetings.

Bad times hit us during this next period: We had to work with two consecutive business school deans who were not concerned about an insurance program. One told me that he would prefer not having one. I was certainly glad that the money raised was restricted to our use. During this time, our insurance professor, Dr. Murray, resigned.

The next dean, Dr. Randy Boxx, was on his first annual business trip, calling on alumni. While in Natchez, he visited with a local insurance agent, Jack Stevens, who filled him in on the fact that Mississippi State had an "Insurance Day" and Ole Miss did not. Jack gave him my name, and shortly thereafter he was in my office inquiring about an "Insurance Day." Dean Boxx became interested and gave us his full support. He also persuaded "Bouncer" Robinson to establish a "Chair of Insurance" in honor of his wife and father. This was also a big step forward for us.

Then, another big event took place that opened another opportunity for our program. An industrywide meeting of insurance educators was being held at Point Clear, Alabama, where several prospective insurance professors would be available for interviews. Fortunately, we were in a position to appoint someone to represent us at this meeting, along with some Ole Miss people, to interview interested professors.

We chose Tom Quaka to represent us, though it required him to get up early enough to ride to Point Clear and make a 9:30 meeting that morning. Tom reported to us that only one applicant would be of interest to us: a young man named Larry Cox, who was a former colleague of Dr. Luck at his New Mexico school. This was our same Dr. Luck who we thought had retired.

We were now in a position to fulfill our purpose with a top-notch professor, Larry Cox, a great and supporting Dean Cyree, and a group of leaders on the advisory committee that knew how to get things done. The only thing lacking was a room full of outstanding students, and Larry Cox was on that from the start. Larry, with the support of Dean Cyree and the current advisory committee, ushered us to success, and our program keeps getting better.

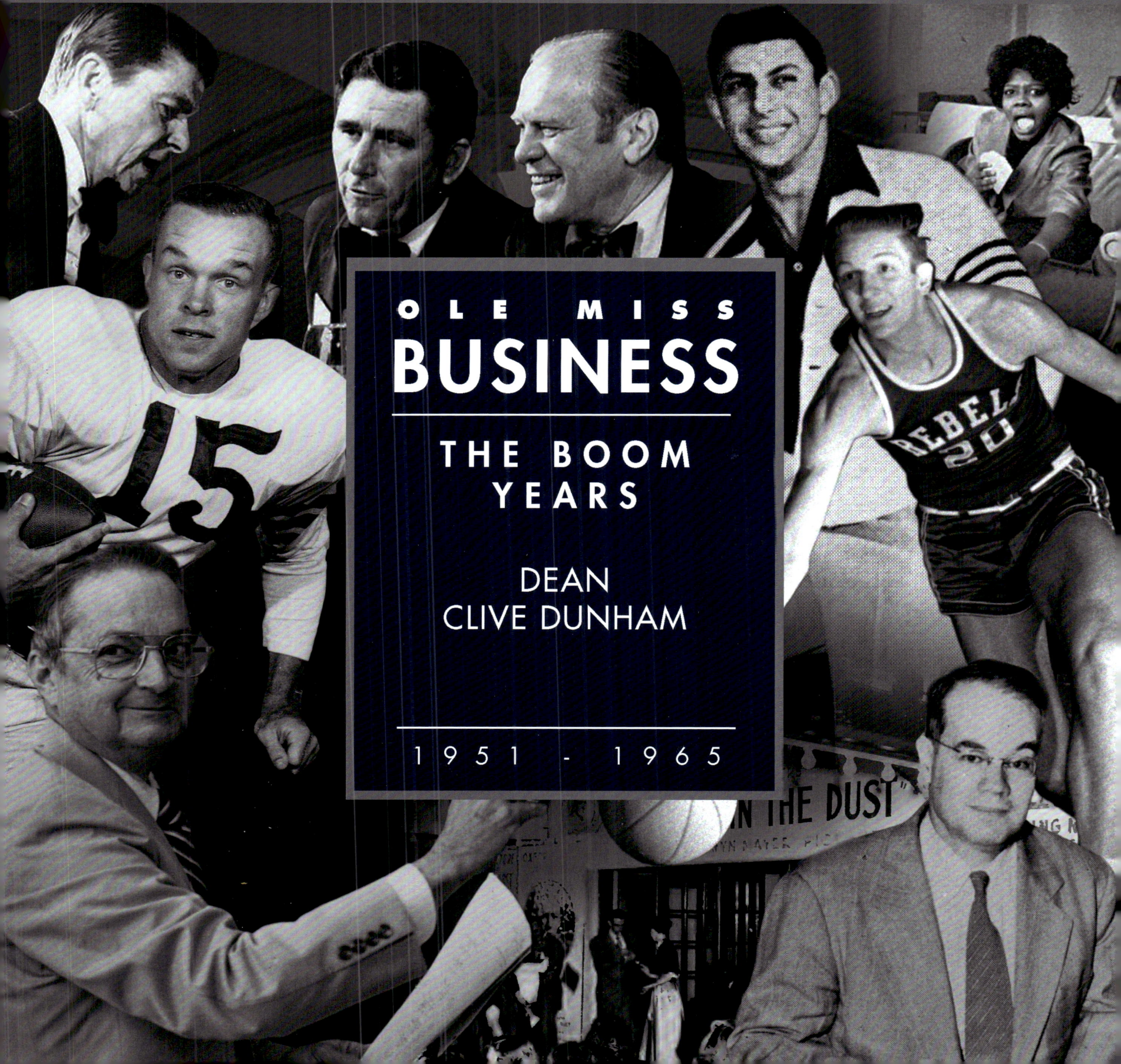

# OLE MISS
# BUSINESS

## THE BOOM YEARS

### DEAN
### CLIVE DUNHAM

1951 - 1965

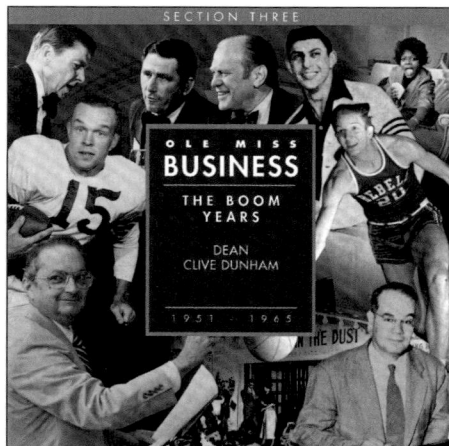

Clockwise from top left: President Ronald Reagan, Governor Winfield Dunn, and President Gerald Ford, Henry Paris, Joyce O'Neal Jones, Hon. John Palmer, Dean Clive Dunham, the Oxford premiere of *Intruder in the Dust*, Professor Eugene Peery.

# CLIVE F. DUNHAM
## DEAN 1950-1965

"The soft-spoken, amiable personality of Dr. Clive F. Dunham…
is as much a part of the Ole Miss campus as the Lyceum."

Whit Thrower, *The Oxford Eagle*, February 13, 1964

When Dean Bell hired Clive Dunham to head the Department of Accountancy, the job came with a starting salary of $2,400 a year — a paltry one for a department chair even by 1937 standards. Regardless, Dunham, who had never lived in the South, was immediately enamored with Ole Miss.

Dunham was the first professor in Mississippi to hold both a CPA and a Ph.D. He did some part-time accounting in Tupelo before becoming dean (probably to supplement his meager pay). Teaching was Dunham's true passion, which was probably for the best. As one of his coworkers at M.M. Winkler and Company in Tupelo put it, "he had very poor handwriting, and thus made a poor staff accountant. But he was a great teacher."

Dunham's teaching acumen was apparent in the high esteem students held for the professor. On at least one occasion, he was the highest rated teacher in student evaluations across the entire university.

Dunham became dean in 1950. By all accounts, he was a more

Clive Dunham was hired as a professor in 1937. In 1950, he was appointed Dean of the School of Commerce.

reserved dean than some of his predecessors, most notably the folksy and animated Bell.

His steady leadership oversaw unprecedented progress within the business school — enrollment gains, new construction, the expansion of technology, and the beginnings of equal opportunities for women and minorities all took place under his watch. During Dunham's tenure, the School of Commerce produced some of its most successful graduates — men and women who would change the face of business, technology, and politics.

Dunham accomplished all this even as the university endured its most tragic and infamous chapter and became the subject of national scrutiny and, for a time, ignominy.

Through all those difficult years, Dunham's high opinion of Ole Miss and his optimism about its future never wavered.

### Mixed Signals

As Dunham was transitioning to the deanship, Mississippi, and

# HON. WINFIELD C. DUNN

## 1950 • BBA, BUSINESS ADMINISTRATION • MERIDIAN, MISSISSIPPI

Winfield Dunn received his bachelor's degree in business administration from Ole Miss in 1950 and his D.D.S. from the University of Tennessee Medical Units in Memphis in 1955. Dunn served with the U.S. Navy in the Asia-Pacific Theater during World War II. He was also a reserve lieutenant in the U.S. Air Force.

Dunn established a dental practice after completing dental school and became involved in the grassroots politics of the Shelby County Republican Party in the early 1960s. Friends were encouraging Dunn to run for Congress — a suggestion that "amazed" him when he first heard it. The idea wasn't quite as enthusiastically received by his closest advisor, though.

"I took that amazement home to my wife, who very wisely said, 'that's the silliest thing I ever heard of, you with a dental practice,'" Dunn recalled. "She talked me out of even thinking about it. But that was kind of a start."

After winning the Republican nomination for governor in 1970, Dunn became the first Republican governor of Tennessee in half a century, serving from 1971-75.

When asked about his most important accomplishments, Dunn said the statewide kindergarten program, the creation of the Ten-

Dunn in the governor's office

nessee Housing and Development Authority, the Department of Economic and Community Development, and the centralizing of the state's purchasing system under the Department of General Services.

In 1975, Dunn joined the board of directors and executive department of Hospital Corporation of America. He has served on numerous corporate boards and presidential commissions. His presidential appointments include the advisory committee to the director of the National Institutes of Health and the National Committee on Highway Safety. He has been active with the Nashville Chamber of Commerce, Nashville Heart Association, Nashville Conference of Christians and Jews, United Way and was three times named Tennessee's Man of the Year by the state's newspaper editors, television news directors, and heads of chambers of commerce. He served two terms as crusade chairman of Character Counts! Nashville.

Dunn with presidents Reagan and Ford

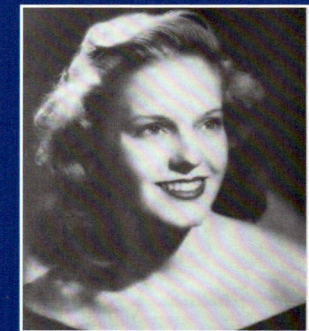

Dunn met his wife, Betty Prichard, while campaigning for president of the School of Commerce. She said of his thoughts of running for governor, "that's the silliest thing I've ever heard of . . ."

Oxford in particular, had been in the national spotlight. In 1949, William Faulkner won the Nobel Prize in Literature "for his powerful and artistically unique contribution to the modern American novel." He was only the fourth American to win the award. The premiere of the film *Intruder in the Dust* took place in Oxford's Lyric Theater just three weeks after the Nobel announcement.

In 1948, the year before Faulkner's Nobel Prize was announced, Mississippi native Tennessee Williams had won the Pulitzer Prize for his stage play "A Streetcar Named Desire."

At a time when the nation was looking at Mississippi's contributions in a positive fashion, the real beginnings of the integration conflict at the university began. In 1950, the *Mississippian* reported that black students might soon begin applying for admission. The controversy was palpable — editorials on both sides of the issue filled the paper's pages. Cross burnings were reported on campus. That same year, a tradition known as "Dixie Week" was initiated, which noted Mississippi historian and Ole Miss Professor Emeritus David Sansing summed up this way:

"...a seven-day celebration of their Southern heritage during which Colonel Rebel and Miss Ole Miss reigned. The opening ceremony of Dixie Week was the reading of the Ordinance of Secession, usually by the president of the student body, from the balcony of the student union

The premiere of the film Intruder in the Dust at the Lyric Theatre in downtown Oxford.
Photo from the 1949 Ole Miss annual.

or from the courthouse on the square. Enlistment of the University Greys, ceremonial consumption of mint juleps, speeches in praise of Robert E. Lee, beard-growing contests, and mule races were the rituals of Dixie Week. One of the most popular events was the auctioning of cheerleaders who served as slaves for the week to their buyers."

Ole Miss, along with Oxford and the entire state of Mississippi, was falling behind the times, a mistake that would cost the university dearly in the early 1960s — casting a pall over the institution that would take generations to lift.

Many university faculty members, as well as Chancellor John D. Williams, were sympathetic to the cause of admitting black students. In response, the legislature launched an investigation into the issue, accusing Ole Miss faculty of teaching integration, apostasy, and attempting to subvert Mississippi's way of life.

That the university in many ways thrived during this tumultuous period for the institution, the state, and indeed the world, is a testament to its resilience. The business school was no exception — growing, improving, and even promoting progressive changes like the elevating of women in direct opposition to the more negative forces impacting the campus at that time.

### Money and Space

The 1950 annual report to the chancellor opened, "The year just past was one of deep discouragement for the

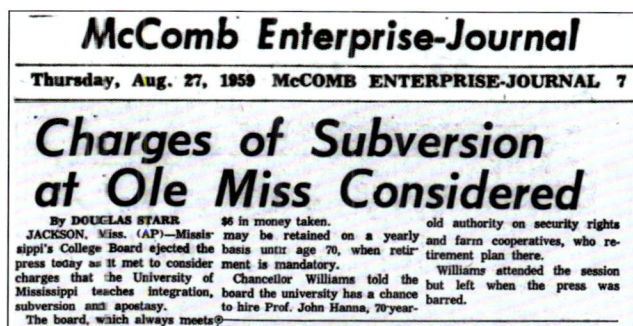

**McComb Enterprise-Journal**

Thursday, Aug. 27, 1959  McCOMB ENTERPRISE-JOURNAL  7

## Charges of Subversion at Ole Miss Considered

By DOUGLAS STARR

JACKSON, Miss. (AP)—Mississippi's College Board ejected the press today as it met to consider charges that the University of Mississippi teaches integration, subversion and apostasy. The board, which always meets

$6 in money taken. may be retained on a yearly basis until age 70, when retirement is mandatory.

Chancellor Williams told the board the university has a chance to hire Prof. John Hanna, 70-year-old authority on security rights and farm cooperatives, who retired but left when the press was barred.

Williams attended the session

# GEORGE P. HEWES

George Hewes with friends and fellow Ole Miss alums.
L to R, Sherman Muths, Hewes, Hunter Gholson,
Howard McMillan, David Arnold, and Jim Ingram

George P. Hewes (BBA '50, LLB '54), a native of Jackson, was a 1950 graduate of the Ole Miss business school. After serving two years in the U.S. Marine Corps, Hewes returned to the campus and graduated from law school in 1954. While at Ole Miss, he was president of the M Club, law school, the YMCA, and was selected for the student Hall of Fame.

He practiced in the Jackson law firm of Brunini, Grantham, Grower & Hewes, where he was engaged in civil trial practice. He was president of the Young Lawyers Section of the Mississippi Bar and the Mississippi Bar Foundation. He was also elected a Fellow of the American College of Trial Lawyers and served as

Regent of that organization from 1984-1988. He also served for twelve years as a Mississippi Commissioner to the National Conference of Commissioners on Uniform State Laws.

In his community he served as president of the boards of Magnolia Speech School, New Stage Theater, Mississippi Symphony Orchestra, the Metropolitan YMCA, the Jackson Country Club and as campaign chairman of the United Way. He has also served as vestryman and warden of St. Andrews Episcopal Church and also served as chancellor of the Episcopal Diocese of Mississippi. He was a member of the board of directors of Trustmark National Bank.

Hewes was very active in alumni affairs at Ole Miss. He served as president of the Ole Miss Alumni Association, the Law Alumni Chapter, and The University of Mississippi Foundation. He received the Distinguished American Award of the Ole Miss chapter of the National Football Foundation. He served as co-chair of the Commitment to Excellence Campaign.

He was married to the late Helen Morrison (BA '54) of Vicksburg and they had three children, Jimmy Hewes and Russell Hewes of Jackson and Laura Hewes Bell of Atlanta.

George Hewes as president of the YMCA

School of Commerce and Business Administration, because of the State's failure to face the critical need for a building to accommodate the work of its 835 students and 49 faculty members. Despite this blow to morale and efficiency, the school achieved a measure of progress in certain fields."

The report went on to note: "At present, the departments are scattered in four separate buildings on the campus. At least one of these, Temporary Classroom Building A, is suited only for emergency use. The great service that the school is capable of contributing to business in the state would be made nearer realization were its quarters more in keeping with its potentialities."

H. Eugene Peery was hired in 1951. The familiar pose above is from the 1970s.

### Journalism Thrived Under Gerald Forbes

In 1951, the Department of Journalism instituted several new initiatives, including awarding the first master's degree by the department, hosting a successful Editor's Short Course, hosting a large Press Institute for high school students, conducting a series of advertising lectures, establishing a scholarship loan fund for women students, and taking a field trip to the *Clarion-Ledger*.

The first master's degree in journalism was awarded to Mr. Rudolph Gandy of Pine Bluff, Arkansas. Gandy's thesis focused on college public relations at Mississippi junior colleges.

Also, in 1951, the members of Lambda Sigma conferred an award of merit to Mr. Hodding Carter of the *Delta Democrat Times* (Carter won the 1946 Pulitzer prize for his editorials on social and economic injustice).

### Two Hats For Dunham

Dunham, in addition to serving as Dean of the school, continued to chair the accountancy program for the duration of his time at Ole Miss. In 1951, he hired H. Eugene Peery, who quickly developed a reputation as an outstanding teacher. Dunham once said that Peery was the best teacher on the faculty in the 1950s.

Though Dunham's first love was accounting, he fought for all departments in the school. In 1952, he instituted a series of "Business Talks" from businessmen who addressed specific problems faced by business owners and managers. According to Dunham, the average attendance for the talks "ranged from 75-100 students."

Dunham also promoted journalism (enrollment grew over fifty percent in the early 1950s), political science, the bureau of business research, the department of economics, among others. He championed for new personnel in marketing, management, and finance.

And, of course, he pled with the administration for a new building. "There continues to be a great need for a modern building designed and equipped for the teaching needs of the school," he wrote. "On a much smaller scale it is urged that asphalt tile be put on the floors of the classrooms in the Lyceum and that the old chairs in the classrooms be replaced."

Despite the deplorable conditions and tight budget, the School of Commerce and Business Administration produced remarkable graduates in the 1950s and 1960s.

# HENRY PARIS

MISS OLE MISS
CISSY WESTBROOK

COLONEL REBEL
HENRY PARIS

Henry Paris was born in Lexington, Mississippi, in 1930. Paris' father was a vice president in the Lewis Grocer Company. As a teenager, Paris spent his summer months working in the Lewis Grocer Company's vinegar plant in Durant.

After he graduated from Lexington High School, Paris enrolled in Ole Miss and majored in business administration. He was head cheerleader for three years. He was also a member of ODK. His senior year, he was selected to the Ole Miss Hall of Fame. And he was elected by his fellow students as Colonel Rebel.

After a two years in the Air Force, Paris returned to the Delta to work for the Lewis Grocer Company — with the understanding that the company would send him to work on an MBA at Michigan State University (MSU was one of only two schools that offered a course of study in food distribution).

He earned his MBA in 1955, graduating Magna Cum Laude.

Paris worked for Lewis in a number of capacities for more than two decades. Eventually, he moved up the corporate ladder and was named vice president.

## A Second Career in Banking

In 1975, Paris was appointed president of Planters Bank. His first order of business was to hire top-notch bankers — men and women who brought banking and finance savvy to the operation. Under Paris' guidance, the assets of Planters Bank increased five fold and his outside interest in the food and gas business thrived.

## A Life of Service

Paris served as president of the University of Mississippi foundation. He was a board member of Indianola Academy for 19 years. And he was active in building the Children's Cancer Clinic in Jackson.

Perhaps Paris' proudest accomplishment was partnering with Bill Yates to build the Paris-Yates Chapel at Ole Miss. "The chapel is for all denominations," Paris said.

Paris and his wife, Rose, have three children and nine grandchildren.

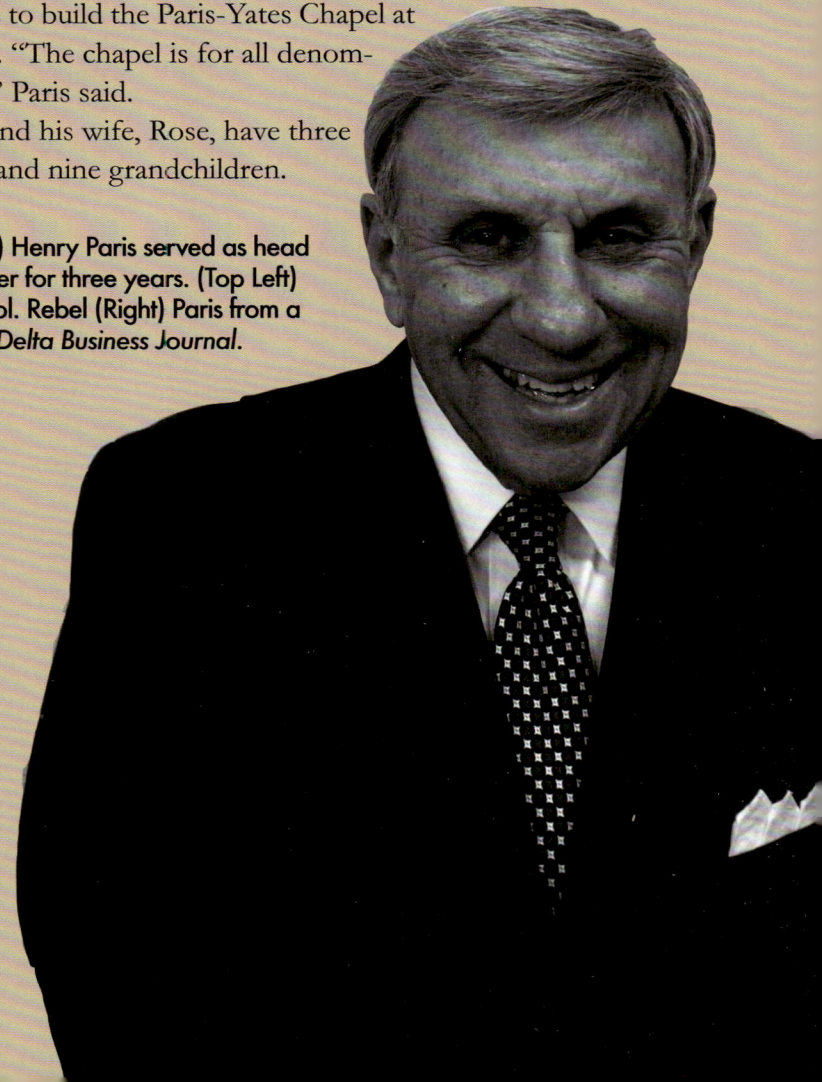

(Top Right) Henry Paris served as head cheerleader for three years. (Top Left) Paris as Col. Rebel (Right) Paris from a feature in *Delta Business Journal*.

## Early Politicians

In the 1950s, the school saw the birth of two politicians — Winfield Dunn and Brad Dye.

Dunn, from Meridian, Mississippi, met his future wife, Betty Prichard, in 1950 while he was campaigning for class president of the School of Commerce.

Dunn was no stranger to politics. He recounted, "My father Albert Dunn was a popular man in Meridian. He was frequently stopped on the street and drawn into conversations with friends. He would bring me into those conversations by introducing me and asking me to say something intelligent. He would put me on the spot like that with his friends and his purpose obviously was to find little inhibitions in me that could be released so I could be a spokesman."

Winfield Dunn from the 1950 annual. Dunn went on to be Governor of the State of Tennessee

Dunn's father was elected to Congress in 1935 and his family spent a year living in Washington D.C. Young Winfield chatted up people in the elevator of the D.C. apartment building where they lived. His neighbors would tip him just for a chance to listen to the boy's Mississippi accent.

Lifelong friend and political consultant Harry Wellford said, "Dunn just had a natural charm or magnetism that appealed to people. He's a very likeable person and has more personal charm than just about anybody I know. And I've known a lot of politicians in my lifetime."

Dunn won the presidency of the School of Commerce in 1950. It was to be a foreshadowing of a successful life in politics. In 1970, Dunn was elected governor of Tennessee (see profile on page 56).

A native of Charleston, Mississippi, Brad Dye arrived at Ole Miss in 1953. He quickly became involved in student govern-ment. First, he was elected Associated Student Body treasurer; the following year, Dye was elected president.

When Dye was ASB president, he explained, some students wanted access to the proceeds from the hamburgers and sandwiches sold in the dorms.. The funds had been directed toward athletics.

"So," Dye said, "I arranged for a meeting between Chancellor Williams and the protesting students." Williams listened to the students' arguments and rationale.

"Thank you all for coming," Chancellor Williams said, "and thank you, Mr. Dye, for organizing the meeting."

As Dye started to leave the Lyceum, Chancellor Williams said, "Mr. Dye, would you stay behind for a moment.'"

After all the other students left, Williams said, "Brad, sit down." Dye sat and the chancellor continued, "I don't know why, but when a football team is winning, your diploma is worth more, the legislature is more generous, and alumni give more. This is more prominent in Southern states. Brad, I'm not about to take any money from John Vaught."

Dye went on to have a wildly successful career in law and politics in Mississippi. He is the only elected official to have served twelve consecutive years as lieutenant governor of the state of Mississippi (see profile on page 72)

Brad Dye, Jr. as ASB Treasurer in 1956. Dye serves for twelve years as Mississippi's Lt. Governor.

## Bankers, Bankers, Bankers

The tenure of Clive Dunham saw no fewer than seven graduates who became bank founders, presidents, and CEOs.

Henry Paris (B.B.A 1952) came to Ole Miss from Lexington,

# W. EMMETT MARSTON, JR.

## 1952 • BBA BUSINESS ADMINISTRATION

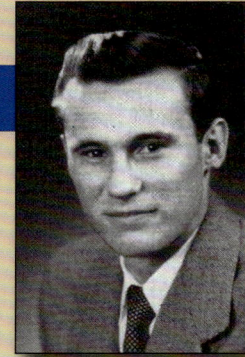

W. Emmett Marston, Jr., was a partner in the Memphis law firm of Martin, Tate, Morrow & Marston, P.C. He also was a key figure in the campaign to renovate the Alumni Center on the University's Oxford campus.

Named campaign chairman of the Alumni Center Challenge in 1992, Marston worked to obtain funds for the $2.3 million project.

Marston, who received a bachelor of business administration degree from Ole Miss in 1952 and a law degree with distinction in 1953, was appointed in 1989 by the Tennessee Supreme Court to chair its Commission on Continuing Legal Education and Specialization. He also was the state chair and life member of the Tennessee Fellows of the American Bar Foundation; chair of the American Bar Association's Standing Committee on Specialization; a member of the American Bar Association's House of Delegates; a life member of the Sixth Judicial Conference; a member of the American College of Real Estate Lawyers and the American College of Mortgage Attorneys; charter member of the Tennessee Bar Foundation; a member of the American Bar Association's Task Force on Applying Federal Legislation to Congress; chairman of the Board of Directors of Security Title Co. Inc. in Memphis; and a director of Mississippi Valley Title Insurance Co. of Jackson.

Marston also was a member of the Mississippi State Bar Association and the Tennessee Bar Association (he served as president). He was also president of the Memphis & Shelby County Bar Association and a director of the American Judicature Society.

For Ole Miss, Marston served as Alumni Association president, Law Alumni president, Lamar Order chairman, director of the University Foundation, and Athletic Committee member. He was the recipient of the Phi Delta Phi Outstanding Senior Award upon graduation from Law School. He also received the Law Alumnus of the Year Award in 1982. He served on the search committees for law school deans and was a representative to NCAA hearings for the University.

Henry Paris served as president of Planters Bank and Trust in Indianola.

Robert P. Guyton served as president and CEO of Bank South Corporation.

Frank R. Day served as chairman and CEO of Trustmark National Bank.

Howard McMillan served as president and CEO of Deposit Guaranty Bank.

Patrick McNarny served on the Federal Reserve Bank of Chicago.

Thomas Colbert serves as chairman of Community Bancshares of Mississippi.

Mississippi. He was cut from all the traditional fraternities because he was Jewish. Not to be deterred, Paris threw himself into the Ole Miss culture. He served as head cheerleader for three years, was inducted into ODK, and elected a member of the Hall of Fame. His senior year, he was elected Colonel Rebel by the student body. Paris went on to a successful career as an entrepreneur and president of Planters Bank and Trust in Indianola (profile on page 60).

Frank Rogers Day, a native of Aberdeen, obtained the bachelor of business administration degree from Ole Miss in 1953 and attended LSU's School of Banking. In addition to funding philanthropic endeavors through the Luckyday Foundation, he served as Chairman and CEO of Trustmark National Bank (profile on page 68).

Robert P. Guyton earned a B.B.A. (insurance) from Ole Miss in 1958 and an MBA from Harvard. He served as president and CEO of Bank South Corporation headquartered in Atlanta (profile on page 81).

Patrick McNarny received his M.B.A. in Business Administration (product management) in 1959. He served as president of National City Bank in Logansport, IN. McNarny also served on the Chicago Federal Reserve Board. He is the only Ole Miss graduate to serve as a member of the Fed (profile on page 82).

Howard J. McMillan, a native of Jackson, graduated from Ole miss in 1960 with a bachelor of business administration degree in banking and finance. He also graduated from the School of Banking of the South at Louisiana State University and the Harvard Business School's Advanced Management Program. He served as president and chief operating officer of Deposit Guaranty Corporation, as well as president of the American Bankers Association (profile on page 84).

Thomas Colbert received a B.B.A. with a major in banking and finance from the University of Mississippi in 1962 and graduated from the Graduate School of Banking of the South at Louisiana State University in 1966. In 1968, he accepted the position of chief executive officer of Farmers and Merchants Bank in Forest, making him the first graduate under the direction of the then recently formed Chair of Banking at Ole Miss to become CEO of a bank. In 1973, Colbert formed (and serves as chairman) of Community Bancshares of Mississippi Inc., a multibank holding company with locations in Mississippi, Alabama, Tennessee and Florida (profile on page 89).

Aubrey B. Patterson (B.B.A. '64) was chairman and chief executive officer of BancorpSouth, Inc., a $9.3 billion-asset bank

# CHARLES S. LOCKE

Charles Stanley Locke of Chicago, Ill., served as chairman of the board and chief executive officer of Morton Thiokol Inc., which started in 1848 as a salt marketer with the generations-old slogan "When it rains, it pours."

Morton Thiokol, a diversified-portfolio company, had sales of about $3 billion among its adhesives and coatings, table and ice-control salt, and aerospace units when Locke retired.

Locke earned a bachelor of business administration degree in 1952 and a master's of business administration in 1955, both from Ole Miss. After graduation, Locke sped through a series of jobs at Price Waterhouse & Co., Westvaco, A.E. Staley, Brown Co. and Allen Group. In 1975, he joined Morton Thiokol, then called Morton-Norwich, Inc., as chief financial officer. Five years later he moved into the CEO's office, where he reshaped the company.

By the time he took over, the company had diversified into chemicals and pharmaceuticals. Locke sold the pharmaceuticals division of the business in 1982 and soon after bought Thiokol Corp., a specialty chemicals business. When he bought Thiokol, he also bought into the aerospace industry. Morton Thiokol Inc.'s aerospace division designed and produced the booster rockets for NASA's space shuttle program (it also built MX missiles).

He led the company through a breakup, two mergers, and a catastrophic incident when the Space Shuttle Challenger exploded.

Locke retired in 1994 and resides in Chicago.

holding company whose subsidiary bank operated 234 banking locations in Mississippi, Tennessee, Alabama, Arkansas, Texas and Louisiana (profile on page 91).

## Technology and Communications

Under Dean Dunham's leadership, the School of Commerce and Business Administration also produced a number of leaders in the field of communications and technology.

John Palmer, (B.B.A., 1956; M.B.A., 1959), said, "Technology is all about making life easier. Every invention from fire to the big-screen TV has been about improving man's quality of life. If you deliver a service that makes life easier and better, people will use it; the service will sell." Palmer added, "Technology makes the world a better place, but when you forget for a moment about making money, achieving success, and outhustling the competition, it's important to remember that the true measure of a company's success is in its integrity and contribution to society."

Palmer, an early pioneer in the communications and cellular telephone business, founded two communications companies — Mobile Communications Corporation of America and SkyTel Communication. Both companies sold for over $1 billion (see profile on page 76).

Sherman Muths (B.B.A., 1954; L.L.B., 1960) has been a lawyer, entrepreneur, and philanthropist. In the early 1980s, Muths heard John Palmer talk about the potential value of cellular telephones — "if you could simply harness the wasted time of individuals

Aubrey Patterson served as chairman and CEO of Bancorp South.

Sherman Muths had early insights into the potential for cellular communications.

John Palmer sold two communications companies for over $1 billion each.

stuck commuting, nonproductively in the Los Angeles area" he said, "the value would be enormous."

Muths studied the burgeoning cellular communications business and in 1983 the FCC began choosing people to run cellular systems For the first 305 U.S. metropolitan areas, winners were based on competing applications (these required loads of paperwork and cost an average $250,000 to prepare). Then, congress authorized a lottery. Sherman Muths applied (individually or as part of an investment group) to all 428 rural areas. According to Muths, the application cost for each one was approximately $40. He and several investment groups won lotteries and were on their way to building (or selling) cellular telephone territories and licenses across the country (see profile on page 70).

Wade H. Creekmore, Jr (B.B.A., 1956; J.D., 1967) and James H. Creekmore (B.B.A., 1959, JD, 1968) were in the local and long distance telephone business until they too entered the FCC lottery for cellular telephone territory and licenses. Wade is president and Jimmy is vice president of Telapex Inc. (they are both directors of the company), the parent company of CSpire, the largest privately-held wireless provider in the United States (see profile on page 74).

Edward O. Fritts (1961) borrowed money from his mother to buy a down and out

Wade and Jimmy Creekmore are directors for the largest privately-owned wireless company in the U.S.

# JOHN H. GEARY

John H. "Jack" Geary is a native of Vicksburg, Miss., and a 1952 graduate of the School of Business at Ole Miss. While a student, he was president of the student body, president of Kappa Alpha Order and inducted into Omicron Delta Kappa and the student Hall of Fame.

After two years as first lieutenant in the U.S. Air Force, he worked for Mississippi Power & Light Co. in Jackson. A few years later, he entered the investment business with Equitable Securities Corp. (ESC), which later became the investment securities arm of American Express. Geary served as a senior vice president and a director of ESC. In 1971, he opened the first office in the Southeast for Paine Webber. He opened his own firm in 1978, which was merged with Morgan Keegan in 1998. Geary retired as a managing director of Morgan Keegan.

Geary has served as an officer and director of a number of organizations within the business, political, educational and religious communities of Mississippi. He was one of a small group in the late 1950s and early 1960s that reorganized and revitalized the Mississippi Republican Party. He served as membership chairman, as a member of the State Executive Committee, and he played a leadership role in most of the early statewide races. With others, he worked to develop a viable two-party system in Mississippi. He was the founding president of the Catholic Foundation of the Diocese of Jackson and served as member of the executive committee and chairman of the investment committee for more than 30 years.

Geary is a past president of the Ole Miss Alumni Association and a past president and former director of the UM Foundation. He also served as co-chairman of the university's first major gifts campaign in 1984 and was a director of the Business School Advisory Board and a longtime member of the Joint Committee on University Investments.

Geary is married to the former Shirley Hester. They have four married children and 12 grandchildren. All four children and two daughters-in-law attended Ole Miss. Geary and his wife are proud that three of their grandsons are current Ole Miss students.

Eddie Fritts served as chairman of the National Association of Broadcasters.

radio station in Indianola, Mississippi. After twenty years of hard work and acquisitors, he was elected president and CEO of the National Association of Broadcasters. His influence on legislation for television, cable, and satellite led to the conversion from analog to digital transmissions. **Fritts also helped secure the regulatory reform of radio and television in the 1995 Communications Act** (see profile on page 87).

James L. Barksdale (B.B.A., 1965) served as CEO of AT&T Wireless Services, following the merger of AT&T and McCaw Cellular Communications. He joined Netscape Communications in 1995, and as its president and CEO oversaw the release of the first major internet browser, the development of JavaScript and Mozilla, and a transaction with AOL valued at $10 billion (see profile on page 92).

### Dunham Gets Aggressive

Dunham was, by all accounts, kind and demure when dealing with students, faculty, staff, and alumni. However, by the mid-1950s, his frustration with the administration and legislature was reaching a boiling point.

His communications with the chancellor bordered on combative.

Excerpts from Dunham's notes and reports include —

■ "The needs of the school to those who are close to the situation are desperate."

■ "Can this state afford not to provide at least one outstanding

Jim Barksdale led Netscape as it changed the way the world browsed the internet.

school of business?"

■ "The implications in the Brewton report is that the School of Commerce and Business Administration is a school that can be run cheaply, simply because the one at the University of Mississippi is being run cheaply. Nothing could be further from the truth. The loss is to the State and its people."

■ "The faculty of the School comprises a group of men who in loyalty to their obligation, in willingness to work their hearts out at a difficult task, in goodwill, in attainment and ability cannot be equaled in any institution of higher education. The student body is superlatively good. Such men in such a cause merit better instruments to work with."

■ "The school has found ways of stretching its manpower to cover a 40 percent increase in teaching load. This has been done by eliminating peripheral courses and by increasing class size. This resort has been exhausted."

■ "Lovely as the old Lyceum is, the interior environment does not impart any suggestion of the dignity or value of the instruction that the student is receiving."

■ "Fine talent will continue to be lost to the State, and accreditation will be delayed until a more adequate, more attractive, and more comfortable physical plant can be obtained."

### More Growth and a Bond Issue

Enrollment in the School of Commerce and Business Administration continued to grow at a frenetic pace. By 1956, the school had become the second largest at the University of Mississippi, trailing only the College of Liberal Arts. The number of courses offered was six times the initial catalog in 1917. By 1956, four degrees were offered: a Bachelor of Business Administration, Bachelor of Public Administration, Bachelor of Science in Commerce, and Bachelor of Science in Journalism.

The Bureau of Business Research (along with faculty members

# FRANK ROGERS DAY

Frank Rogers Day was born in Aberdeen, Mississippi, attended the University of Mississippi, the Graduate School of Banking at Louisiana State University, and served as a 2nd Lieutenant in the U.S. Army in Augsburg, Germany.

Day began his banking career in 1958 with the First National Bank of Jackson, predecessor to Trustmark National Bank. He advanced through various positions over the years and in 1976 was named president of First Capital Corporation, holding company for First National Bank. In 1981, he was named chairman and CEO of First National Bank and retired as chairman of the board of Trustmark National Corporation in 1999. The bank experienced extraordinary growth under his leadership. He led in the acquisitions of fifteen financial institutions across Mississippi to make Trustmark the largest bank in the state. Assets increased fivefold from $1.3 billion to $6 billion, while earnings per share increased for seventeen straight years.

Day exemplified the life of a philanthropist. In 1978, he established the Luckyday Foundation to provide college scholarships for Mississippi residents. Luckyday scholarship programs provide support to hundreds of Mississippi residents each year. More than 3,500 students have received scholarship awards to offset the cost of college attendance. The Christine and Clarence Day Scholarship in the University of Mississippi School of Business is the largest business scholarship in the state.

The Luckyday Foundation joined with the Mississippi Bankers Association in 2001 to honor Mr. Day's legacy in banking by endowing the Frank R. Day/Mississippi Bankers Association Chair of Banking at the University of Mississippi, representing a major investment in the education of future bankers and ensuring the permanence and stability of the chair.

Frank Day died on December 9, 1999, from Lou Gehrig's disease.

Over 3,500 students have received scholarships through the Luckyday Foundation to offset the cost of going to college.

from economics) continued to publish periodicals and studies at an impressive clip.

The department of journalism thrived, in spite of its founding chair Gerald Forbes' resignation in July 1956. Jere Hoar joined the journalism faculty in 1956 and Samuel Talbert stepped in as chair. For the tenth year in a row, the department sponsored the Mississippi Scholastic Press Association meeting. Hundreds of high school students and journalists attended the conference. In 1956, Journalism students also started working for the University News Bureau. They contributed stories, photographs, illustrations, and interviews to the bureau. Between 1956-1958, students had written over 150 articles that had been published in newspapers and magazines.

In 1956, students in the department of political science initiated Governor J.P. Coleman into Pi Sigma Alpha, the national honorary society for political science students.

As early as 1957, students were being taught to use "computing machines" for bookkeeping, signaling the end of the old days of endless hours putting pen to paper in massive ledgers. Space had been allotted in the Lyceum to include an accounting laboratory, a statistics laboratory, a type-writing laboratory, an office laboratory, and a calculating machine laboratory.

Three huge developments in 1958 would forever change the course of the school. First, the legislature passed a resolution authorizing a bond issue to fund the building of a new facility to house the School of Commerce and Business Administration.

Second, the Mississippi Bankers Association funded a faculty position — a chair in banking. It was the first faculty position in university history to be funded by outside sources. Third, an appropriation for salary increases was received by the university. In his annual report to the chancellor in 1958, Dean Dunham expressed gratitude for all three.

Dunham put a great deal of effort into the design and construction of the new building. He wrote, "Shape, height, lighting, acoustical properties, ventilation, seating equipment, and classroom aids influence the capacity of the teacher to hold the attention of the students and to get them to think along with him."

Dunham could be seen carrying architectural renders and blueprints from 1958-1961.

A young accounting student from Sardis, Mississippi, James Davis, recalled the transition from the Lyceum to the new building to be christened Conner Hall in 1961.

"My first accounting class was in the Lyceum," David said. "We hadn't even noticed across the street that Conner Hall was coming out of the ground. My first intermediate accounting class was taught in the new building, so I was one of the last who had business classes in the Lyceum and one of the first to have them in Conner Hall."

Davis continued, "Getting Conner Hall was a major addition to this campus. Dr. Clive Dunham was dean, and he planned and he budgeted and it was probably the most economical building they ever built. Every square inch was useful. There were no ar-

Conner Hall opened in 1961 to great fanfare. It was one of the few buildings on campus with air conditioning.

# SHERMAN MUTHS, JR.

**1954 • BBA, BUSINESS ADMINISTRATION • GULFPORT, MISSISSIPPI**

Sherman Muths (BBA 54, LLB 60) practiced law in Gulfport, was a quietly successful businessman, and for more than 60 years served as one of Ole Miss' most dedicated and outspoken ambassadors.

Attorney Muths was a member of Harrison County, Mississippi and American bar associations, Mississippi Trial Lawyers Association and Association of Trial Lawyers of America. A fellow of Mississippi and American bar foundations, he was president of the Mississippi Junior Bar, Harrison County Bar and Mississippi Bar Foundation Board of Trustees. He also served as chairman of the State of Mississippi Judicial Nominating Committee, member of the Mississippi House of Representatives and member of the U.S. Gulf of Mexico Fishery Management Council.

Businessman Muths was a developer of downtown Gulfport property, vice president of Mississippi Coast Marine, Inc., and a former owner of a rural Illinois telephone system. He was president of the Gulfport Chamber of Commerce and chaired the Mississippi Commission on Marine Resources and the Board of Directors of the Mississippi Housing Finance Corporation. He founded the Gulfport Business Club and the Coast Wine Society, as well as Visions Gulf Coast, which studies race relations and seeks solutions. He also was also co-founder and owner of the Mississippi Sea Wolves, the state's first professional hockey team.

"Ambassador" Muths was president of the Ole Miss Alumni Association, president of the Law Alumni Chapter, chair of the Lamar Order, and president of the Gulf Coast Alumni Club. He also has been a member of the Ole Miss Loyalty Foundation since its inception, the Athletics Committee, Ole Miss Associates, Circle Society, University Foundation's Board of Directors, and Trent Lott Leadership Steering Committee.

As one alumnus put it, "No one loves Ole Miss better than Sherman. He has done about everything that can be done for the University." Another said, "You couldn't find many people who love Ole Miss more than Sherman does. He has shown that love and support through commitment of time, effort and money."

Sherman Muths in the early 1950s with Professor Wendell Trumbull.

Sherman and Celia Muths standing outside the apartment they occupied when Sherman was in law school.

Sherman Muths has given his time, effort, and resources to Ole Miss. One alum said, "He's done about everything that can be done for the university."

chitectural wonders that would cost a lot of money. There was no opulence in the building. It was down to business."

In 1960, a time-and-motion study laboratory was installed to teach students about production and personnel management.

Jimmy Davis in 1962. Davis took classes in the Lyceum as well as Conner Hall.

Time-motion studies involved testing how to lay out factory or other production floors to allow for the most efficient completion of tasks. Students would create miniatures using models of tables and other equipment to determine the most effective manufacturing flow. Though time-motion had been taught previously, this was the first time the study had a dedicated space, in response to rising popularity of factory design as a topic of study in the late 1950s.

The move to Conner Hall would provide even more space, and gradually shift more of that space toward ever more modern machines—particularly computers, which, at the time, were more like large pieces of furniture than the miniaturized machines of the modern day. Computing in the 1960s required a real commitment in terms of square footage.

With the rapid growth in enrollment, it appeared that Conner Hall would be completely full by the time it opened in 1961.

In the annual report prior to the move to Conner, Dunham wrote, "When this building was planned, it was believed that Journalism would be quartered with the rest of the School. This proved to be impossible. The Department of Journalism is to be in Brady Hall. This building is in deplorable condition, but relocating certain partitions, new floors, paint, new wiring, and new plumbing will make it usable for a few years, after which time perhaps a new building will materialize."

The physical separation of the journalism department would

# THE PURE ECONOMIC VALUE OF A HOUSEWIFE

Franklin Howard taught economics at Ole Miss in the 1959 fall semester and the 1960 spring semester. He was 32 at the time and was by far the youngest prof I had in undergraduate school. He did undergrad studies at the University of Connecticut and graduate work at Connecticut and the University of Virginia. Professor Howard was energetic, of average height, had sandy hair, and usually wore a cord jacket with leather elbows. He had a ruddy complexion and drank with his students.

He once devoted a class hour to a lecture on the pure economic value of a housewife, using his own wife and children as the example. He had at least three young children, some of whom were in school and some younger. Mrs. Howard was a beautiful young woman, from Austria, as I recall. He theorized the scene of the death of Mrs. Howard. What if he had to go into the open market to hire people to perform the tasks which were previously taken care of by Mrs. Howard?

He then went to the blackboard and began writing down names and numbers, lecturing all the while.

| Job Description | Weekly Salary |
|---|---|
| Cook | $28 |
| Laundress | $26 |
| Cleaning lady | $30 |
| Caretaker of children | $100 |
| Transportation | $26 |
| Prostitute | $22 |
| **Total per week** | **$232** |

Of course, the loving nurture provided by a mother is priceless and irreplaceable. Nonetheless, Frank calculated that the annual pure economic value of a housewife in 1959/1960 was approximately $12,048

Frank was the best undergrad professor I ever had. He died in Vicksburg in 2012.

**Submitted by Neil White, Jr.**
*BBA 1961, major in Economic Analysis, Ole Miss*
*LLB 1963, Ole Miss*

**Editor's Note:** Dean Ken Cyree calculated that $12,048 in 1959 is equal to $101,324.51 in 2017 dollars

# HON. BRAD J. DYE, JR.

**1956 • BBA, BUSINESS ADMINISTRATION • 1959 LLB, LAW**

vocational-technical education and universities.

Dye served eleven years on the board of the Federal Home Loan Bank of Dallas. Prior to 1980, he was elected as a state representative, state senator, and state treasurer. He was chairman of the State Retirement Board, executive director of the State Agricultural and Industrial Board (now the Mississippi Development Authority), and commissioner of the Workmen's Compensation Commission.

As a student, Dye was named to the Ole Miss Hall of Fame and served as treasurer and then president of the Associated Student Body. Twice president of Pi Kappa Alpha fraternity, he chaired the group's National Convention after graduating from Ole Miss.

Dye is charter president of the UM Business Alumni Association, a life member of the Ole Miss Alumni Association and a member of the UMAA Foundation.

Dye and his wife, Donna, are members of Christ United Methodist Church in Jackson. They have three sons, Hamp, Ford, and Rick, and five grandchildren. Dye, his sons, and daughters-in-law together hold ten degrees from The University of Mississippi.

Brad J. Dye Jr. (BBA 56, LLB 59) practiced with Danks, Dye, Mills & Pittman in Ridgeland, Mississippi.

Dye was lieutenant governor of Mississippi for three terms, from 1980 to 1992, the only person in state history to hold that position for twelve consecutive years. He presided over the passage of legislation of immense importance, including the Education Reform Act (1982), the creation of a statewide personnel system, the creation of the Institute of Technology Development, economic development acts (1989) and the state's first comprehensive four-lane highway program (1987). He was also known for his strong support of The University of Mississippi Medical Center, the Department of Mental Health, Archives and History,

Brad Dye (second from left) pictured with the ASB Cabinet from 1955.

prove, ultimately, to be the first step toward a more permanent dissolution between the department and the school.

### A New Home; A New Hire

In 1961, Conner Hall opened. Enrollment exploded to nearly 1,100 (Conner Hall was one of the few buildings on campus that had air conditioning). Students, faculty, staff, alumni, and visiting business men and women were enamored with the facility.

A new faculty member was also hired. Dr. Bennie McNew, a recent Ph.D. graduate of the University of Texas, would join the

James Meredith in 1962 being escorted by federal agents and a member of the national guard in front of Conner Hall.

faculty to fill the Chair of Banking — the chair that was fully funded by the Mississippi Bankers Association.

There was much cause for celebration from faculty, students, staff, and administration, but the fervor and enthusiasm surrounding this new era would soon be overshadowed.

### Integration

Meredith was not the first black student to attempt the feat of entering Ole Miss — only the first to succeed. So great were the lengths Mississippi politicians were willing to go to prevent integration, Clennon King, who applied for admission in 1958, was committed by the state "lunacy panel" to Whitfield asylum.

Dunham's tenure coincided with the most heated years of the Civil Rights Movement, which famously had one of its defining moments right in front of the Lyceum with the admission of James Meredith as the university's first black student. The riots that accompanied that event, as well as the nearly two-year legal and social battle between Meredith, the NAACP, Governor Ross Barnett, and President John F. Kennedy, made Ole Miss a topic of national discussion.

### An evolving purpose

In addition to growing in size, the business school grew its purpose to meet the changing times, in response not only to the social upheaval happening all over the United States but to the advent of new technology that would forever change the business world.

Demographics were shifting as well. Women had been a part of the school dating back nearly to its inception, but had been slow in growing their numbers. By the end of Dunham's tenure, the female portion of the student body had risen to fifteen percent, still well short of the roughly thirty-five percent of 2017, but a significant milestone nonetheless.

Even more important than the numbers of women enrolling was their changing role, both as business students and as career women post-graduation. Secretarial Science was still by far the most popular course of study for women in the 50s and 60s, but by the end of Dunham's tenure the opportunities for female students were beginning to open up, the first wave of what would

# WADE & JAMES CREEKMORE

**WADE 1956 BBA; 1967 JD, LAW ■ JAMES 1959 BBA; 1968 JD, LAW**

In 1947, Wade H. Creekmore, Sr. and his cousin, Edward, acquired a small telephone company in Calhoun County. Wade, Sr.'s sons – Jimmy and Wade, Jr. – joined the family business after graduation from Ole Miss.

In 1959, the family launched Delta Telephone Company and in 1960 the Franklin Telephone Company. Jimmy managed the Louise-based Delta Telephone Company; Wade, Jr. ran the Meadville-based Franklin Telephone Company. For the next quarter century the Creekmores managed these rural telephone exchanges in several Mississippi counties – a fact that would ultimately prove crucial to the future of the company.

In 1988, the Creekmores stepped into the yet-to-be-proven mobile telephone market. They formed Cellular South and the company started with a small retail office in Gulfport, Mississippi.

In fewer than five years after the FCC began awarding licenses in the wireless industry, Cellular South had acquired several and was positioned to implement the new wireless technology.

Over the last quarter century, Cellular South (later rebranded as CSpire) has expanded in tandem with the astonishing growth of the wireless industry. The company has led the industry with innovative voice and data services. And the Creekmores continue their commitment to provide the same advanced services in rural areas that are available in metropolitan areas.

Community service is a top priority and a core value for CSpire. The company established the CSpire Foundation, an organization that has donated more than $2 million to Mississippi's eight public universities for scholarships and endowments. CSpire also sponsors awards for the top Mississippi collegiate athlete in football, basketball, and baseball.

Since 1999, CSpire has invested more than $700 million in network infrastructure. The company is the largest privately held wireless provider in the United States. Not bad for a family business that started with a rural phone exchange in Calhoun County.

> **CSpire is the largest privately-held wireless provider in the United States.**

be a true revolution in the decades to come.

During this era, a female Ole Miss graduate earned a spot as a principal partner at one of the largest CPA firms in New York City. She was not the only woman from Ole Miss securing high-ranking positions formerly open only to men.

Perhaps even more significant was the enrollment in the fall of 1965 of Ernest Watson of Moss Point, Mississippi, and Joyce O'Neal Jones of Jackson, Mississippi. Watson and Jones were the first two African-American students to enroll and claim majors in business.

Ernest Watson of Moss Point (left) and Joyce O'Neal Jones of Jackson (right) enrolled as freshmen in the school of business in 1965. Prior to their enrollment, only two black students had been admitted to Ole Miss.

**A broad curriculum**

Despite the modernization and social reform that was happening in the late 1950s and early 1960s, the curriculum during Dunham's tenure was still a far cry from what one would expect in a modern business school. A much broader scope of subjects fell under the purview of what was known starting in 1961 as the School of Business and Government. The coming decades would see these, as well as more closely-related fields like accountancy, branch off to form their own schools.

The 1950 catalog (the year Dunham took over as dean) stated that the goal of the school was to serve three distinct groups of students:

"(Those who) look forward to careers in various fields of business, including accountancy, banking, business education, insurance, merchandising, industrial management, newspaper management, office management, personnel management, and secretarial science.

The students who look forward to careers in public administration

The business firms, community groups, and public agencies of Mississippi, which need appropriate technical guidance from a university staff of specialists in business and public administration."

The courses offered provide a glimpse into the very different world that was the business curriculum at the time — some with a level of specificity that speaks to what a different world the mid-century business graduates were entering from that of today's. Courses included:

- Rail Transportation
- Motor, Water, Air Transportation
- Business Opportunity in Mississippi
- Public Utilities
- Resources of Latin America
- Timber Economics
- Factory Planning and Layout
- Fire, Marine, and Inland Marine Insurance
- Management of the Weekly Newspaper
- News Photography
- Public Opinion and the Press
- Elementary and Advanced Typewriting

# HON. JOHN N. PALMER

O n November 9, 2001, Corinth native John Palmer was sworn in as ambassador to Portugal. Prior to being appointed as ambassador by President George W. Bush, Palmers list of accomplishments were nothing short of extraordinary.

Palmer founded two telecommunications companies — each eventually sold for over $1 billion.

He was co-founder of Northminster Baptist Church in Jackson. He was also the founder of The MIND Center at UMMC. He served as chairman of the trustees of the National Symphony Orchestra.

Palmer sat on the Board of Directors of three New York Stock Exchange companies – Entergy, EastGroup, and AmSouth. He served as second president of CTIA, a group that represents the U.S. wireless industry. And he was president-elect of the Mississippi Economic Council, though he resigned to go Portugal for ambassadorial appointment.

Palmer was also chairman of Gulf-South Capital, Inc. in Jackson, Mississippi, and served as the chairman of SkyTel from 1989 until its sale to MCI WorldCom in 1999 for $1.3 billion. He was appointed by President Bush to sit on the President's Export Council as a Private Sector Advisor to the Secretary of Commerce and by President Reagan as the Private Sector Trade Advisor to the Office of the U.S. Trade Representative.

In addition to starting his own companies, Palmer is a quiet angel investor for entrepreneurs in the region. His seed money has catapulted many technology companies to the next level.

"John Palmer is a good citizen, as well as a true pioneer in the telecommunications industry," U. S. Senator Trent Lott said. "He's a real innovator. He takes risks; he moves into areas where others have feared to tread, and it's made him a very successful businessman.

U.S. Senator Thad Cochran added that Palmer's success "gave us a deep sense of confidence in the state."

Palmer is a director of The University of Mississippi Foundation and led in the creation of the Center for Telecommunications and the Mobile Communications Corporation of America Fellowship and Assistantship Program. The fellowships and assistantships were created with a $1 million gift from the corporation and was designed to enhance the quality of the Ole Miss MBA program.

He also was a primary donor for the Palmer-Salloum Tennis Center.

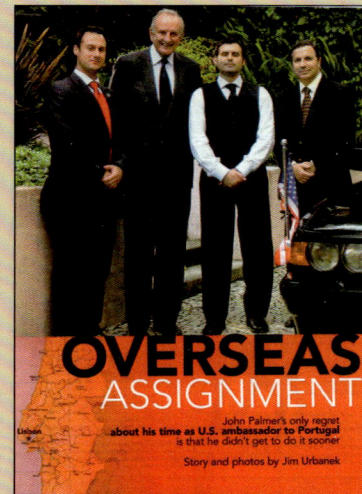

- Elementary and Advanced Shorthand
- Dictation and Transcription
- Municipal Government and Administration

In 1950-1965, 19 courses of study were offered:

- Accountancy
- Advertising
- Banking and Finance
- Business Education
- General Business Concentration
- Secretarial Science Concentration
- Combined Curriculum in Accountancy and Law
- Combined Curriculum in Business and Law
- Combined Curriculum in Public Administration and Law
- General Business
- Industrial Management
- Insurance
- Journalism
- Marketing
- Office Management
- Personnel Management
- Public Administration
- Secretarial Science
- Statistics

The 19 courses of study offered (as opposed to the 11 offered in 2017), reflect a period in which the idea of what constituted "business" was much broader than it is today. The list was surprisingly similar to that of the very first 1920 School of Commerce catalog.

The end of the Dunham era, however, coincided with the beginning of a decades-long restructuring of the curriculum and the sharpening of the school's focus as it adapted to changes in culture and technology.

**A virtuous cycle**

It is important to note that the growth of the business school during the 1950s and 1960s was not merely in size. The increase in the quality of the programs offered was tremendous as well. Dean Dunham noted in an interview with the *Oxford Eagle* in 1964 that the success the school enjoyed was the result of attracting better students. Those students built up the school's reputation and, in turn, brought ever-better human resources to Oxford.

Around 90 percent of the faculty at the time held degrees from top-tier business schools, including Harvard, Northwestern, and Columbia. Of that 90 percent, more than half were native Mississippians who returned home, often making the same personal financial sacrifice that Dunham made when he committed himself to Ole Miss.

And that increase in the quality of instruction not only attracted more qualified students, it produced more qualified graduates. Those graduates, in large numbers, stayed to work and apply their talents in Mississippi, making the business school an invaluable resource to a state that badly needed it.

Even through all the growth and change, some things stayed the same — basic tuition in 1950 was $80 per semester. In 1965, it was $79.50.

**An Eloquent Goodbye
and One Final Act**

Dunham had been a fixture in the School of Commerce since 1937. The period of his deanship, from 1950 to 1965, saw five Mississippi governors and four United States presidents come and go, including John F. Kennedy, who would be assassinated just over a year after forcing Meredith's admission to the university.

# TOM PAPA

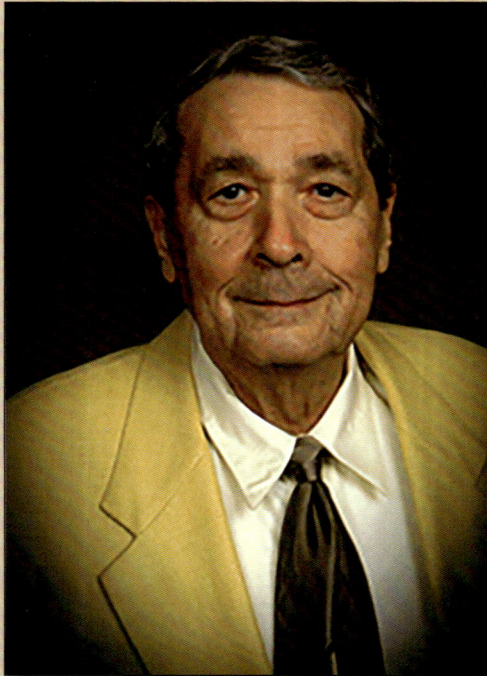

Tom Papa was instrumental in establishing the Gertrude C. Ford Foundation. The group has given Ole Miss millions of dollars.

Tom Papa was born and raised in Helena, Arkansas. He graduated high school from Subiaco Academy in May 1947 and joined the United States Armed Forces, where he proudly served in the Navy. He went on to attend the University of Mississippi where he received a bachelor of business administration. While at Ole Miss, Papa was an active member of Kappa Sigma Fraternity. Tom is often heard saying that some of the fondest memories he has are from his time spent as an undergraduate at Ole Miss.

After graduation, Papa returned to Jackson, to work for the Internal Revenue Service. Shortly thereafter he began his private practice accounting career at Touche Ross & Co from where he later retired. Upon retirement, Papa helped form the Gertrude C. Ford Foundation where he served as president for many years. In 1998, the Ford Foundation awarded The University of Mississippi $20 million to design and build the Gertrude C. Ford Center for the Performing Arts on the Oxford campus. Through his work at the Foundation, Papa has been instrumental in the foundation's support of the university, including gifts to the new state of the art science building and the UMMC Mind Center.

He lives in Jackson, MS with his wife, Gayle. He is the father of two children and proud grandfather of four.

The beginnings of the space race and perhaps the most turbulent period of the Cold War took place as well, culminating in the Cuban Missile Crisis in 1962.

In reflecting on his tenure at Ole Miss, Dunham paraphrased the remarks of a noted college president in his final report to Chancellor Williams:

"What a man ought never to forget with regard to a college is that it is a nursery of principle and of honor . . . I cannot admit that a man establishes his right to call himself a college graduate by showing me his diploma. The only way he can prove it is by showing that his eyes are lifted to some horizon which other men less instructed than he have not been privileged to see. Unless he carries freight of the spirit, he has not been bred where spirits are bred . . . Students are in college in order to enable the world to live more amply, with greater vision, with a finer spirit of hope and achievement. They are there to enrich the world, and they impoverish themselves if they forget the errand."

In 1965, Jimmy Davis (B.B.A., 1962; M.A., 1963) was visiting his parents after a long tax season working for Arthur Andersen in their Houston, Texas, office.

Clive Dunham's official portrait

"I was visiting friends and faculty at Ole Miss, including my former professor J.D. Holmes," Davis said. "Holmes said, 'Jimmy, I'm taking a leave of absence next year. Why don't you apply for this job?' I asked, 'and teach!?' He said, 'Yes!' I had never thought of such a thing as an academic career, but that very afternoon I went down to Dean Dunham's office, and I said, 'Mr. Dunham, Mr. Holmes tells me he's leaving and he thinks I should apply for this job.' Dean Dunham looked across his desk and said, 'We just might have a place for you.'"

Later that year, Chancellor Williams asked Dean Dunham to step down. Rather than stay on as a professor, Dunham decided to leave the university.

Davis recounted a conversation from the summer of 1965. "Dean Dunham and I talked on the phone numerous times working out details of my hiring. On one of those phone calls during the summer, Dean Dunham said, 'Now Jimmy, I will not be here. I have resigned my position as dean, and I will be teaching this fall at my alma mater, University of Illinois.'"

When Dunham hired James Davis as a professor of accountancy, it was his last act as dean at Ole Miss.

# RAYMOND BROWN

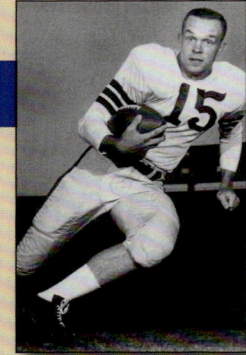

Raymond Brown (BBA '58, LLB '62) enrolled at Ole Miss in 1954 after earning a football scholarship. He also played baseball and helped the Rebels earn Southeastern Conference titles in both sports. As a quarterback, Brown was named SEC passing leader in 1956 and SEC total offense leader and All-SEC in 1957 as well as Most Valuable Player in the 1958 Sugar Bowl victory over Texas. In baseball, he played on the 1956 College World Series Team.

A member of the M-Club and vice president of Sigma Chi fraternity, Brown served as president of the School of Commerce and Business Administration in 1957-1958. He was named to the undergrad Hall of Fame and to Omicron Delta Kappa.

After graduating, Brown was signed by the Baltimore Colts and played on the team's 1958 and 1959 world championship teams.

During his three years in professional football, Brown enrolled in law school at The University of Maryland, but finished his law degree at Ole Miss, after serving as editor and business manager for the Mississippi Law Journal. He was then appointed to clerk for U.S. Supreme Court Justice Tom C. Clark, the first such clerkship for an Ole Miss Law School graduate.

Brown, an instrument-rated pilot, served as president of Brown, Watt & Buchanan law firm in Pascagoula. He has served as president of the Mississippi Bar Association, president of the Bar's Young Lawyers' Association, chair of the Southern Conference of Bar Presidents, and Mississippi chair of the American College of Trial Lawyers.

A former UM Foundation board member, Brown has served as president of both the M-Club and Law Alumni Chapters. He is a member of the Lamar Order and the Chancellor's Trust and has served several terms on the Alumni Association board of directors, as president in 1991-92.

## SUGAR BOWL CHAMPIONS

With a clarity of purpose, Ole Miss flattened Texas 39-7 in the 24th annual Sugar Bowl classic. It was a date —January 1, 1958—the Rebels will long remember, as will the stunned Longhorns.

Quarterback Ray Brown, the game's outstanding player by unanimous press box choice, highlighted proceedings when he ran 92 yards from punt formation for his second touchdown of the chilled afternoon. He counted the opening marker from a yard out, and passed for the second, a three-yard play, to end Don Williams.

The Rebs led 6-0 at the quarter, 19-0 at the half and 26-0 after three periods of play. The third touchdown was entered by HB Kent Lovelace on a nine-yard tour at left end. The fourth marker went to QB Bobby Franklin on a four-yard turn of the same left flank.

The Longhorns had scored midway the final quarter for 26-7 and had the Rebs, backed up by penalties, in real trouble when Brown, scheduling a punt, saw that the kick would be blocked. He set sail to his port side, drew a terrific block from FB Charlie Flowers, was in the clear and under full convoy at midfield. Afoot, he traveled 103 yards. The official yardage was 92 for the longest run ever in a Sugar Bowl game.

Raymond Brown, quarterback, received the Warren V. Miller Memorial Trophy as outstanding player in the Sugar Bowl.

# ROBERT P. GUYTON

Robert P. Guyton of Atlanta was president and chief executive officer of Bank South Corporation. Under his leadership, the bank tripled in size and as of 1987 had $3.7 billion in assets. *Forbes* magazine listed Bank South as one of 300 "Up and Coming" companies in the country, and *Business Week* included it among its 1,000 most-valuable companies.

Guyton earned his BBA degree from Ole Miss in 1958 and his MBA degree from Harvard.

Guyton's banking career began with the Bank of Blue Mountain, where he worked during summers while he was in school. He then moved to Deposit Guaranty National Bank in Jackson, which he joined in 1960. From there, he joined Irving Trust Company of New York during the summers of 1964 and 1965, and finally he settled with the National Bank of Georgia in Atlanta. He served as the president and member of the bank's board of directors form 1971 to 1974. At age 37, Guyton was elected president of First Mississippi National Bank.

Guyton was a director of First Mississippi Corporation, Business Council of Georgia, Atlanta Arts Alliance, and the High Museum of Art. He was a director and treasurer of Central Atlanta Progress, directed the Atlanta Chamber of Commerce's $3.7 million New Forward Atlanta campaign, and chaired the $7.5 million Westminster Schools campaign.

Guyton was vice president of the Georgia Bankers Political Action Committee, the Young Presidents' Organization, Association of Reserve City Bankers, Chief Executive Organization, and World Business Council. He was named the 1968 Mississippi Outstanding Young Man of the Year, was the 1969 recipient of the Junior Chamber of Commerce Distinguished Service Award, and in 1987, he was inducted into the Ole Miss Alumni Association Hall of Fame.

Guyton is married to the former Katherine Cole Taylor of New Albany, and they have two sons.

# PATRICK MCNARNY

Pat McNarny served as area president of National City Bank in Logansport, Indiana. But he also carries the outstanding distinction of being the only bank president in the Ole Miss Alumni Association who has served on the Chicago Federal Reserve Board.

McNarny earned his bachelor of business administration degree in 1958 and his master of business administration degree in 1959, both from the University of Mississippi. He went on to earn his doctor of jurisprudence degree in 1966 from the Indiana University School of Law-Indianapolis.

In June 1958, McNarny was commissioned as a 2nd lieutenant is the U.S. Army. After ten years of service, he was release with the reserve rank of captain.

McNarny had a steady climb to the top. His career quickly escalated from starting in 1961 as assistant cashier at Indiana National Bank in Indianapolis to vice president of the First Trust and Savings Bank in Kankakee, Illinois, in 1968. He joined the Beverly Bank of Chicago in 1971 as vice president, and only a year later he was hired as senior vice president, secretary, and member of the board of directors of First Illinois Corp. and the First National Bank and Trust Co. of Evanston, Illinois. In 1972, he became chairman of the board, president, and chief executive officer of the same bank – a position he held until 1993. McNarny has been a member of five bar associations and was admitted to practice law in Indiana and Illinois. He was also a member of the American Bankers Association Council and was the chairman of the board of directors for the Indiana Bankers Association.

McNarny was a member of Phi Delta Phi at Indiana University and in 1993 was inducted into the Ole Miss Alumni Association Hall of Fame. He has also been a member of Omicron Delta Kappa and Delta Sigma Phi.

McNarny has held numerous faculty positions at universities in Illinois, Indiana, and Wisconsin and has had a number of articles published in business journals and banking bulletins. He also served as an Otho Smith Fellow Guest Lecturer at the University of Mississippi. He has served on nine different boards of directors, and he is an active member of professional organizations and fraternal associations. He has served as an elder, a trustee, and a deacon in the Presbyterian Church.

> McNarny is the only bank president in the Ole Miss Alumni Association who has served on the Chicago Federal Reserve Board.

# JIMMY HILL

**1960 • BBA, BUSINESS ADMINISTRATION • RIPLEY, MISSISSIPPI**

Jimmy L. Hill retired in 2000 as treasurer of Hill Brothers Construction Company, Inc., and president of Hill Brothers Leasing Company, Inc. He previously served with the Biltrite Corporation as plant comptroller. He has served as board member and treasurer of the Tippah County Good Samaritan Center. In addition, Hill serves as a member of the board of directors of the Tippah County Hospital.

Hill Brothers Construction Company worked on such projects as expanding Highway 49 to a four-lane highway and building a portion of the Mississippi River levee.

Hill was the founding president of the Tippah County Ole Miss Club and also served as director and treasurer. He, among others, has helped the club attain the largest endowment among all alumni club scholarship endowments. Hill was instrumental in making possible the memorial garden outside Paris-Yates Chapel on the Ole Miss campus, which is dedicated to remembering former Ole Miss students who have lost their lives.

Hill helped establish a program that allows high school seniors from Tippah County to take trips to the university each fall. The seniors meet with representatives from admissions, financial aid, and housing, and are given a campus tour. Tippah County enrollment at Ole Miss has increased more than 100 percent since the scholarship program began.

Hill was awarded the Ole Miss Alumni Association Alumni Service Award in 2005. He and his wife, Beth, have three sons, Jimmy Hill, Jr.; Rev. Steven Hill; and Dr. Thomas G. Hill, all of whom graduated from or attended Ole Miss.

> Jimmy helped establish a program that allows high school seniors from Tippah County to make visits to Ole Miss each fall to meet with representatives from admissions, financial aid, and housing.

# HOWARD L. MCMILLAN, JR.

## 1960 • BBA, BUSINESS ADMINISTRATION • JACKSON, MISSISSIPPI

Howard McMillan (third from left) with fellow Ole Miss and business school alums

Howard Lamar McMillan, Jr. of Jackson graduated from the University of Mississippi in 1960 with a bachelor of business administration degree in banking and finance. He also graduated from the School of Banking of the South Louisiana State University and the Harvard Business School's Advanced Management Program.

Upon his graduation, McMillan found employment with Deposit Guaranty National Bank, a company he would go on to work for nearly four decades. He became vice president of the Commercial Loan Department in 1967, a senior vice president in 1975, and executive vice president in 1977. By the time of his retirement in 1998, he was president and chief operating officer. The scope of McMillan's reputation as a banker was national. Perhaps his most impressive accomplishment was being chosen, in 1994, to serve a term as the president of the American Banking Association. Harry M. Walker, then the president and chief operating officer of Trustmark National Bank, applauded the decision.

"We can all be proud that a Mississippian has been chosen to represent… the state in this important position," said Walker. "He is well qualified to lead the ABA in the coming year."

The ABA's membership represents about 90 percent of the commercial banking industry's total assets.

In addition to his passion for business, McMillan served his various communities, holding a stunning array of volunteer positions for Jackson, the state of Mississippi, and Ole Miss. He served as president of the Ole Miss Alumni Association and was a member of the University of Mississippi Foundation executive committee.

In 2006, McMillan brought his years of experience to academia, accepting a position as dean of the Else School of Management at Millsaps College. Then-president Frances Lucas heralded his arrival with enthusiasm.

"His expertise in business, leadership, and community support will enrich the education of hundreds of future leaders," said Lucas.

When Lucas stepped down as college president in 2009, McMillan was tapped to serve a year as acting president while a national search was conducted.

"Howard McMillan is a dynamic leader and a wonderful mentor to many people, including me," said Lucas.

# JOHN WARNER ALFORD, JR

1960 • BBA; 1966, MA • MCCOMB, MISSISSIPPI

McComb native Warner Alford, Jr. was already destined for Ole Miss fame when he finished his college career in 1960. He was co-captain of that year's undefeated national champion team. That would have been enough to make him a campus sports legend. It was only the beginning, however, of a life-long relationship with the university.

Alford would go on to be a coach, athletic director, and, later, executive director of the alumni association in a career that included work not only in the college sports world but also in business.

During Alford's years as athletics director, which ran from 1978 to 1994, Ole Miss experienced tremendous growth in both facilities and fundraising. Alford also helped expand athletic opportunities for both men and women at the university during this period, increasing the number of varsity sports from eight to 15. He was largely credited with bringing women's sports greater prominence, especially the young women's basketball team, whom he hired Van Chancellor to coach.

"Nobody cares more about the student-athlete than Warner Alford," said Chancellor. "Nobody. People would not believe all of what he's done to make sure every kid who comes to play a sport here is given every opportunity, every encouragement possible to graduate."

From 1994-99, he worked as a vice president for Mississippi Diversified Corporation, which provides insurance and related products to more than 300 auto dealers. In 1999, he was named athletics director for The University of Louisiana-Monroe and served in that position until he was named vice president and national sales manager of Assurant Group's Indirect Auto in 2001. Alford returned to Ole Miss and held positions as executive assistant for development for the UM Foundation and coordinator of external programs for the Lott Leadership Institute; he also worked with the Ole Miss First scholars program.

He was always a welcome face to see stepping into positions of responsibility on campus, which is why he was greeted back to helm the alumni association.

"We were looking for someone with the deep friendships and close associations already in place who could fill the void left by Herb (Dewees') retirement and add to an already superior staff," said Mary Sharp Rayner, president of the alumni association and chair of the 19-member search committee that recommended Alford. "It was a unanimous decision." Alford led the association during the $21 million expansion of The Inn at Ole Miss.

He was inducted into the M-Club Alumni Hall of Fame in 1999 and the Mississippi Sports Hall of Fame in 2003.

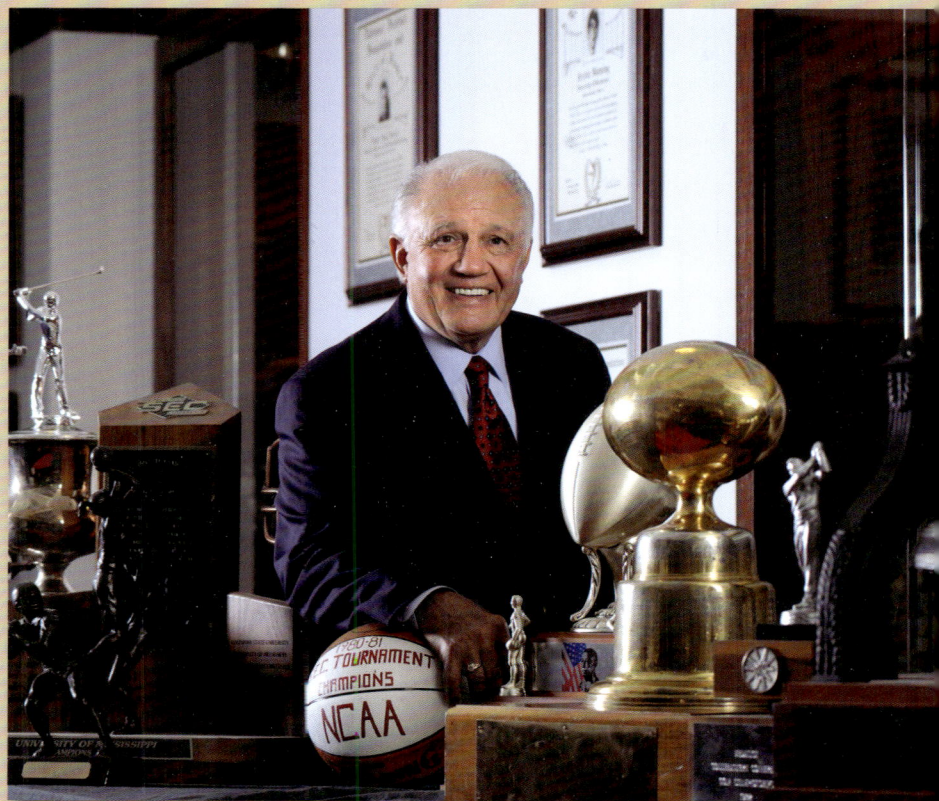

# CAROLE LYNN MEADOWS

## 1960 • BSC; 1964 MB ED • LUCEDALE, MISSISSIPPI

Carole Lynn Meadows of Gulfport earned a B.S. and a master's degree in business education from the University of Mississippi. She has more than 25 years of teaching experience at Mississippi Gulf Coast Community College. She also worked for five years as an investment broker with JC Bradford.

Meadows is co-founder of the Lynn Meadows Discovery Center, the first children's museum in Mississippi, and serves as chair of the building committee for the forthcoming WINGS Children's Performing Arts and Education facility at the Discovery Center. She was awarded the Rotary International Paul Harris Fellow Award in recognition of her work for children.

Such an educational pursuit is fitting for a woman who is by profession a teacher. Her career includes classrooms at the high school and collegiate levels, and five years as a stock broker. She also teaches at church. But for Meadows, teaching is more a calling than a job. "Whether teaching a Sunday School class of 5-year-olds or adults, students at the community college or women in investment clubs, I am happy. There is such joy in helping someone learn and grow."

A native of Lucedale, Meadows was elected the first woman president of the Ole Miss Alumni Association in 1994 and was a 1999 inductee into The University of Mississippi Alumni Hall of Fame. She was a member of the university search committees for the vice chancellor for student affairs, athletic director, and chancellor. She served as annual fund chair for four years and currently serves as chair of the Alumni and Friends of The Inn at Ole Miss Campaign.

Her former community service includes serving as president of the Gulfport chapter of the National Association of Junior Auxiliaries, the first woman executive committee member for the Gulfport Chamber of Commerce, PTA president, co-chair of the American Cancer Tennis Tournament, and chair of the Mother's March for the Harrison County March of Dimes.

Meadows served as secretary of the executive committee of the Gulfport Main Street Association, board member of the Gulf Coast Business Council, and board member of Mississippi Council on Economic Education.

# EDWARD O. FRITTS

Edward O. "Eddie" Fritts was first elected as National Association of Broadcasters president and chief executive officer in 1982. Since then, he has grown the NAB into one of the most respected and effective lobbying organizations in the country. Fritts' former ownership of a mid-south radio station group and his prior service on the NAB board have enhanced his ability to forward a progressive agenda for radio and television broadcasters in the nation's capital.

Fritts is known for promoting the public service commitments of broadcasters. He has actively furthered the number of opportunities for station community efforts by serving on the boards of the Advertising Council, the National Commission Against Drunk Driving, and the "Committee of 100" of the U.S. Chamber of Commerce. He has also served on the Individual Advisors Committee of the New York Stock Exchange.

As an advocate of the NAB's growing international involvement, Fritts has served as vice chairman of the State Department's International Media Fund, assisting Eastern European nations in establishing private broadcast systems. He also founded Fritts Broadcasting Group, which includes six radio stations in Louisiana, Mississippi, and Arkansas and advises their clients on lobbying strategy for federal law changes.

The Indianola native was vice chairman of President Ronald Reagan's White House sector initiatives board and is the recipient of numerous national and international awards.

Fritts, a previous member of The University of Mississippi Foundation board, was the first recipient of the Ole Miss Silver Mike Award for significant contributions to broadcast journalism. The national Sigma Alpha Epsilon fraternity honored him with their Highest Effort Award. And in 1999, the Media Institute presented him with their prestigious American Horizon Award for leadership in promoting the vitality of American Media and Communications.

Throughout his years in Washington, Fritts always looked for ways to advance the university. He led a Washington committee that established the Jamie Whitten Chair for Law and Government at Ole Miss. He and his wife, Martha Dale, worked with Tricia Lott in raising funds to help restore William Faulkner's Rowan Oak home in Oxford. He chaired a Washington committee that organized the successful effort to honor Senator Thad Cochran by raising funds for a future Congressional Archives Building to be located at Ole Miss, and he helped organize the Kennedy Center Gala for the establishment of a Trent Lott Institute of Leadership on campus.

Fritts was inducted into the Ole Miss Alumni Association Hall of Fame in 1999. He and his wife live in Arlington, Virginia, where they have been active in various Washington civic, educational, and charitable organizations. They have three children, Kimberly, Timothy, and Jennifer — all Ole Miss alumni.

# JAMES W. DAVIS

James W. Davis, a native of Panola County, joined the Houston, Texas, office of Arthur Andersen & Co. after earning his bachelor's and master's degrees from the University of Mississippi.

After two years in Houston, he was hired as an assistant professor of accountancy and pursued his doctorate at Ole Miss. In 1985, Davis received the university's Outstanding Teacher Award, now the Elsie M. Hood Outstanding Teacher Award. He served as president of the Mississippi Society of CPAs in 1983-84 and received its Outstanding Educator Award in 1993. He won the Patterson School of Accountancy's Outstanding Teacher Award five times and was named the Peery Professor of Accountancy in 1995.

Davis served as dean of the Patterson School from 1993-2002. During that time Conner Hall was completely renovated along with the construction of Holman Hall, a project that received the largest amount of donor funding in the history of Ole Miss at that point. While Davis was dean, the university received the collections of the American Institute of CPAs, or AICPA, library in New York City, making the J.D. Williams Library the library of the accounting profession in the U.S. and the largest accounting library in the world.

Davis officially retired in 2009, but he has continued to teach part-time and retains the title of Peery Professor Emeritus of Accountancy. He estimates he has taught more than 10,000 students during his tenure at Ole Miss.

He is a member of St. Peter's Episcopal Church, Sigma Nu Fraternity, Beta Alpha Psi, Beta Gamma Sigma, and Phi Kappa Phi.

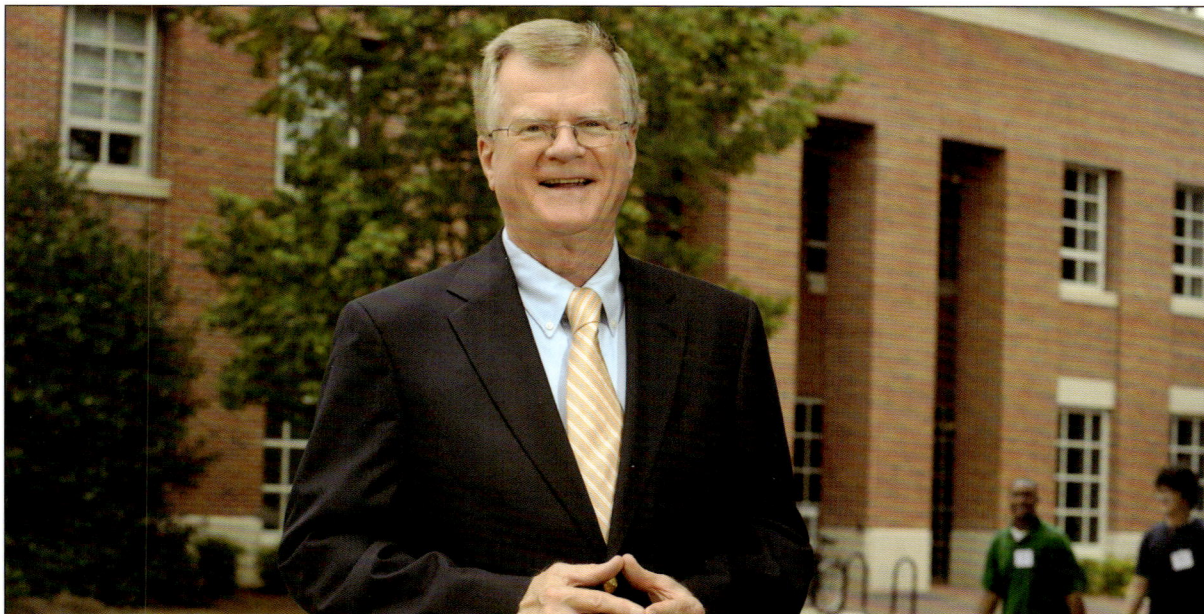

Although officially retired, Davis teaches part-time. During his 52-year tenure in the classroom, Davis estimates he has taught more than 10,000 students at Ole Miss.

# THOMAS W. COLBERT

Thomas W. Colbert Sr. of Flowood is chairman of Community Bancshares of Mississippi Inc., a multibank holding company with locations in Mississippi, Alabama, Tennessee, and Florida. He received a B.B.A. with a major in banking and finance from the University of Mississippi in 1962 and graduated from the Graduate School of Banking of the South at Louisiana State University in 1966.

In 1968, he accepted the position of chief executive officer of Farmers and Merchants Bank in Forest, making him the first graduate under the direction of the then recently formed Chair of Banking at Ole Miss to become CEO of a bank.

In 1973, Colbert formed Mississippi's first bank holding company, Community Bancshares of Mississippi. Today, Community Bancshares has grown from $6 million in assets to more than $2.3 billion in assets and continues to be named one of Mississippi's fastest-growing companies.

Colbert has served as president of the Board of Trustees of State Institutions of Higher Learning; chairman of the Belhaven College Foundation board; chairman of the Colbert Family Foundation; chairman of the Mississippi School of Banking; and director of the University of Mississippi Foundation.

He also has served as a member of the Mississippi contingent of the John C. Stennis Commissioning Committee; Southern Baptist Convention Annuity Board; and In Touch Foundation board of Atlanta, Ga. He was a recipient of the 1984 Boy Scouts of America Silver Beaver Award. In 2005, Colbert was inducted into the Mississippi Business Hall of Fame.

THOMAS and ANN COLBERT FOUNDERS HALL

## Gentleman banker

### Community Bank's chairman proves nice guys can—and should—finish first

Thomas Colbert has been a supporter of education and Ole Miss at every level.

# ROGER M. FLYNT, JR.

## 1962 • BBA; 1964, LLB, LAW • MERIDIAN, MISSISSIPPI

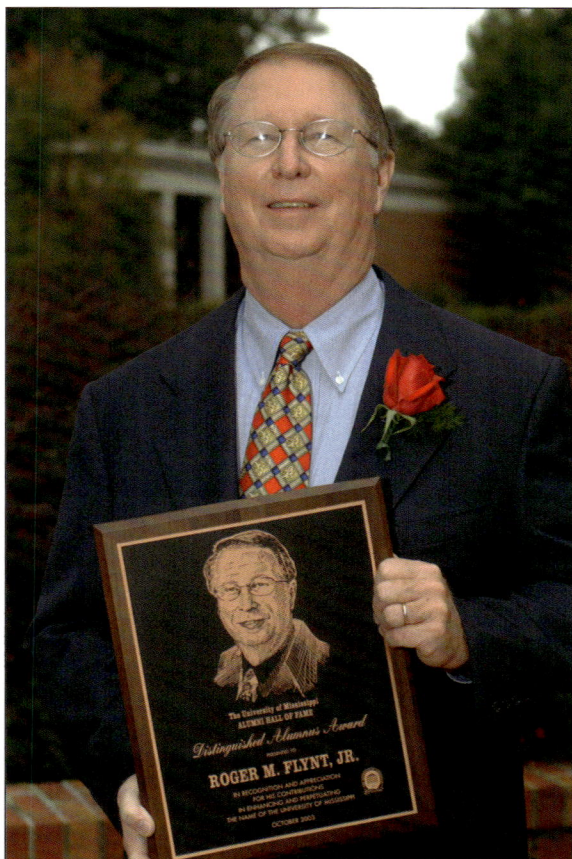

Roger Flynt earned his bachelor of business administration degree in 1962 and a law degree in 1964, both from Ole Miss. The nearly 40-year career that followed included work putting both degrees to use.

He began his career in private legal practice and then worked as assistant U.S. attorney for the Northern District of Mississippi for three years. Then, the Meridian native shifted course toward business. He joined BellSouth in 1968, moving to different offices throughout the South as his career advanced. Flynt also served as vice president of the United States Telephone Association, representing all Bell and independent telephone companies on legal,

legislative, and regulatory matters. He retired from BellSouth corporate headquarters in Atlanta in early 1999.

After his daughter graduated from high school, Flynt and his wife, Gaye, moved to Oxford in 2002 to enjoy retirement. It wasn't to be a retirement spent in leisure, however. He immediately made supporting his alma mater a top priority.

"After his retirement, he volunteered to help the university in any way, and I asked him to assume leadership in the recruitment of Chancellor's Trust members," said Chancellor Robert Khayat. "He enthusiastically accepted the request and [was] remarkably successful in calling on Ole Miss friends and colleagues to join in the effort to strengthen Ole Miss through membership in the Chancellor's Trust."

When it was decided by officials at his former company, BellSouth, to give financial support to several universities, Flynt made sure Ole Miss was included. The result was a $100,000 corporate gift from BellSouth to the University's Commitment to Excellence Campaign for the Chancellor's Trust Program.

"Roger Flynt has had a spectacular career and is respected by all who know him," said Khayat, who became friends with Flynt when the two were college students. "Even as a young person, Roger demonstrated qualities of a successful leader. Through the years, Roger has actively supported alumni association activities, law school programs, and university foundation work. We are deeply grateful for his commitment of time, energy, and resources."

Flynt's love of the university was passed on to his three sons. All three—Mayo Flynt, John Flynt, and Russell Parks—attended the university for their undergraduate careers.

# AUBREY PATTERSON

## 1964 • BBA, BUSINESS ADMINISTRATION

When Aubrey Patterson started work for the Bank of Mississippi in 1972 as an assistant vice president, no one could have guessed he would lead a relatively small northeast Mississippi community bank through a series of mergers, acquisitions, and growth that would place the bank, known today as BancorpSouth, in the top 75 commercial banks chartered in the United States.

Under Patterson's leadership – and vision – BancorpSouth has grown into a full-service financial services company with over $13 billion in assets, more than 4,000 employees, and approximately 300 locations in nine states.

Having once been described by an industry journalist as possessing "a quiet demeanor, but with an analytical mind, a competitive spirit, and clearly formed ideas about banking," Patterson views his career as a calling and his life's chosen work. Patterson also serves on the Financial Services Roundtable Board of Directors (the Roundtable represents 100 of the largest integrated financial services companies providing banking, insurance, and investment products and services to the American consumer).

Robert Khayat said, "Concurrently with Aubrey's leadership of the bank, he has emerged as a leader in Tupelo – and across the state and the nation." Patterson, who has held innumerable civic and industry positions, served as chairman of the American Bankers Association in 2002. Passionate about efforts to improve education, he was appointed by Governor Haley Barbour in 2004 to an eleven-year term on the Mississippi Board of Trustees of Institutions of Higher Learning, the governing board for Mississippi's eight state universities.

# JAMES L. BARKSDALE

Jim Barksdale (BA '65) was a key player in the university's progress toward becoming a Phi Beta Kappa institution. A crucial factor in securing a coveted Phi Beta Kappa chapter was increasing the number of high-ability students enrolled. To help with this goal, Jim and Sally McDonnell Barksdale (BSC '65), gave the University $5.4 million to establish an Honors College on campus

Ole Miss Chancellor Emeritus Robert Khayat noted, "Most of Jim's gifts are made anonymously, and therefore, no accurate measure of his financial contributions can be made."

When Barksdale was president and CEO at Netscape Communications Corp. in Mountain View, Calif., he managed all aspects of the Internet software company.

Barksdale has served as CEO of AT&T Wireless Services, following the merger of AT&T and McCaw Cellular Communications, Inc. From January 1992 until the merger, he held the position of president and COO of the $2 billion McCaw.

Prior to McCaw, Barksdale spent 12 years with Federal Express Corp. of Memphis. From 1979 to 1983 he served as chief information officer, overseeing the development and implementation of the company's world-renowned customer service and package tracking systems. In 1983, he became executive vice president and chief operating officer.

After his appointment to that role, the company grew from $1 billion to $7.7 billion in revenues and expanded operations to 135 countries. Under his leadership, Federal Express also became the first service company to receive the Malcolm Baldridge National Quality Award.

One of his most recent ventures, Spread Networks, is a super-fast fiber-cable network that creates a new link for speed-obsessed traders who trade between Chicago and New York.

Barksdale served on the boards of 3Com Corp., @Home, Harrah's Entertainment, Robert Mondavi Corp., and Netscape Communications.

> Under Jim Barksdale's leadership as COO of FedEx, company revenues increased from $1 billion to $7.7 billion.

# OLE MISS
# BUSINESS

## A TIME OF CHANGE

### DEAN BEN MCNEW

1965 - 1979

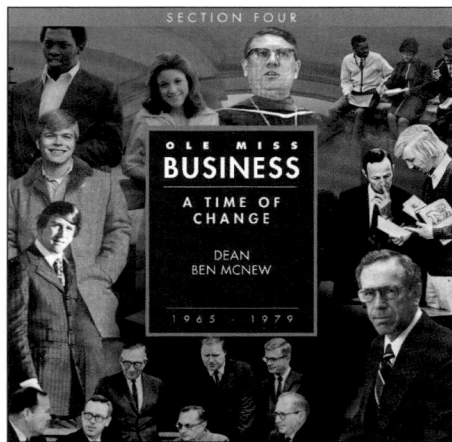

SECTION FOUR

OLE MISS
BUSINESS

A TIME OF
CHANGE

DEAN
BEN MCNEW

1965 · 1979

Clockwise from top left: Col. Reb "Gentle" Ben Williams and Miss Ole Miss Barbara Biggs, Chancellor Porter Fortune, Joyce O'Neal Jones with fellow classmates in 1965, Dean McNew helps a student, Dean McNew, McNew meets with accountancy faculty, Archie Manning, Dick Molpus.

# BEN "BENNIE" MCNEW
## DEAN 1965-1979

"Buying Mississippi products is good economic citizenship."

Ben McNew, *Clarion-Ledger*, October 30, 1968

## A More Candid Dean

If J.D. Williams hoped the next dean of the School of Business and Government would be more dynamic and assertive than Clive Dunham, his wish came true in the form of Ben McNew.

McNew, a graduate of the University of Texas's Ph.D. program, had been hired as a professor in 1961 to fill the Chair of Banking, a position sponsored by the Mississippi Bankers' Association.

McNew was appointed "Acting Dean" — and act he did. Dean McNew made his thoughts, ideas, and beliefs clear from the very beginning of his tenure — he wanted better teaching, better research, and better credentials for the faculty. He also made clear to everyone who was in charge. When one faculty member complained about appropriation of department resources, McNew said, "I'll allocate funds as I see fit."

McNew was also direct and candid in how he communicated with the chancellor and IHL board members. In an early report

Ben McNew was hired as the Chair of Banking, a faculty position endowed by the Mississippi Bankers Association.

to the chancellor, he pointed out the strengths and weaknesses of the business school.

"Areas of strength that might be listed in the School of Business Administration include —

- a diverse student body
- high admission standards
- varied course offerings
- student counseling procedures
- placement services
- public relations, and
- faculty interest in student welfare.

Conversely, weaknesses that might be listed include —

- poor performance in the classroom and in research by some faculty members
- insufficient course offerings in some areas
- poor administration by some department chairmen
- lack of interest by a few faculty members in nonteaching responsibilities, and
- excessive teaching assignments."

## McNew Named Acting Dean At Ole Miss

UNIVERSITY — Dr. Ben B. McNew, who occupies the Mississippi Bankers Association

Dr. McNew was a lecturer in the Department of Finance at the University of Texas. For the

"However," McNew added, "these conditions are thought to exist (to some degree) in all schools of business and do not go beyond normal limits at the University of Mississippi."

## A Closed Society

In 1966, Senator Robert F. Kennedy came to Ole Miss to speak as a part of the law school's speaker's series. The speech was originally scheduled for an auditorium in the law school, but interest was so tremendous they moved the event to Tad Smith Coliseum. Senator Kennedy and his wife were greeted to a standing ovation by the estimated five thousand attendees. According to historian David Sansing, one Mississippi journalist wrote that this ovation was proof that Ole Miss was a "hotbed of liberalism."

Kennedy was introduced by Ed Ellington, chairman of the speaker's series. Ellington announced, "After this day, never again let it be uttered that this is a closed society."

Watson and Joyce O'Neal Jones, the first African American students enrolled in the School of Business and Government, were sophomore accounting majors when Kennedy delivered his speech. Both would agree that Ellington's proclamation was premature.

Watson, a Moss Point native, recalled, "All the classes had a seating chart and the professors made sure no one sat in front of me, behind me, or directly to the right or left of me."

Accounting major Joyce O'Neal Jones (center) was one of three black female undergraduates at Ole Miss in 1965. There were five undergraduate males.

Watson added that all the professors had discussed the seating arrangement and decided to place students similarly in every class. "It was like I sat on an island."

Watson also had a dormitory room completely to himself for three and a half years.

"There were only fourteen black students at Ole Miss that year, and only eight undergraduates. So we all met in my dorm room."

Watson said his dorm, as well as the lobby of the women's dorm, was where the black students gathered from 1965-1968 (this was before the Black Student Union was formed in 1969).

"My father was president of the NAACP in Moss Point," Watson said. "We were activists. We knew it was important to have more black students at Ole Miss, and I knew it would be difficult. But I also expected to get a good education."

Watson said that professors, for the most part, taught classes as if nothing had changed. A few, he said, ignored the minority students, while others acknowledged their presence.

Joyce O'Neal Jones, a Jackson native who had also been involved in the Civil Rights Movements prior to enrolling at Ole Miss, said one professor called her to the side after class.

"I don't know what to call you," the professor said to Jones, "I've never had a colored person in my class." Then he asked, "Should I call you nigger, niggress, colored?"

Jones responded, "How about calling me Joyce?"

Watson and Jones both had an upper-level accounting class under Joseph Cerny. Watson said his relationship with Cerny illustrated the complexity of the era.

"We called Professor Cerny 'Papa Joe'," Watson said. "He liked me. Professor Cerny always included me in class discussions. If we went on a field trip to visit an accounting firm in Memphis, he made sure I was included and felt welcomed. But every so often, when you'd least expect it, Papa Joe would use 'the magic word'."

Both Watson and Jones graduated in 1968 with degrees in accounting. Watson was hired by IBM to work in their Huntsville, Alabama, division. Jones had a long career with General Electric (see profiles on page 98).

### The Search for a New Chancellor

When J.D. Williams announced his retirement in 1967, a national search was conducted to find a replacement for the man who had led the university for twenty-two years.

A July 7 edition of the *Clarion-Ledger* reported that the search had been narrowed to six men. The newspaper reported that "Dr. Ben McNew, acting dean of the Ole Miss business school is said to be the first choice by a thin vote with the [IHL] subcommittee…"

The report mentioned that McNew

Ben McNew was backed by the Mississippi Bankers Association (and one prominent IHL board member) for the position of Chancellor at Ole Miss. Ultimately, Porter Fortune was selected by the board.

GOLDEN ANNIVERSARY — Celebrating the 50th anniversary of the founding of the School of Business and Government at the University of Mississippi were (from left) Dr. Ben B. McNew, acting dean of the school; James George of Monticello, class of 1930; Dean Horace B. Brown Jr. of the University of Oklahoma College of Business Administration, former dean at Ole Miss; Robert M. Hearin, president of the First National Bank of Jackson; and John R. Nunnery of Meridian, class of 1927.

Ben McNew (left) led a "Golden Anniversary" celebration for the School of Business and Government in 1977. Robert M. Hearin (second from right), who attended the 50th anniversary event, would play a significant role in the school's future.

Photo from *Clarion-Ledger*

was backed by most of the state financial institutions.

The *Ledger* story ended with, "One report indicated McNew would accept the post if offered, in spite of the strong opposition from several members of the board."

James Davis, a young professor of accounting in 1967, said that McNew had the support of one powerful member of the board of trustees (a banker) and that most within the university assumed he would not be named chancellor.

Even McNew, in a 2017 interview, admitted, "there were some negotiations about the chancellorship, but I was somewhat skeptical even at the time that I would go into that position."

The IHL eventually chose Porter Fortune to succeed J.D. Williams as chancellor. In what some described as an extension of an olive branch, Chancellor Fortune promoted McNew's status from acting dean to dean.

### Golden Anniversary

On October 26, 1967, McNew presided over a 50th anniversary celebration of the business school.

The theme of the anniversary program was "Leadership for the Future."

The principal speakers at the event were Dr. Horace B. Brown Jr., dean of the University of Oklahoma College Business Administration and former dean at Ole Miss; Dr. Porter L. Fortune Jr., Ole Miss chancellor-elect; and Robert

*Continued on page 103*

# INTERVIEW WITH ERNEST WATSON
## CO-FIRST BLACK GRADUATE OF THE SCHOOL OF BUSINESS

**What was life like on the Ole Miss campus when you arrived in 1965?**

I arrived two years after Meredith. Prior to our arrival, there were only two blacks on campus. We arrived in '65. It was something like eight undergraduates. Then we had a few grad students and a couple in law school.

**How did the professor react to you?**

The professors in the business school for the first two, maybe two-and-a-half years, they didn't acknowledge our presence really, to be honest with you. My major was accounting. So all my classes were in Conner Hall. At that time everyone used seating charts. And what they would do — this would really make it tough on us — is that no one would be assigned to sit behind me, in front of me, or on both sides of me. You could tell they had gotten together and said, "We're just going to leave that area around them open."

Ernest Watson (on top bunk) and friends gathered in his dorm room since he wasn't assigned a roommate for three-and-a-half years.
Photo from *Ebony* magazine

**That must have been strange?**

Yes. In the early days, they didn't acknowledge me being in there. As time went by, it got a little better. The earlier years were pretty rough. I also had a dorm room to myself in Garland Hall for three-and-a-half years. I had a roommate for one semester, Irvin Walker, who was the fourth black to enroll at Ole Miss, and he was my roommate for one semester. He got married and moved off campus, and from that point on, I didn't have a roommate at all.

**So it was sort of like the desk. Giving you space . . . or taking space?**

Yes. So whenever someone was on campus and wanted to chit-chat, we'd all meet in my room. If you look at the photograph in

*Ebony* magazine from 1966, you'll see everyone is in my room. That's me on the bed in top bunk. A few months later, *Mademoiselle* wrote an article. They were questioning us about what we thought of Ole Miss and everything. And really, we liked Ole Miss. We started talking about going to ball games. I said, "I would love to go, if they just wouldn't play Dixie so much." And that's the name of the article, "If They Wouldn't Play 'Dixie' So Much."

**So, what was your social life like?**

We didn't have a social life, not on campus. We went to one football game our first year there, and we got drinks thrown all over us, so we didn't go to football games anymore. I did play intermural basketball my senior year. A new group came to Garland, and they asked me to play because I'm about 6'3", and at the time that was kind of tall, so I played for my dorm team. I had a car on campus, so on weekends we would jump in my car and go to Holly Springs.

**Did you spend much time in the city of Oxford?**

My roommate Irvin Walker and I went to a store on the Square. The old guy in the store asked me, "Do you all need anything? Do you want anything?" And I said, "No. We're looking." I was supposed to say *no, sir*. And because I just said *no*, it got out of hand in that store. We had to be escorted back to campus. This was my first few days on in Oxford. After that happened, we didn't do too much in Oxford. Like I said, I just went to the business school, Conner Hall, and took all my classes.

**What brought you to Ole Miss? And did you know what to expect?**

We knew what we were up against. I'm from Moss Point. My dad was president of the local NAACP chapter, and we were active. I went to Washington and marched. And the Mississippi March during that time, I participated in that. Marched from Tougaloo to Jackson. So there was a push for someone to go to Ole Miss. We looked at it as something that needed to be done. "There are only two guys at Ole Miss right now. Someone's gotta go." It was a tough decision, but I said, "Okay, I'm going."

### You know Chancellor Emeritus Robert Khayat is from Moss Point?

Sure was! The Khayats took care of us. You know my grandmother worked for the Khayats, and anything you wanted, you had to go through my grandmother. To be honest with you, we lived like kings down there because my grandmother knew the Khayats.

### Were there any professors who reached out and were kind?

Yes. There was a professor named Joe Cerny; everybody called him Papa Joe. Now, he was a little weird. I had him when I started taking some of the 400 and 500 level classes. He would always try and include me in the classwork. If we took a field trip, he would make sure that we went on those field trips together. We would go to Memphis to accounting firms, and he made sure I was included. He didn't show any hard feelings or bad feelings in the classroom. But he *would* call you the magic word every once in a while.

Ernest Watson (right) and his team at General Electric's aircraft engine division.

### What about other professors?

I had Intermediate Accounting from Gene Perry. Now, Gene Perry was hard. He was there teaching Intermediate Accounting. Some's gonna fail; some's gonna pass.

### What did you do when you graduated?

I went to work for IBM in Huntsville, Alabama, in the space system program. The space program was really getting started then — to get it to go to the moon. IBM built all of the computers on the rocket, the Saturn V rocket.

I couldn't ask for a better education than I received at the business school at Ole Miss. It was great. I left IBM, worked for Kaiser Aluminum, and then I worked for General Electric in the aircraft engine division in Cincinnati, Ohio. Worked for General Electric for twenty-eight years and retired. I live here in Mesa, Arizona. I golf a lot.

You're not going to ever hear me say, "I hate that I went to Ole Miss," because it meant a lot for me in my later life. It worked out pretty good. Here's the only problem; it was great, but do you know I've only been on that campus one time since 1968.

### You should come back.

I have a nephew who graduated this past May. They bought a brick for me. It's got my name and everything. I don't miss the football games or the basketball games. If they're televised, I'm watching them. I joined the Alumni Association, but I just never go back. I know it's beautiful.

### It is beautiful, and it's a different place, as it should be. A lot of that is because of brave folks like you.

Yeah, from what I see. I know people out here who graduated from Ole Miss who I see on the golf course all the time laughing and talking to me. It's totally different, so it worked out pretty good for me, I think.

*Ernest Watson Interview conducted August 27, 2017*

# INTERVIEW WITH JOYCE O'NEAL JONES
## CO-FIRST BLACK GRADUATE OF THE SCHOOL OF BUSINESS

**Why did you decide to come to Ole Miss in '65, when the year before there were only two black students at the school?**
I grew up in Jackson, Mississippi. Since I was twelve or thirteen years old, I have been actively involved in civil rights and the NAACP. My older sister and cousin were heavily involved in the movement. And often they would go on marches, and I would go along. I was young, so I would go along and be "the camera person." People from Tougaloo College were very active back in the `60s in the Civil Rights Movement. Back then, blacks couldn't sit on the benches at the Jackson Zoo, so we marched over it, and they closed the zoo down for a year.

I lived one street over from Lynch Street, where there was a Masonic Temple. Medgar Evers was the adult supervisor to our youth NAACP chapter. We would go on marches. Medgar would take us. He instructed us; he guided us. I was arrested two or three times; got thrown in jail. The last time I marched and got thrown in jail was when Medgar Evars was assassinated. Our youth chapter went out, and we marched, and they kept us there for about two or three days.

Joyce Jones playing cards
in New Dorm in 1965
Photo from *Ebony* magazine

I've always been actively involved. My first year, I went to Tougaloo College my freshman year then I decided that if I was going to stay in Mississippi, I was going to stay and get a degree at a college that was well-known to Mississippians. So, I went to Ole Miss my sophomore year.

**Was there any trouble or struggle with your application? Or were you accepted with any fanfare?**
Let me tell you, three black females all applied in 1965. It is so funny. We were accepted, but when we went up to pre-register (we didn't go the day school started; we went up maybe a month or so before), they knew when we entered town. There was a police presence at the hotel we stayed in that night. They spotted us on the interstate going up. When we went to the Lyceum the next day to register, they had it circled with police officers.

We're going, "Oh my gosh, what is this?" But we went in; we did not have problems. If there were any, I was not aware of it. I don't know what was done behind the scenes. We were followed everywhere we went by a police squad.

**What was it like in the early days?**
The first day that school started, they had a "Welcome Rebel Party" at the town square. And we went. It was, I think, nine blacks, six males and three females. The band was playing. As the night went on, people drank and it was very rowdy, and the thing I remember most was the crowd turned on us. They surrounded us; they backed us up to the bandstand, because I'll never forget this, the band started playing Bob Dylan's "Like a Rolling Stone." And the more — "how does it feel to be alone" — they just went wild. They started throwing stuff at us; they backed us up; we looked to the police for help, and they walked away.

So we're going, "Oh my God. We're going to have to fight these hundreds of people to get out of here," and then out of nowhere, again this is something I would never forget, a minister came, and his name was Jim Jones, and he was from the Wesley Foundation. But the students knew him, and he said to them, "Let us through," and they parted, and he led us out of there.

It made the papers, because my mom called me the next morning and told me to come home. But I didn't. I stayed.

All three years, there was always something going on, some commotion; if we went to the local theatre, at that time blacks sat upstairs; we would sit downstairs, and they had little symbols. They would hiss like a snake if any of what they called "the Ole Miss blacks," or "colored folks" was anywhere. It happened in restaurants, at the movies, but we were never afraid.

**What about your classes?**

Nobody would sit in front of us, behind us, or on either side. That's a fact.

**That must have been hard?**

We knew what we were getting into; it's not like we went up there blind. So no, to me, it was sort of amusing. I remember once in an organization and theory class I had, it was an older white professor, and the whole class was that you worked in a group and you did organization and theory; you would come up and pick a project that you worked on it the whole year, and obviously I was not in a group. I was by myself, and he made a joke in front of the whole class, "Nobody selected Joyce, and everyone's given up their group name, so I guess her group name would have to be the 'Lone Ranger.'" So I said, "Oh, okay." After class he asked me, he said, "I don't know what to call you. Should I call you 'nigger' or should I call you 'nigress' or should I call you 'colored girl'? I've never taught a colored before." And I just smiled and said, "You can just call me Joyce."

So it was always something like that the whole time we were there.

**What about your professors?**

There were professors we always talked about while we were at the business school. Peery — we had classes with him. And our "beloved" Papa Joe Cerny. I remember those three. The other people, there was one that taught me a marketing class that like twenty-five percent of your grade was class participation, and he never would call on me. I'd hold my hand up and he'd go down the aisle and skip over me. The highest I got out of that class was like a 75. I think he may have given me like five percent or something like that, but it was always stuff like that. So those are the ones I remembered.

I had problems with Mr. Cerny. He assumed you should have been set in your major and knowledge, and for some reason, one day in the class we were talking about commodities and cotton, and he would turn and look at me and Ernie and say, "Why don't you guys tell us about cotton?" Then we would have to say, "I've never seen cotton in my life." He always made little digs like that. He didn't shy away from doing or saying discriminatory things.

Between Ernie and me, I was the studious one. I studied from mid-day to like six or seven o'clock at night; and I got it out of the way. So one day, Cerny asked us how we studied, and I told him I study till six or seven o'clock for your class. Ernie said, "Oh, I stay up all night."

That is all Cerny wanted to hear. He loved Ernie. Ernie got A's out of him; I got C's. No matter what I did, that man gave me a C, and no matter what Ernie did, Ernie got an A because he was "more dedicated."

**Were there support faculty or staff?**

The dean of women. I don't know if maybe she felt overwhelmed that there were black females that she was responsible for for the first time. She was very sympathetic. That I do remember, because I'd just think, "This poor woman is going to have a heart attack." Because we were always getting threats, and she would call at like one o'clock in the morning and say, "I think y'all better leave your rooms because I just got wind that they're going to come over and do so-and-so.'" So we would have to get up out of the bed, leave the dormitory until it was all-clear, but she was always looking out for us. I give her credit for that.

**What did you do after Ole Miss?**

After I graduated from Ole Miss, Ernie and I were married, so for the first couple of years we moved with his advancements. Then in 1970, we moved to Cincinnati, Ohio, and I got hired at General Electric. I worked there for about twenty-nine-and-a-half years. I was always in finance. I guess they thought, "We have a black that can add 1 and 1" and they pushed me. Once I went to Naples, Italy, and closed a revenue sharing deal. I wanted to tell them, "Are you kidding? Do you think I can do that job!?" But this company sent me as *the* finance person to close the deal in Italy.

*Joyce Jones Interview conducted on September 4, 2017*

*Headline from the Enterprise-Journal
(McComb), September 17, 1965*

## Negroes Jeered at Rebel Dance

OXFORD, Miss. (AP) — A street dance for returning University of Mississippi students ended abruptly Thursday night when nine Negro students were surrounded and jeered.

The "Welcome Rebel" party for new and returning Ole Miss milling white students and asked the Negroes to return to the campus a mile away "in order to prevent an ugly incident from erupting."

Oxford police surrounded the Negroes, who then returned to the campus

# HON. DAVID W. HOUSTON III

1966 • BBA; 1969 • JD, LAW • ABERDEEN, MISSISSIPPI

David W. Houston III served as U.S. bankruptcy judge for the Northern District of Mississippi from 1983 to 2013. Prior to assuming the bench, he was a partner for 11 years in the Aberdeen law firm of Houston, Chamberlain and Houston. He also served as a special agent with the Federal Bureau of Investigation in Washington, D.C., Tampa, Fla., and New York City.

Houston served two terms on the board of directors of the American Bankruptcy Institute and chaired its legislative committee for 11 years. From 1995 to 2003, he was the judicial chair of the American Bankruptcy Institute's Southeast Bankruptcy Workshop.

From 1997 to 2013, Houston served as a member of the Committee on the Budget for the Judicial Conference of the United States and for two years chaired that committee's Subcommittee on Congressional Outreach. He was a member of the Judicial Conference Committee on the Administrative Office of the United States Courts for nine years.

At Ole Miss, Houston was a member of Phi Kappa Phi, Omicron Delta Kappa, Beta Gamma Sigma, Beta Alpha Psi and Sigma Chi fraternity. He served as Associated Student Body Judicial Council chairman.

In 2011, Houston was the recipient of the Mississippi State Bar Association Judicial Excellence Award. He was selected a fellow of both the Mississippi Bar Foundation and the American College of Bankruptcy. In 2003, he received the Bierce Distinguished Service Award.

Houston retired from the federal bench in 2013 and joined the law firm of Mitchell, McNutt & Sams in its Tupelo office.

M. Hearin, president of the First National Bank of Jackson (Hearin's foundation would have a lasting impact on the business school).

Dr. Fortune cited the school for molding outstanding leaders in its fifty years of existence. "I promise you as the new chancellor," Fortune said, "to endeavor in every way to make this school even greater in its contributions to the young people, to industry, to business, to government, and to the state of Mississippi."

Dean Brown addressed a group in Fulton Chapel and said, "Proof of how well a school is performing is not only how its graduates do in the business and professional world but is also in the performance of graduate students…Graduate students from the University of Mississippi School of Business and Government do well."

"If there was ever a time when there was more need for strong and dedicated leadership for the future," Brown added, "I don't know when it was. Schools of business and government are in a strong position to supply that leadership."

Mr. Hearin, stressing the necessity and qualities of good management, challenged the present student body to meet responsibilities of preparing for future leadership.

Archie Manning (#18) started taking classes in Conner Hall long before he was a household name.

Dean McNew cared about his students and wanted the most rigorous education for all students in the school.

"You must prepare yourselves to lead, to manage, to succeed," the banking executive said. "And education is the foundation of preparation."

Interestingly, the contributions of founding dean James Bell weren't featured at the 50th anniversary event.

## A Computer Era Began

McNew wrote, "During 1968, curricula changes were made at both the undergraduate and graduate levels. The principal change occurring at the undergraduate level involved General Business 307, Business Data Processing I. This course, which covers both FORTRAN and COBOL programming language, was made a required course in all curricula except Business Education. The pervasive influence of computers makes it imperative that every student of business and economics be able to recognize computer problems and have some familiarity with their solutions, and this required course in data processing will introduce students to computer operations and potentials."

## A Football Star Majors in Business

When a freckle-faced freshman from Drew, Mississippi, started taking classes in Conner Hall in 1968, no one could have imagined

# GEN. WILLIAM FREEMAN

**1967 • BBA, BUSINESS ADMINISTRATION • NEWTON, MISSISSIPPI**

William L. Freeman Jr. has served as the adjutant general for Mississippi and also served as the commanding general for the Mississippi Army and Air National Guard. He was responsible for providing Mississippi and the United States with a ready force of approximately 13,000 citizen soldiers and airmen equipped and trained to respond to any contingency, natural or man-made. Freeman also directed the Mississippi Military Department and oversaw the development and coordination of all policies, plans, and programs of the Mississippi National Guard in concert with the governor and state legislature.

Freeman enlisted in the Mississippi Army National guard in 1966 as an artilleryman. Following the completion of Officer Candidate School at the Mississippi Military academy, he was commissioned in 1969 as an artillery officer. He has commanded on the battalion and brigade levels and was promoted to brigadier general in 1996 and appointed as the adjutant general by Governor Haley R. Barbour in 2008.

Freeman has more than 35 years of service in uniform. He is a Hall of Fame member of the Mississippi Military Academy's Officer Candidate School and is an honorary member of the Ole Miss Army ROTC Alumni Board.

The Newton native has earned numerous military decorations and awards, including the Legion of Merit, awarded for exceptionally meritorious conduct in the performance of outstanding services and achievements, and the Magnolia Medal, awarded in 1978.

In addition to his career in the military, Freeman has achieved success in the banking industry and also served in local government with the city of Newton.

He retired as the senior vice president and chief operating officer of Newton County Bank in 2008 with almost 40 years of service in the banking industry.

Freeman also served on the city of Newton's board of aldermen for three years prior to being elected mayor in 1980. He held that office for more than seven years.

Freeman is a past president of the East Mississippi Ole Miss Alumni Club. He has served on the board of directors and as treasurer for the Newton County chapter for many years and as a key contact for the Alumni Association for more than a decade. He is married to Karen McEntyre Freeman of Meridian, and they have two sons, Stanley and Daniel. When both sons joined the Mississippi Army National Guard in 1977, Freeman was the one to swear them in.

the impact he would have on Ole Miss. Freshmen weren't allowed to play on the varsity squad in 1968, so Archie Manning made his football debut in the 1969 season.

Manning recalled, "Although it was kind of an up-and-down season for us, it turned out to be a memorable season. It was also the 100th year of college football, which was pretty special. All the teams wore a "100" decal on their helmets. We were predicted to be pretty good, but we lost our second and third games by one point — conference games. We got upset by Kentucky, and then we lost a very memorable game to Alabama in Birmingham. It was a high-scoring game. Big numbers, record numbers, which was unusual for the SEC in 1969. That was probably the best game I ever had. It was one of the first college games ever televised at night on national television. They beat us 33-32. So we were kind of in bad shape early in the season."

The Alabama game put Archie Manning in the national spotlight. After the game Alabama coach Bear Bryant said, "That's the best college quarterback I've ever seen."

Archie continued, "We went on to beat three nationally-ranked, undefeated teams that year. We beat undefeated (No. 6) Georgia, we beat undefeated (No. 8) LSU, and we beat undefeated (No. 3) Tennessee, so we were playing very well by the end of the year."

The Ole Miss team went to the Sugar Bowl that year and defeated Arkansas 27-22. In 1969, Manning won the hearts of college football fans everywhere.

*Dean McNew*

With rapid inflation underway, how can Man protect himself and at the same time make a meaningful contribution to society? What will be the result of increasing U.S. reliance on foreign resources when they are scarce and subject to political-economic manipulation? How, in fact, can Man survive that inevitable day of reckoning in economics, in the environment, and in politics? Such questions aren't susceptible of easy answers, but they come up again and again in business school courses. Obviously, specialized knowledge in administration, business, and economics is needed to deal with these and similar questions; but a broad education is also needed and it involves knowledge of geopolitics, mathematics, and science. Keeping that in mind, the School of Business Administration has designed its curricula responsive to changing needs.
*Bennie M. McNew*
*Dean, School of Business Administration*

**Dean McNew in the 1975 annual**

Manning graduated with a B.P.A. in business Administration with an emphasis in city management (Note: Archie's son, Eli, was an honor's student in the business school. He graduated with a degree in marketing and a GPA of 3.44).

## External Ambassador and Internal Strife

Dean McNew was a wildly successful ambassador to the Mississippi business community. He immersed himself in service to the state. In the late 1960s, McNew traveled the towns across the state making speeches on the importance of "Buying Mississippi."

In a speech to the Jackson Civitan Club, McNew said, "Buying Mississippi products is good economic citizenship." Noting Mississippi's low-ranking in per capita income, he said, "We've got a duty to utilize our strength and energy to bring the state up to what we want it to be." He added, "a dollar spent in Mississippi turns over seven or eight times before it leaves the state."

In 1970, McNew established a new banking program at Ole Miss to train individuals who wanted to enter the banking industry. The first class had seventy students.

McNew also worked to plan an "Institute for School Heads" that would train superintendents, principals, and members of school boards. In an article published by *The Star Herald*, McNew revealed something about his personal nature. "Conflict in a free society is inevitable," McNew said, "especially in the field of education where public employees and administrators are confronted with the possibility of changing and uncertain

# DON FRUGÉ

## 1967 • BBA; 1970 • JD, LAW • MERIDIAN, MISSISSIPPI

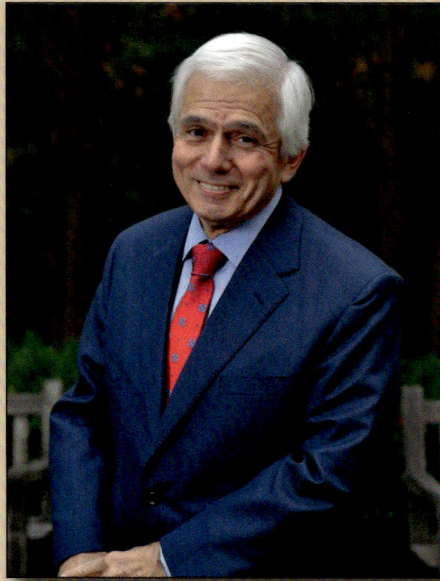

**D**on L. Frugé is currently chairman and CEO of Frugé Capital Advisors, LLC, an independently registered investment advisory firm. He and his partner son, Don Jr., provide wealth management services to individuals, families, and nonprofits. Don is also of counsel at the Frugé Law Firm, PLLC, of Oxford Mississippi.

Don, a 1963 graduate of Meridian High School, received his BBA, accounting (1967) and JD (1970) from the University of Mississippi followed by a masters of law degree in taxation from New York University in 1971. He joined the law faculty in 1971 and has continued to teach courses in estate planning, taxation and nonprofit organizations.

For 22 years, Don oversaw the growth of the University of Mississippi Foundation. During that time the university endowment grew from $8 million in 1984 to over $420 million when he retired, ranking it 35th nationally in endowment per student at public universities.

Don has served the University of Mississippi in a number of capacities throughout the years, including Professor of Law, Ex-

ecutive director of development, vice chancellor for university affairs, vice chancellor for university advancement, head golf coach and as president/CEO of the University of Mississippi Foundation. Currently, he serves the university as chairman of the Ole Miss Athletics Foundation (2005 to present), a Board Member of the University of Mississippi Foundation, a member of the joint committee on university investments (1984 to present) , and professor emeritus of law.

Don is a past-president of the Oxford-Lafayette County Economic Development Foundation and a board member for 16 years. Frugé holds memberships in the Mississippi State Bar, the American Bar Association and is a Fellow of the Mississippi State Bar Foundation. He is the author of several books including the *Mississippi Wills and Trust Manual* (1979) and *Estate Planning for Retarded Persons and Their Families* (with Green) (1982). Frugé served as a Director of Home Savings Bank, Meridian, Mississippi, and of Hancock Fabrics, Inc., Tupelo, Mississippi. A member of Phi Kappa Phi, Frugé was named Alumnus of the Year, Beta Alpha Psi, 1991, and Law Alumnus of the Year, 2013. Don is an Eagle Scout and a former member of the Boy Scout Council.

Don and his wife, Mary Ann, are active members of St. Peter's Episcopal Church in Oxford. They have enjoyed working with college students in various capacities and have co-chaired programs statewide for engaged and married couples.

As a student at Ole Miss, Frugé served as president of Omicron Delta Kappa, treasurer of Sigma Chi Fraternity, captain of the Ole Miss Golf Team, a member of the "M" Club and of Beta Alpha Psi and as chairman of the Law School Moot Court Board. Don's wife, Mary Ann (BA 1966, MA 1970), and their son, Don, Jr. (JD 1996) are also graduates of Ole Miss.

relationship." He added, "Conflict, although inevitable, need not be irrational. We have learned that the professionalization of industrial relations alleviates conflict in the private sector, the same will hold true in the public sector."

McNew was also a staunch supporter of the Mississippi Economic Council (MEC) — the statewide chamber of commerce. He was appointed as chair of the council's committee that studied and analyzed the state's business climate. He spoke on behalf of the MEC at assemblies of tax assessors and collectors, criticizing the lack of uniformity of tax assessments across the state. And he was named to the MEC's committee that studied the state's financial institutions.

While the private sector embraced McNew and his business acumen, he continued to agitate certain members of the faculty — primarily in the accounting department.

Professor James Davis recalled defending his dissertation in 1971 when McNew was on the review committee. Davis' dissertation subject was the history of accounting in the state of Mississippi.

"My department chair said to me, 'Someone at the University of Tennessee has written a dissertation on the development of the CPA profession in Tennessee; same thing happened in Missouri.' So, being a native Mississippian, I thought it would be great to create the same history for this state."

McNew, apparently, didn't respect historical dissertations.

"During my review, Dean McNew threatened not to sign my dissertation," Davis said. "He felt I should have picked some accounting principle or theory."

Several other committee members, all of whom worked under McNew, enthusiastically stated, "I'll sign it!" and McNew finally backed down.

Davis added, "Ben was a study in contention."

McNew with some of the accounting faculty before they left the school of business. Front Row (L to R, front row) Charles Taylor (acting chair of accounting), McNew, Eugene Peery, Carl Nabors, (L to R, back row) William Joor (business law), Albert Craven, and James Davis.

# MICHAEL STARNES

1968 • BBA, BUSINESS ADMINISTRATION • OXFORD, MISSISSIPPI

**M**ike Starnes was chairman and chief executive officer of M.S. Carriers, Inc., of Memphis. He received a bachelor of business administration degree from Ole Miss in 1968, and he boasts over twenty-five years of experience in the transportation industry. As of 1990, M.S. Carriers had an annual revenue of $110 million, more than $8 million in profits, and a listing on *Forbes* magazine's 1990 list of America's 200 best small companies.

In 1984, Starnes received the Small Business Executive of the Year in the Mid-South Award, followed by the Wall Street Transcript Gold Award in 1987, the Wall Street Transcript Bronze Award in 1988, and the Master of Free Enterprise Award in 1991. In 1995, he received the Contribution to Amateur Football award from the Ole Miss chapter of the National Football Foundation and the College Hall of Fame. The Ole Miss athletic training center bears his name to honor his $1 million donation, which helped to complete the center. As of 1994, it was the biggest single donation the Ole Miss athletic department had ever received. Starnes said he wanted to help the school be able to compete with schools in the SEC.

In 2002, Starnes donated another $1 million to create an endowment for academic scholarships. The endowment was named in honor of Robert Khayat, the then-chancellor of the University of Mississippi, and was intended to "kick off the $100 million Ole Miss First campaign." He also contributed to the Lott Leadership Institute at Ole Miss.

Starnes also served as a director on the following boards: the Chickasaw Council of the Boy Scouts of America; the Nations Bank of Memphis; The University of Mississippi Foundation; the Memphis Area Chamber of Commerce; the Memphis Food Bank; and the Interstate Truckload Carriers Conference.

He was also on the board of trustees of St. Mary's Episcopal School; the Executive Committee of the American Trucking Association; and he was a member of the Young Presidents' Organization.

### Another player; a different experience

In 1972, Ben Williams, the first black football player to dress for a varsity game, enrolled in the business school. Williams, who stood 6'4" and weighed 230 pounds, was wildly popular among the students.

Williams said, "I really didn't have any problems with racism. Everyone treated me kindly and had a degree of respect for me."

Williams was not only successful on the playing field (he was an All-America selection in 1975), he was elected by the student body as Col. Rebel (a popularity contest that equated to Mr. Ole Miss).

Williams graduated in 1976 with a B.B.A. in general business.

Business major Ben Williams (pictured here as Col. Rebel with Miss Ole Miss Barbara Biggs) experienced a very different Ole Miss from what Ernest Watson and Joyce Jones endured.

### The 70s Economic Crisis & Journalism

McNew and his faculty were remarkably nimble in adjusting coursework to meet the needs of students, and the U.S. marketplace.

Dr. S. Cabell Skull, chairman of the Department of Economics and Finance, wrote in the school's annual report, "The state of the American economy reached a crisis point during 1971-1972, culminating in the dollar devaluation and a staggering federal budget deficit. Although each American is affected by these and other economic developments, the true significance is not generally understood by the public. The task of enlightening our citizens on the operation of the competitive price system, its virtues and limitations remains an unending challenge to economic faculties. In an attempt to reach a greater student audience, the department faculty has recommended important revisions in the curriculum, including changes in course content, course require-ments, and the addition of new courses that are considered especially 'relevant' for today's concerned students."

As the school was adapting to the new economies, the Department of Journalism was growing faster than any other division of the school.

McNew pleaded for new facility for the department.

Jere Hoar, acting chair, wrote, "Journalism students are encouraged to have double or triple majors, additional majors being in subject matter fields likely to prove valuable in broadening the intellectual base and providing information necessary for the reporting of today's complex society.

"Not neglected in this attempt has been the effort to provide training for specific careers in journalism fields. It is no idle boast that the record of achievement of University of Mississippi journalism graduates is equaled by the graduates of no other comparable unit in the mid-South." In 1974, Hoar was named Outstanding Teacher of the Year.

### Dismantling the School

In 1949, Joseph Cerny (yes, "Papa Joe") published an article in *The Mississippi Certified Public Accountant,* a quarterly publication of the Mississippi Society of CPAs, advocating the need for separate schools to teach accountancy. Cerny wrote, "The trend [in separate accounting schools] is very similar to the one in law and medicine, and it is almost certain that in the next decade or two there will be several recognized schools of accountancy as there are schools of law, etc."

Cerny's prognostication was early by two decades, but as

# LARRY MARTINDALE

Larry Martindale ('68) was a partner with Atlanta-based W.B. Johnson Properties LLC, a real estate development and management company, which owned NorthLake Foods Inc., the nation's largest Waffle House franchise.

Under the name J.P. Hotels, the company also acquired the Ritz-Carlton Hotel Co. and owned and operated franchises in Holiday Inn and Marriott hotels.

In 1983, the Ritz-Carlton Hotel Co. consisted of four domestic hotels. When W.B. Johnson Properties sold the company in 1996, it had expanded internationally with 34 hotels. In 1992, the company was the first in the hospitality industry to win the prestigious Malcolm Baldrige National Quality Award.

A Grand Junction, Tenn., native, Martindale arrived at Ole Miss on a basketball scholarship. After four great years at Ole Miss, he served in the U.S. Marine Corps in California and launched his career in 1970 by affiliating with Waffle House Inc.

In 1976, he joined W.B. Johnson Properties as president and CEO of NorthLake Foods, and in 1978 was selected to take on the added responsibilities as chairman and CEO of J.P. Hotels. When W.B. Johnson Properties bought Ritz-Carlton Hotel Co., Martindale was promoted to vice chairman and COO of the parent company.

Martindale and his wife, Susan, became involved with Chancellor Emeritus Robert Khayat's initiative to revitalize campus with a long-term landscaping plan. Because of his experience in the hotel industry, Martindale recognized the impact of an institution's appearance in the recruitment of students, faculty, and staff and believed it built the morale of a university community.

In addition, the couple's generosity supported renovations to the Old Gym, which he calls his "Madison Square Garden," referring to his time on the Rebel basketball team. In October 1998, after a $7 million facelift, the Old Gym was renamed the Martindale Student Services Center.

Mirroring their involvement in Atlanta civic organizations and charities, the Martindales have become advocates for many Ole miss programs. Susan Martindale is a founding director of the Ole Miss Women's Council for Philanthropy. Larry Martindale has provided leadership on the UM Foundation.

Dale Flesher wrote in his *Accountancy at Ole Miss: A Sesquicentennial Salute*, "The smoldering ember was there, and eventually that ember became a flame."

Flesher continued, "Because most business administration programs emphasized management-related training, there was little room for addressing the rapid growth in the body of accounting knowledge. Thus, separating accountancy from the School of Business came under discussion."

Grover Porter, chair of the Department of Accountancy in 1975, gave a speech in Tupelo suggesting that every state school should have a separate school of accountancy. The *Tupelo Journal* quoted Porter, and McNew read the story. He was furious. According to Flesher's work, McNew called Porter to his office and declared, "You better hope you get a separate school of accountancy because you will never get tenure in the School of Business Administration as long as I am dean!"

N. Kenneth Nail, a CPA in Tupelo, hosted a luncheon for the accountancy faculty, the Professional Accountancy Advisory Council (made up of Ole Miss accounting alumni), the chancellor, the vice chancellor, and Dean McNew. The Council members — most of whom supported a separate school of accountancy — thoroughly grilled Dean McNew in front of his superiors and his underlings.

Nail, who had been previously been supplied with departmental budgets, said, "We are donating 'big bucks' to the Department of Accountancy to help it enhance its programs. Now, we have learned that these donations are in effect being diverted to other departments in the School of Business Administration. We want a stop put to these practices."

McNew was not pleased with the meeting. According to Professor Davis, after that meeting it was all-out political warfare between McNew and the accounting faculty.

In the late 1960s, the Department of Political Science (along with the Bureau of Government Research) had been relocated to the School of Liberal Arts. Then, in 1976, the thriving Department of Journalism had also been removed from the school of business. Now, McNew stood to lose the Department of Accountancy.

The friction between the dean and the faculty was so great that it made recruiting faculty almost impossible.

Flesher wrote about his own experience interviewing for a faculty position:

*I came for an interview in the spring of 1977 and was told by Vice Chancellor Harvey Lewis that if I wanted a job at Ole Miss, I should express no opinion on the subject of schools of accountancy. Lewis told me that the dean, Ben B. McNew, would not hire anyone who was in any way supportive of a separate school. On the other hand, the faculty would not hire anyone who was not supportive of a separate school. When asked, I pled ignorance on the subject and was approved by both factions.*

Charles W. Taylor, chairman of the Department of Accountancy, wrote: "It is paradoxical that during this period in which the University has suffered a serious decline in enrollment, the Department of Accountancy has attained a dramatic increase in both course and major enrollment, yet . . . the accountancy program at the University of Mississippi should be curtailed by administrative fiat. The curtailment has been accomplished by an absolute failure to give special administrative recognition to the unique situation existing in the accounting Ph.D. marketplace. [This] has created a serious faculty shortage. This lack of balance in faculty positions within the School of Business Administration has resulted in conducting senior level courses with enrollment levels that are unconscionable and has resulted in a disservice to accountancy majors."

In an attempt to gain leverage with the administration and the IHL board of trustees, McNew wrote in his 1978 annual report, "Over the last five years, Business at the University of Mississippi has grown more than any other college, school, or division in the entire state. In fact, the School of Business Administration at the University of Mississippi accounted for some sixty-three percent of the growth at this institution from 1973 to 1978.

## McNew Outnumbered

With growing support for a separate school of accountancy, and the growth in the number of accountancy majors, in November 1977, Chancellor Porter Fortune appointed a campus-wide committee to consider the feasibility of a separate school. After thorough study, the committee submitted a report strongly urging the establishment of a separate School of Accountancy. The chancellor endorsed the idea and sent it to the Board of Trustees.

Because of the support given by the administration and alumni, the board approved on June 15, 1978, the establishment of a separate School of Accountancy.

Perhaps the administration and alumni supported the separation based upon the merits of such a move. But McNew's demeanor and demanding nature didn't help his cause to keep the two schools together.

## MEC Will Examine The State Business Climate

Examination of factors affecting Mississippi's business climate was launched this week by the Mississippi Economic Council. The examination is being made by members of the Council's Business Climate Committee, headed by Dr. Ben McNew, dean of the School of Business Administration at the University of Mississippi.

Some 50 MEC members, all business leaders in their local communities, are involved in the study. The committee, in the coming 12 months, will be

Tennessee; Dr. D. H. Arner, Mississippi State University; Carl Black, Jr., Jackson; Ellis Bodron, Vicksburg; Dan Bowling, Monticello; E. L. Boyce, Brookhaven; Frank Buehler, Cincinnati, Ohio; T. O. Burris, Jr., Jackson; Jim Carraway, Monticello; Natie Caraway, Jackson; Don Chumney, Jackson; W. K. Clark, Starkville; Curtis Coker, Jackson; J. D. Cox, Jackson; V. J. Daniel Jr.,

Dean McNew chaired a number of committees for the Mississippi Economic Council to examine taxation, banks, and the business climate in the state.

In his final report, McNew wrote, "As overwhelming as these achievements may seem, they cannot be viewed in context without additional information. Much of this progress and development took place while the business unit was being partitioned. In the late sixties, shortly after the law enforcement program had been obtained, the School of Business and Government was separated from the Department of Political Science and the Bureau of Governmental Research. This action, however, did not prevent the business unit from securing full accreditation for its graduate programs in 1972. Then, in 1976, the Department of Journalism was withdrawn. These units were transferred to the College of Liberal Arts. In 1978, the Department of Accountancy was authorized to become a school completely separate from the School of Business Administration. In addition, many attempts have been made to transfer such courses as economic statistics to the Department of Mathematics and business data processing to the School of Engineering. To be sure, these demands for transfer can be expected when a particular unit is undergoing substantial growth while others are not, but it must be realized that such transfers can diminish student demand and be detrimental to educational effectiveness."

McNew left Ole Miss in 1979. He went on to have a successful career as an administrator and professor, including a ten-year stint at his alma mater, University of Central Arkansas, from 1988-1999, where he established the McNew Banking Lectureship Endowment Fund.

# GERALD M. ABDALLA

1969 • BBA; 1973 • JD, LAW • MCCOMB, MISSISSIPPI

Gerald M. Abdalla (BBA 69, JD 73) was the chairman, president, and CEO of Croft, LLC, a manufacturer of aluminum and vinyl windows and doors in McComb.

While at Ole Miss, Abdalla was a member of the Beta Alpha Psi accounting fraternity, Phi Eta Sigma scholastic honorary and Phi Delta Theta social fraternity. He was also on the Moot Court Board and a member of the Phi Delta Phi legal fraternity while in law school.

After receiving his LLM in taxation from New York University School of Law in 1974, he served as an attorney for Carlton Fields in Orlando, Fla., for four years before moving to Croft.

He currently is a member of the Chancellor's Trust, Accountancy Order and Patterson School of Accountancy Professional Advisory Council at Ole Miss.

In the 1990s, Abdalla approached then-Chancellor Robert Khayat about making a donation to the university. As the two men talked, Chancellor Khayat asked about the range of the gift. Abdalla responded, "In the $60 million range."

Khayat recounted, "I had no idea what to do with $60 million. I called Provost Carolyn Staton to the office to get her input. Without missing a beat, she suggested an institute of international studies."

Abdalla was involved in the formation and development of the Croft Institute for International Studies and served as chairman, president, and trustee of the Croft Institute. Abdalla also was involved in the formation and development of the Joseph C. Bancroft Educational and Charitable Fund, for which he currently serves as executive director.

Abdalla and his wife, Jennifer (BA 72), have two sons, Jerry Jr. (BA 00, JD 03) and Tom (BA 03), and one daughter, Elise.

# INTERVIEW WITH BEN "BENNIE" MCNEW
## DEAN, SCHOOL OF BUSINESS & GOVERNMENT
## 1965-1979

**Talk about the state of the business school (positives and negatives) when you took over.**

The school was in good shape when I became acting dean. It had established a Chair of Banking fully supported by the Mississippi Bankers Association, and it had been accredited for many years. Its reputation was one of quality, with graduates taking their places in outstanding businesses, governments, publishing companies, educational institutions, and other organizations. At that time, the name of our division was the School of Business and Government, and it included the Department of Political Science and the Department of Journalism. Accreditation, at that time, had been modified to allow business schools separate recognition at the graduate level. The University of Mississippi had not been accredited separately at the graduate level, and this was viewed by some as a negative factor.

**What were some of the obstacles you faced? What was your greatest challenge?**

Obstacles began with inadequate financial resources that affected virtually everything from faculty to publicity. The academic areas of economics, finance, management, and marketing were in one department, and that arrangement was thought to be cumbersome. In accounting, which was a separate department, faculty holding a CPA certificate and a master's degree had long been counted by the accreditation agency as having a terminal degree. The accreditation agency changed that terminal-degree provision to require a doctorate. And the outgoing dean [Clive Dunham] was the only accounting faculty with a doctorate at that time. Working to establish a department of management and marketing, to recruit accounting faculty with doctorates, and to secure graduate accreditation was indeed a challenge. However, inadequate financing was probably the greatest challenge, and despite successful efforts to attract private funds for the areas of industry, insurance, and other disciplines, financial resources remained problematic over the years.

**Of what are you most proud during your tenure as dean?**

The graduates and what they have accomplished in their chosen endeavors. It was pleasing to me that the School of Business Administration, with meager resources, attracted a growing body of students. At one time our enrollment was only a few students less than the largest division of the university.

**What was the genesis/motivation for the accounting school to split from the business school?**

Again, I do not have complete information about this matter, but I believe one or more of the national accounting organizations encouraged separate accounting schools, and that was probably a strong force for the movement. I believe the accounting faculty, the state accounting association, and the central administration at the university wanted the separation.

> "It was my job to abide by the accrediting agency's rules and regulations. In many instances, enforcing these tenets caused problems for which I seemed to get blame."

**Looking back, would you be supportive of (or opposed to) a separate accountancy school?**

I would be opposed.

**Throughout history, political pressures have been put on deans at universities. Did you feel any pressures from outside sources about curriculum, agendas, admissions, etc.?**

Yes. In keeping accreditation, it was my job to abide by the agency's rules and regulations. In many instances, enforcing these tenets caused problems for which I seemed to get the blame.

And I remember one troublesome newspaper article stemming from a study I did. My study had to do with financial resources in Mississippi, and my conclusion was that the state would need outside resources. The release from the university indicated that Mississippi had sufficient resources within its own borders to do what it needed. When that hit the papers, I had much explaining to do. Fortunately, I was able to ameliorate the situation by sending out a copy of the study.

**What was your vision for the business school when you took over?**

It was a surprise to me that the office became open. Therefore, I had not established a vision at the time. However, my goals soon became to increase enrollment and to provide an outstanding educational experience in diverse areas of business administration.

**Did you notice any change in students (behavior, quality, interests) during your time as dean?**

I believe I detected a slight change in aspirations from traditional academic pursuits to preparation for employment. That change was not pronounced, but it may have been present.

**Did you have any memorable speakers?**

We had some distinguished speakers come in from time to time. On one occasion on Commerce Day, we had the president of

**Bennie Banks McNew stands by the mailbox of his parents' old homeplace in Centerville in north-central Faulkner County, Arkansas. The McNew Charter Farm has been named a 2014 Century Farm by the Arkansas Department of Agriculture.**

Georgia Pacific as our guest, Mr. Robert Pamplin. His headquarters were in Oregon, and he came in through the Oxford airport in an executive jet, and that was kind of unusual for Oxford. The night before Commerce Day, the student body heard a jet come in. We had a good attendance. Some of the students told me that I could attribute that to their being aware that they came in on that executive jet.

*Interview with Dr. Ben McNew conducted August 2017*

# GEN. PAUL HESTER

General Paul V. Hester, a native of West Point, Mississippi, was commander of Air Force Special Operations Command in Hurlburt Field, Florida, a position that gave him responsibility for 20,000 active duty, Reserve, Air National Guard, and civilian professionals. The command provided Air Force Special Operations Forces and combat search and rescue for worldwide deployment and assignment to unified combatant commanders.

While at Ole Miss, Hester was a member of Kappa Sigma fraternity and was its National Man of the Year in 2002. He was the cadet wing commander of the Air Force ROTC program, and, after commissioning, entered the Air Force in January 1971, earning his wings in December of the same year at Columbus Air Force Base. His aviation career, including a combat tour in Southeast Asia, has been spread over the A-7D, F-4, F-15, F-16, and MC-130 aircraft.

He commanded seven different units in his thirty-plus-year career, including commander of the U.S. Forces in Japan and 5th Air Force at Yokota Air Base, Japan.

Hester's staff tours include duty in the Tactical Air Command's Directorate of Plans and the Commander's Action Group; chief of the Air Force's Legislative Liaison Office at the U.S. House of Representatives; division chief in J-5 of the Joint Staff; Joint Chiefs of Staff representative to the Organization for Security and Cooperation in Europe; and director of Air Force legislative liaison for the secretary and the chief of staff of the Air Force. Hester was inducted into the Ole Miss Alumni Association Hall of Fame in 2004. He and his wife live in San Antonio, Texas.

# RICHARD MOLPUS, JR.

## 1971 • BBA • PHILADELPHIA, MISSISSIPPI

Dick Molpus is founder and president of Molpus Woodlands Group, a timberland investment management organization headquartered in Jackson. Molpus has had a long career in public service and business. In 1980, he became executive director of the Governor's Office of Federal-State Programs under Mississippi Gov. William F. Winter and worked as part of Winter's team to pass the historic Mississippi Education Reform Act of 1982.

In 1983, Molpus was elected secretary of state of Mississippi, spearheading improved Mississippi election laws, strengthening public disclosure laws for lobbyists, and forcing renegotiations of 10,000 below-market 16th Section land leases. In 1995, Molpus ran unsuccessfully as the Democratic nominee for governor of Mississippi.

After his third term as secretary of state, Molpus began Molpus Woodlands Group, which manages more than 1.5 million acres of timberland across 17 states. Molpus and his wife, Sally, founded Parents for Public Schools, which has spread to 17 chapters across 12 states. He co-chaired the 2006 Jackson Public School Bond Campaign, bringing $150 million for new schools and renovations.

Molpus received the H. Council Trenholm Memorial Award from the National Education Association, was inducted into the Mississippi Business Hall of Fame in 2005, and was honored in 2008 as a Champion of Justice by the Mississippi Center of Justice. In 2007, he organized and founded the U.S. Endowment for Forestry and Communities, a $200 million endowment to improve forest health and assist timber-reliant communities, and he is a founding board member of the National Alliance of Forest Owners.

# GEORGE T. LOTTERHOS

## 1971 • BBA • GERMANTOWN, TENNESSEE

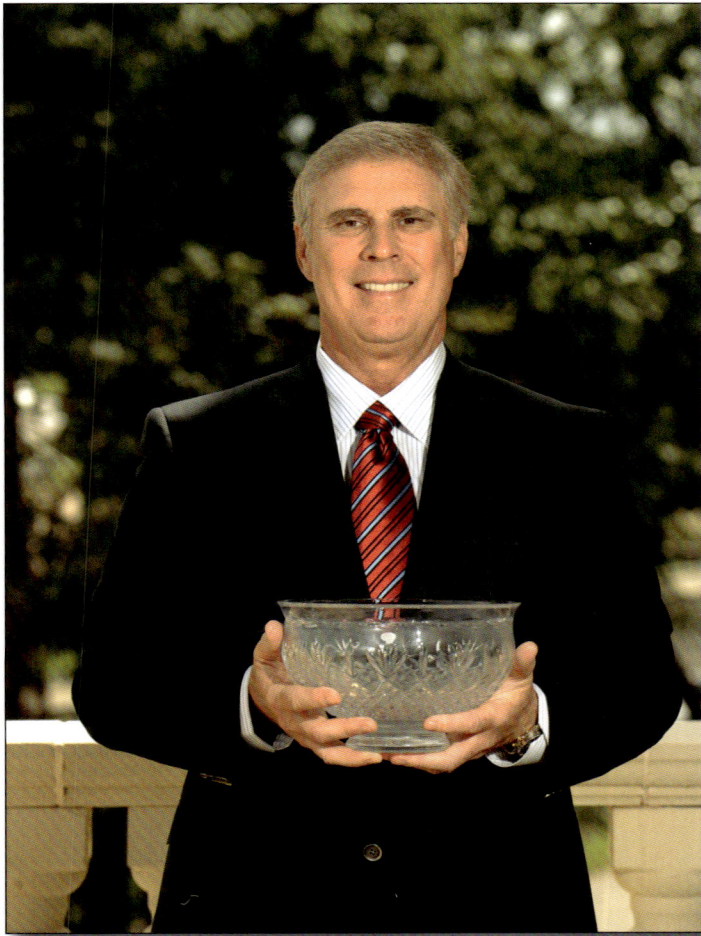

George Lotterhos of Germantown, Tennessee, is a 1971 graduate of the University of Mississippi School of Business. While at Ole Miss, he was a member of the football team for four years as a defensive end and was a member of Pi Kappa Alpha fraternity.

Upon graduation from Ole Miss, he married Carolyn Jones, his high school and college sweetheart. They have two children. Lotterhos entered the financial world in 1971 and, after over forty years, is managing director at Raymond James Morgan Keegan. He is the recipient of the 2008 M-Club Alumni Chapter Service Award. Based on leadership, service, and commitment to the M-Club, the award was named after him that same year.

Lotterhos is a past president of the M-Club Alumni Chapter and a past president of the Rebel Club of Memphis. He served as one of the founders of the Grove Bowl in 1989 and was also instrumental in the establishment of the M-Club Athletic Hall of Fame. He was also a member of the President's Club of UMIC, Inc., a Memphis-based investment banking firm.

Lotterhos received the Bill Wade Unsung Hero Award from the All American Football Foundation and has served on the board of directors of the M-Club Alumni Chapter as a board member emeritus.

He has served on the advisory board for Germantown Methodist Hospital and serves on the banking and finance advisory board for the University of Mississippi School of Business Administration. Lotterhos was given the Ole Miss Alumni Association Alumni Service Award in 2012.

# WALTON GRESHAM

**1971 • BUSINESS ADMINISTRATION • INDIANOLA, MISSISSIPPI**

W alton Gresham III is a businessman from Indianola, where he is a life-long resident.

He serves as president of Gresham Petroleum Co., secretary of Double Quick, secretary of Delta Terminal, and director and member of the executive committee of Planters Bank & Trust Company.

He is active in his community and profession, serving as a past president of Delta Council, the Indianola Rotary Club, the Indianola Educational Foundation, and the Indianola Chamber of Commerce. He is currently chairman of the Community Foundation of Sunflower County. Gresham is past president of the Mississippi Propane Gas Association and Mississippi Petroleum Marketers & Convenience Store Association. He has been the Mississippi director to the National Propane Gas Association.

Additionally, Gresham has served in other organizations and entities during his career as a volunteer leader, and his passion has been to promote economic development and a better infrastructure in the Mississippi Delta and the state of Mississippi.

A graduate of Indianola High School (1967) and the University of Mississippi (1971), Gresham has served on the University of Mississippi Alumni Board as well as the University of Mississippi Foundation Board. He was a member of Phi Delta Theta Fraternity and has remained active as an alumni volunteer.

Gresham is married to the former Laura Ethridge of Oxford, and they have two daughters and five grandchildren.

Gresham is a lifelong member of St. Stephen's Episcopal Church, serving in all offices over the past 45 years, in addition to being a licensed layreader.

# E. ARCHIE MANNING, III

1971 • BPA, BUSINESS ADMINISTRATION • DREW, MISSISSIPPI

Archie Manning was an outstanding professional football player who has also found time for significant service to his community and local and national charities.

After earning his bachelor of public administration degree at Ole Miss in 1971, he quarterbacked the New Orleans Saints for 12 years before going to the Houston Oilers. During his professional career he was named National Football Conference Player of the Year in 1978 by both UPI and Sporting News, Pro Bowl quarterback in 1978 and 1979, and the NFC passing leader in completions and yards in 1980.

He was the winner of the 1978 Justice Byron "Whizzer" White Humanitarian Award, pro football's most prestigious award, for service to team, community, and country. In 1979 the Veterans of Foreign Wars gave him their national Hall of Fame service award, and the Milwaukee Press Club presented him with their Bart Starr Meritorious Service Award. In 1980 the Drew native was named Mississippian of the Year by the Mississippi Broadcasters Association. The New Orleans Jaycees named him their 1978 Outstanding Young Man.

For seven years Manning was honorary chairman of the Big Brothers of New Orleans, and for nine years he was honorary head coach of the Louisiana Special Olympics. He was 1980 Louisiana chairman of the Muscular Dystrophy Association and the 1982 honorary chair of the Mississippi Association for Blindness. He chairs the Archie Manning Cystic Fibrosis Tournament in New Orleans. He is a member of the Multiple Sclerosis National Sports Committee. He has also been actively involved in work with the Ronald McDonald House, the Fellowship of Christian Athletes, the Boy Scouts, and the American Cancer Society, the Mental Health Association, and the United Way.

# G.O. "LANNY" GRIFFITH, JR

Lanny Griffith serves as chief executive officer of BGR Group. He joined the Washington, D.C.-based government affairs and communications firm in 1993 after serving in several roles in former President George H.W. Bush's administration.

Griffith's political career began in the early 1960s, when he volunteered as a junior high school student to work for Republican gubernatorial candidate Rubel Phillips. In the 1980s, he worked for the Republican National Committee, managed former Mississippi Gov. Haley Barbour's U.S. Senate race, and he served as the executive director of the Mississippi Republican Party for three years. In 1988, he served as Southern political director for Bush's presidential campaign.

In 1989, Griffith was sworn in as special assistant to the president, serving as Bush's liaison to governors and other statewide elected officials. In 1991, Bush nominated Griffith to be assistant secretary of education. At the U.S. Department of Education, he directed Secretary Lamar Alexander's effort to build a national consensus around educational standards and testing.

Griffith represented the U.S. on the Education Committee of the Paris-based Organization for Economic Cooperation and Development and served as co-chairman of the Advisory Council on Dependents' Education, which serves as the school board for all dependent schools worldwide under the jurisdiction of the U.S. Department of Defense.

Griffith's work for the Bush family continued with his role as national chairman of the Bush-Cheney 2000 Entertainment Task Force and entertainment coordinator for the 2001 Bush inauguration. He later served as a Bush Ranger and member of the Bush 2004 National Finance Committee.

Griffith is founder of the Trust for the National Mall and currently serves on the board of directors. He serves as national treasurer for the Duke of Edinburgh's Award in the U.S.

# EDITH KELLY-GREEN

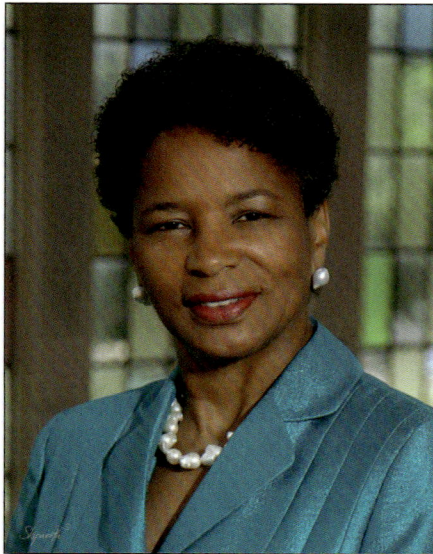

Edith Kelly-Green was vice president of Strategic Sourcing and Supply for Federal Express Corporation. She was responsible for the global supply chain management function, controlling the planning, procurement, storage and distribution of $1.5 billion in corporate inventories and $6.5 billion in annual spending.

Kelly-Green joined FedEx in 1977 as a senior accountant and quickly progressed through the ranks. As managing director of finance, she was the division leader for writing the Malcolm Baldrige National Quality Award application, which FedEx won in 1990. In 1995 and 1997, she received the prestigious FedEx Corporation Five-Star Award.

Prior to joining FedEx, Kelly-Green spent four years in public accounting with Touche Ross (now Deloitte & Touche) in Memphis as a senior auditor. She holds a master's degree in business administration from Vanderbilt University and is a certified public accountant. She is a 1987 graduate of Leadership Memphis and a 1990 graduate of Leadership America.

Kelly-Green has presented to many groups on topics of quality and supply chain management. She serves on the board of trustees for the Center of Advanced Purchasing Studies (CAPS) and is a member of several roundtables focusing on supply chain management. She is also frequently quoted in articles about this topic.

Kelly-Green has also been active in The Make a Wish Foundation, Memphis Zoo, Memphis in May, Senior Citizens Services and the Women's Foundation. A breast cancer survivor, she is committed to national fundraisers that help communicate and reduce the risk of cancer. She is also active in The University of Mississippi Foundation and The University of Mississippi Commitment to Excellence Campaign. She established an endowment fund at Ole Miss to provide scholarships to African American women entering the School of Accountancy. Additionally, she has served as assistant treasurer of the Mississippi Boulevard Christian Church and as a board member of the Christian Disciples of Christ Foundation. Other recognition includes the Women of Achievement Initiative Award, Girls Inc. She Knows Where She's Going Award, March of Dimes White Rose Award, and Simply the Best. She has been recognized in both *Ebony* and *Dollars and Sense* and in 1997, she received the Ambassador Award for Diversity Leadership.

Personally, Kelly-Green tries to focus not so much on "success" but on "significance." In that regard, she tries to keep balanced by spending as much time as possible with her family.

Most recently, Kelly-Green has opened a chain of restaurants.

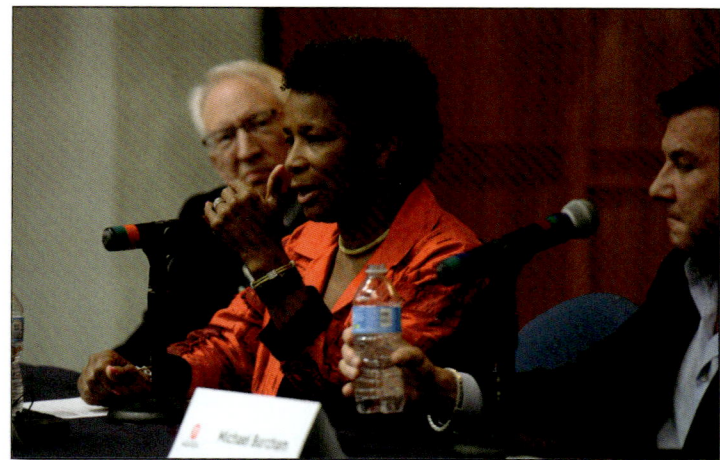

Edith Kelly-Green speaking at the Center for Innovation and Entrepreneurship (Bill Rayburn is to her right)

# JAMES M. ELY

**M**ike Ely is a native of McComb, Mississippi, and a 1977 graduate of the School of Business at The University of Mississippi. During his years at Ole Miss, he was a student manager for the Ole Miss Rebels football team and a member of Sigma Chi fraternity.

In 1977, he joined Allstate Insurance Company as an operations supervisor in the Jackson regional office. During his thirty-four-year career with Allstate, he held many positions, including field product manager and regional underwriting manager. In 1984, he was appointed market analyst for Allstate's five-state regional office. In 1995, he was transferred to Nashville as regional underwriting manager for the Southern Region. He remained there until his retirement from Allstate in June 2011.

Ely earned the Chairman's Award for his organization and design of the Auto Revitalization Program and completed the Executive Leadership Program at Vanderbilt University.

He is a past president and board member of the Middle Tennessee Ole Miss Alumni Club, a past vice president and member of the executive board of the M-Club Alumni Chapter, a life member of the Ole Miss Alumni Association and M-Club Alumni Chapter, a member of the Business Order for the UM School of Business, and a longtime member and past vice president of the UM School of Business Insurance Advisory Council.

Ely was an integral part of the Middle Tennessee Ole Miss Alumni Club's scholarship fundraising events at the Ryman Auditorium in Nashville. The inaugural Mississippi at the Ryman and the Mississippi Rocks the Ryman events, both featuring 3 Doors Down, generated more than $90,000 for the Middle Tennessee/Chris Bonds Ole Miss Alumni Chapter Scholarship Endowment.

Ely was awarded the Ole Miss Alumni Association's Alumni Service Award in 2011. He is married to Peggy Davis Ely. They have two daughters, Julie Ely Cropp and Laura Katherine Ely, both Ole Miss graduates, and they make their home in Oxford.

# WILLIAM R. JORDAN

## 1973 • BBA, BUSINESS ADMINISTRATION • COLUMBUS, GEORGIA

William Jordan, known to his friends as "Bill," came to Ole Miss from his hometown of Columbus, Georgia, in 1969 to get an education and to play football. He caught passes from Archie Manning on the football field, and in the classroom, he acquired the business acumen that would eventually make him a giant in the outdoor apparel industry. He earned his bachelor of business administration degree in 1973.

After graduation, Jordan returned to Columbus and worked in his family's boat business, but by 1983 he was ready to start his first company, Spartan Archery Products, which offered products that hunters found necessary in the woods.

By 1986, Jordan had developed what would become his greatest business success, Realtree Camouflage. Starting with the first pattern of bark, which was literally traced from an old oak in his parents' yard, innovation was the key to Realtree's success. Realtree offers a variety of versatile camo, including patterns for western and waterfowl markets.

After some trying times in the late 1980s, Realtree grew quickly throughout the 1990s, becoming a household name in the hunting industry. Jordan never stopped innovating.

He also never forgot the university that set him on the path to success. Jordan has been recognized by the Alumni Association, was inducted into the Alumni Hall of Fame in 2012, and had a football practice field named in his honor—a thanks given for the $2 million he contributed to the athletics fundraising campaign Forward Together.

"We are so thankful for generous alumni like Bill Jordan who know what it's like to build a business into a national presence," said Keith Carter, senior associate athletics director for development and executive director of the Ole Miss Athletics Foundation. "Essentially, that's what we're doing here. We're building a program that must continually improve in order to be competitive."

Jordan never forgot his humble start with a small company in the back room of his late father's marine dealership, equipped with only the great support and education he received at Ole Miss. Despite many setbacks along the way, he persisted, creating an all-American success story.

# ROBERT "BEN" WILLIAMS

## 1976 • BBA, BUSINESS ADMINISTRATION

Ben Williams was the first African American football player at Ole Miss. A defensive lineman from 1972-1975, he thrilled fans with his athletic abilities, becoming a three-time All-SEC performer recognized with a number of awards. Affectionately dubbed "Gentle Ben," he continued to add to his list of firsts. In 1975, he was the first African American given the designation "Colonel Reb" by the student body. The distinction is the highest honor Ole Miss students bestow on a fellow male student.

After earning a bachelor's degree in business administration in 1976, Williams played professional football for ten years for the Buffalo Bills. During this time, Williams earned All-Pro honors and was named to the Bills' Silver Anniversary All-Time Team. In recognition of his outstanding athletic career, he was inducted this year into the Mississippi Sports Hall of Fame. He also has been inducted into the Alumni Association's M-Club Alumni Hall of Fame and is a recipient of the university's Award of Distinction.

A businessman and owner of LYNCO Construction Co. in Jackson, Williams has served his family, community, and alma mater by giving his loyalty, time, and financial support.

Williams has served as a member of the Black Alumni Advisory Council, The University of Mississippi Alumni Association Board of Directors, the Foundation Board of Directors, the M-Club Board of Directors. and as chair of the Minority Scholarship Endowment fund raising efforts. In March 1996, the scholarship was renamed The Robert "Ben" Williams Minority Scholarship Endowment.

In his community, Williams is active in the Easter Seals Society and in the Multiple Sclerosis Association. Professionally, he is a member of the Association of Building Contractors and is a recipient of the Ralph L. Wilson Leadership Award. He and his wife Linda have three children.

# GEORGE HILLIARD

Georgeﾟ E. Hilliard has served as president and partner in the Memphis independent insurance agency Pete Mitchell and Associates, Inc. As managing partner, he is responsible for the service standards, business practices, and profitability of the agency. He is a native of Hernando, Mississippi, and a 1973 graduate of Hernando High School.

Hilliard is a member of the national, state, and local associations for Professional Insurance Agents. The Tennessee association recognized him as its 2008 Agent of the Year, acknowledging both his professional and personal accomplishments.

He is past president of both the Tennessee and Memphis PIA associations and was the first African American to be elected president of both associations.

He holds both the Certified Insurance Counselor designation and the Certified Professional Insurance Agent designation. He has served as a subject matter expert for Pearson Vue, the firm that administers pre-licensing insurance education and examinations for Tennessee.

Hilliard served as a member of the board of directors for the Memphis Chamber Foundation and as an executive committee member of the Ole Miss Alumni Association board of directors. He also served as the fundraising chairman for the Memphis Alumni Chapter of Phi Beta Sigma Fraternity, Inc., scholarship program.

He has received numerous personal awards and honors, including the Memphis Silver Star New Achievers Award; Phi Beta Sigma Fraternity, Inc., African American Male Image Award; Black Business Association of Memphis Special Recognition for Outstanding Board Service; and Phi Beta Sigma Fraternity, Inc., Southwestern Regional Bigger and Better Businessman Award. He was inducted into the Ole Miss Alumni Association Hall of Fame in 2009.

While at Ole Miss, Hilliard was a member of Phi Beta Sigma Fraternity, Inc. Hilliard and his wife, Malinda, live in Memphis and have three daughters, Sabrina, Melodia, and Brittany

# SCOTT WEGMANN

Scott Wegmann is vice chairman and co-managing director in the Houston, Texas, office of Cushman and Wakefield, the largest privately-held commercial real estate services firm in the world. Wegmann specializes in tenant/user representation. For 30 years, he has represented numerous companies in Houston and across the country. He has completed transactions totaling more than twenty million square feet in more than seventy-five cities in the U.S. and in Asia, Europe, Australia, Canada, and South America. E&Y/Kenneth Leventhal Real Estate Group honored Wegmann with the 1991 and 1997 Legacy Award, "The Deals That Make a Difference," for his representation of Apache Corp. in its 223,000-square-foot corporate headquarters relocation to Houston, and Continental Airlines Inc., in its Houston corporate headquarters relocation/consolidation.

*Houston Business Journal* honored Wegmann as a Most Valuable Player in citywide office brokerage for 2004 and 2005, along with the Landmark Awards as its Project Sale category honoree for the 2006 sale/leaseback of the BMC Software headquarters. The NAIOP Commercial Real Estate Development Association honored Wegmann as Office Broker of the Year in 1997 and 2005. Cushman and Wakefield selected him as one of two Managers of the Year for 2007. Wegmann was inducted into the Ole Miss Alumni Hall of Fame in 2011.

Wegmann has served in leadership roles in numerous associations including the Houston Office Leasing Brokers Association, The Children's Fund, the advisory board of Amegy Bank of Texas, St. Luke's Methodist Church and Episcopal High School.

Wegmann resides in Houston with his wife, Loraine. Their two daughters, Jennifer and Julie, both attended Ole Miss.

# MICHAEL GLENN

In addition, Glenn was a member of the five-person executive committee, which planned and executed the corporate strategy. He also served on the Strategic Management Committee, which oversaw operations of the corporation.

Before FedEx Corporation was formed in January 1998, Glenn was senior vice president of worldwide marketing, customer service and corporate communications for FedEx Express. In that position, he was responsible for directing all marketing, customer service, employee communications and public relations activities. Glenn joined FedEx in 1981 and has held several leadership positions in the sales and marketing divisions.

He currently serves on the board of directors of Pentair, Inc., Renasant Bank, Autism Speaks, and the United Way of the Mid-South. He is also chairman of the board of Madonna Learning Center, a school for special-needs children, and he serves on the executive committee of Christ United Methodist Church, where he and his family are members.

Born in Memphis, Tenn., Glenn is married to Donna Hatley Glenn. They have three children: Hatley, Tucker, and Katherine. He earned his bachelor's degree from the University of Mississippi and his master's degree from the University of Memphis.

T. Michael Glenn was executive vice president of market development and corporate communications for FedEx Corporation. Glenn also served as president and chief executive officer of FedEx Services. In this role, he led all marketing, sales, and communications across the FedEx Office and Global Supply Chain Services business units.

# OLE MISS BUSINESS

## THE 80s

DEAN
M. LYNN SPRUILL

DEAN
REX L. COTTLE

1980 - 1991

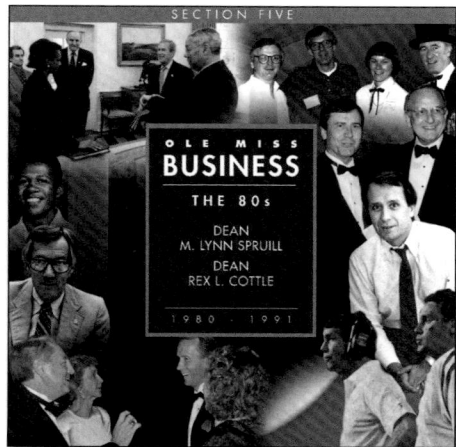

SECTION FIVE

**OLE MISS BUSINESS**

THE 80s

DEAN
M. LYNN SPRUILL
DEAN
REX L. COTTLE

1980 · 1991

Clockwise from top left: John Palmer in the oval office with Condoleezza Rice, President George W. Bush, and Colin Powell; Dean Lynn Spruill at a convention with Don Moak, Susan Spruill, and Bouncer Robinson; Chancellor Gerald Turner and John Palmer; Dean Rex Cottle; Coach Steve Sloan and John Fourcade; Sherman and Celia Muths with Dean Cottle; Dean Spruill; Augustus Leon Collins

# LYNN SPRUILL
## DEAN 1980-1984

"Ole Miss is the intellectual center of the state and we want the best students."

Lynn Spruill, *Enterprise-Journal*, July 27, 1982

Carl Nabors, who had served in the business school in 1961, was appointed interim dean after Ben McNew's departure. He was a member of the accountancy faculty (and officially part of a new school separate from the School of Business Administration), but Nabors had so much institutional knowledge, Chancellor Fortune believed he would serve as the best bridge until a new dean search had been completed.

In 1980, Lynn Spruill was hired away from the University of Kentucky.

"In 1980, the business school at Ole Miss," Spruill explained, "was on the cusp of a transition which was very much the same as the state of most relatively small public universities' business schools in that era. The schools were fairly closed off from the business community. They were insular, not very outward looking. They taught pretty much the same old stuff. They were not — and I don't mean this in a harsh way, but it's true — very distinguished. They were not viewed with a great deal of respect on the campuses. And Ole Miss wanted to change that."

In the 1970s, the trend in business schools, and their deans,

Lynn Spruill was the first full-time dean after the accounting-business school split.

began to shift to an external focus.

"In 1979, after Ben McNew left," Spruill said, "I think the university made a conscious decision to follow what was becoming the model — to look for someone who could create a strong internal structure, but who was *externally* focused."

Spruill was fortunate to have Randy Boxx serve as his associate dean. Spruill referred to Boxx as "absolutely spectacular." And Carl Nabors, "who knew everything," according to Spruill, also helped manage internal affairs.

"I was aided and abetted by these two men who looked after the inside part of the college. So I never had to dig into the intricate details of everything happening in curriculum in the business school, because Randy and Carl knew it backwards and forwards, and had it under control."

The school was facing an accreditation process — now without a School of Accountancy. But according to Spruill, Boxx and Nabors took care of the internal challenges. Spruill's challenge was to generate external support.

In the 1980s, the American Association of Collegiate Schools of Business (AACSB) were scrutinizing the levels of external sup-

An internal memo listing the charter members of
the Business Advisory Council

port.

"So," Spruill said, "it was my job to convince the AACSB a) that there were alumni who were willing to help — that is provide money — and b) that there were outsiders *within* the university who were supportive of what we were trying to do — which meant the deans' council, the chancellor, the vice chancellor."

## An Advisory Council

In 1981, Spruill created a business advisory council comprised of successful businesspeople who had some interest in the success of the school.

"We put together a group of twenty-five people that came from across the country to help us. Some of the members included John Palmer, Jim Barksdale, and Howard McMillan, (see list of inaugural business advisory council at left).

"We didn't raise a ton of money at first," Spruill said, "but we raised lots more than had ever been raised before."

One of the board members asked Spruill to visit his insurance office in downtown Jackson. "He handed me a check for $25,000. I took it back to campus, and we had a great celebration. That was a lot of money. It was a beginning."

But it was only the beginning. More checks would come, in much larger amounts, from members of the business advisory council.

## Dealing with the Split

The School of Accountancy had just been established in 1979. Reflecting on the split in a 2017 interview, Spruill said, "Well, it was an odd set up. I came to it with my eyes wide open. I don't yet, to this day, understand why it took place. When I was interviewing and took the job, I was thirty-eight years old. I'm a good deal wiser, I think, today. I'm not sure I would have taken the job. I think splitting off accounting from business doesn't make a lot of sense to me. I would have fought it, but it was what it was."

The split caused some difficulty with re-accreditation by the

AACSB, but Randy Boxx and Carl Nabors navigated the terrain, and the school received accreditation.

## New Programs

In addition to the establishment of an advisory council, under Spruill's tenure, several new programs were initiated, both internally and externally.

In 1980, the Tom B. Scott, Jr., Savings and Loan Chair, was established with the cooperation and support of the savings and loan industry in Mississippi.

In 1981, the J. Ed Turner Chair of Real Estate was established (partially supported by the real estate industry in Mississippi).

In 1982, the Self Chair of Free Enterprise was endowed by Ole Miss alumni.

In 1983, the Phil B. Hardin Chair of Marketing became the university's first fully endowed chair.

And, in what was perhaps one of the most successful external moves in the history of the School of Business Administration, the Mississippi Small Business Development Center (MSBDC) was established. It was a step in the direction of a greater service commitment by the School of Business Administration to the small business community of the state (which included 99 percent of all businesses in Mississippi [see profile page 140]). The MSBDC's focus was to help launch new businesses, as well as identify the causes of small business problems in existing businesses and to make practical assistance available to businesses encountering those problems.

(L to R) Don Moak, chair of banking, Dean Spruill, Susan Spruill, and Jack "Bouncer" Robertson at a banking convention.

## A New Direction

Spruill titled a 1982 report mailed to alumni "A New Direction." He admitted that his comments might initially sound old fashioned because he was going to discuss the "three r's."

But Spruill's new "three r's" were recruiting, research, and recognition.

Recruiting, Spruill explained, would come in two parts: first, recruit the best faculty; then, recruit the best students. He noted that during his first two years, eight new faculty members had been hired. Spruill called them "top-notch teachers."

Research, which Spruill admitted might not seem important to some, was the only way to achieve high visibility nationally or regionally as a School of Business Administration. He emphasized the strong link between competence in the research arena and competence in the classroom. As evidence of the strides made in research, two major national conferences on research were held on the Ole Miss campus — the Delta Pi Epsilon National Research Conference on Business Education and the American Marketing Association Values Conference. In addition, the Southern Business Administration Association hosted a workshop for deans on the Oxford campus.

"The first two 'r's'", Spruill wrote, "lead directly to the third — recognition." Spruill wanted the School of Business Administration to be recognized as "a school on the move, as well as a place to go if you want a strong, up-to-date, rigorous program in all the business areas."

# GEN. AUGUSTUS LEON COLLINS

1982 • BBA, BUSINESS ADMINISTRATION • OKALONA, MISSISSIPPI

Maj. Gen. Augustus Leon Collins learned a valuable lesson while a student at the UM School of Business Administration — "There will be plenty of opportunities in life," he said, "but if you are not prepared, the opportunities will pass you by and may never return."

Born in Okolona, Collins graduated from the business school in 1982 with a Bachelor of Business Administration.

He was appointed adjutant general of Mississippi by Gov. Phil Bryant in 2012, while also serving as commanding general of both the Mississippi Army and Air National Guard. He began his military career in 1977 with the Mississippi, National Guard, Company B, 1st Battalion, 198th Armor Regiment.

The general became a business major because he believed it would provide him with the best options for his future.

"With a business degree, you are exposed to many areas that will benefit you in the world," he said. "Ole Miss is a nationally renowned university, and I wanted a degree that would speak volumes when asked where I attended college."

Collins said the Ole Miss business school prepared him for many military assignments including his time in Iraq, where he managed a force of almost 5,000 service members from various branches of the military, and the management courses trained him, in part, to supervise workers.

The finance and accounting courses taught him how to develop and manage budgets, and the business law courses gave him an understanding of how to interpret military law. His favorite course was business law.

He relied on the topics he learned when he served as one of the commissioners for the Mississippi Workers' Compensation Commission. Business law also helped him manage personal and family matters.

Some of his fondest memories as an undergrad were the road trips to Jackson with his friends to watch Ole Miss football, including one game in particular. In 1981, Ole Miss was predicted to lose against Mississippi State, but the Rebels scored a touchdown in the final minutes and won the game.

When asked what advice he would give Ole Miss students today, he said, "I would tell them that the world will care very little who you are or where you came from," he said. "What it does care about is whether or not you can produce.

"Those who can will move up the ladder and occupy positions like vice presidents in a short time. Those who can't will find themselves stuck in the entry-level positions or be forced to bounce from one job to another. Ole Miss prepares you for the challenge. Get the most out of your education. That way, when you leave, you will leave knowing that you possess the best tools to be the best at whatever endeavor you choose."

Collins lives in Madison with his wife, Debra, where he enjoys playing golf and spending time with his grandson, Tre. The couple has two sons: William and Benjamin. Benjamin is a personal trainer in Houston, Texas, and William works for security in the Federal Deposit Insurance Corp. in Washington, D.C.

Gen. Collins was featured on the cover of the 2017 edition of *BusinessFirst*

## An Alumnus Named John Palmer

Dean Spruill developed a friendship with Ole Miss alumnus John Palmer. Palmer was president of a rapidly growing company called Mobile Communication Corporation of America, one of the pioneers in the development of cellular telephones.

Palmer recalled, "Lynn Spruill had a wonderful vision for the business school, but he didn't have the budget to buy pencils."

Initially, Palmer, along with the other members of the business advisory council, tried to help with recruiting.

"I called a friend in Clarksdale who was considering going into an MBA program. 'You should consider going to Ole Miss,' I told her. She said, 'Texas is giving me a $2,500 fellowship to go.' So, I said, 'Then, you should go to Texas.'"

As Spruill had hoped, John Palmer, along with the other board members, started to gain a better understanding of the difficulties the dean faced in making his "three r's" become a reality.

## Athletics Committee and Fundraising

Spruill's competence didn't go unnoticed by Chancellor Fortune. First, the chancellor asked Spruill to serve on the Intercollegiate Athletics Committee (the same committee that Dean James Warsaw Bell chaired during his tenure as dean of the School of Commerce).

"Those were not great days," Spruill recounted, "I spent more time than I would have anticipated as a

John Palmer and the MCCA team. Palmer's friendship with Dean Spruill and the company's 1995 windfall would result in a $1 million gift to Ole Miss.

As a member of the athletics committee, Spruill often received phone calls from inebriated alums complaining about coaches.
Above (L to R) Steve Sloan and John Fourcade.

member of the athletics committee."

Spruill received occasional late-night phone calls from inebriated alums complaining about Steve Sloan or Billy Brewer or Bob Weltlich.

"I got tickled at some of them," he said, "but they were interesting and exciting times to be a part of."

In addition to his role on the athletics committee, Spruill was asked by the Chancellor to spearhead a $25,000,000 fundraising campaign. For the last half of his tenure as dean, Spruill split time between running a development operation and serving as dean of the business school.

"I had an office over in the alumni building, fighting the inevitable fight between the foundation and the alumni association over who had access to donors, as well as to being the contact with the Grenzebach consulting firm the foundation had hired," Spruill said.

## A Performer

A dean, a member of the athletics committee, and chair of a fundraising campaign weren't the only roles Spruill filled. He also performed each season in the Ole Miss summer showcase theatre.

"Within two weeks of arriving on campus," Spruill said, "I joined the troupe. I sang and danced and acted in the summer showcase from 1980 through 1984."

A 1980 edition of the *Ole Miss Alumni Review* reported, "Lynn Spruill picked an unusual way to introduce himself to the community: standing before 900 people in Fulton Chapel and

# AN ANOMALY — THAT WORKS
## ACCOUNTING AND BUSINESS: SEPARATE SCHOOLS

### COMMITMENT TO EXCELLENCE

I n their more than 78 years of existence, the School of Business Administration and the School of Accountancy at The University of Mississippi have established an impressive record of achievements in teaching, research, and service activities. Faculty and students have distinguished themselves professionally and scholastically with reputations on par with institutions having much larger facilities and resources. Ole Miss has a reputation for using its resources efficiently, a fact that was noted by the AACSB visitation team at the end of the recent reaccreditation process. They said that we are "the best, little, efficient program" they have seen. We are proud of our reputation for accomplishment, and we are committed to maintaining this high level of quality and efficiency in the future.

We are now pleased to announce approval and partial funding for a new Business and Accountancy complex. This facility will include the construction of entirely new buildings and the complete renovation of Conner Hall, the home of the business and accountancy programs since 1961. The construction of new buildings represents a strong and tangible statement that The University of Mississippi is committed to moving its Schools of Business Administration and Accountancy to the next level in the pursuit of academic excellence.

The learning environment created by the new structure will inspire and support all who teach, study, and conduct research within its walls. Designed to be both visually appealing and technologically advanced, the new buildings will equip faculty to pursue new standards and initiatives in education, research, and service activities. Members of the faculty and the corporate community will be able to unite and pursue strategic goals in a more vigorous manner. Students will develop their skills and abilities in academic facilities among the most advanced in the country. The new business and accountancy complex will enable an already outstanding faculty, staff, and student body to move into a truly competitive position in the region and the nation.

Alumni, friends, and organizations now have the opportunity to join in this momentous endeavor by responding to the challenge to complete the funding for the new building complex. Full funding will make it possible to construct and equip facilities that will dramatically change the stature and future potential of The University of Mississippi.

We know you will want to share in this pursuit of instructional excellence as we strive to make the new building complex a reality. Your financial generosity will be recognized as forming a partnership with us to create the most pivotal and momentous change in the Ole Miss Schools of Accountancy and Business Administration in more than thirty years.

Whether you choose to sponsor a classroom, an office, or another important feature of these facilities, your gift will provide enduring benefits for students, faculty, and the people of Mississippi far into the 21st century.

Please join us and many other generous supporters to make this vision a reality. Your contribution will make a truly important difference. We are eager to move forward to achieve the next level of excellence in business and accountancy education. Will you support us?

*W. Randy Boxx, Dean*
SCHOOL OF BUSINESS ADMINISTRATION

*James W. Davis, Dean*
SCHOOL OF ACCOUNTANCY

I n 1979, when the accounting school and the business school split, the separation was in vogue.

According to Dale Flesher, associate dean of the School of Accountancy, who has written extensively on the subject, "At some universities, the 'school' was an organizational unit in name only. In other words, some universities changed the name of the organizational unit from 'department' to 'school,' without there being any organizational change.

Flesher recalled the national landscape in 1979.

"At the time we separated at Ole Miss," he said, "the AICPA had gone on record to encourage and support such an organizational structure. However, the only truly operational separate school of accountancy was at C.W. Post College on Long Island."

At about the same time Ole Miss separated, the University of Florida and the University of Southern California established programs similar to Ole Miss.

Dean Lynn Spruill, the first dean hired after the School of Accountancy was its own "school," said, "Well, it was an odd set up, but I came to it with my eyes wide open. It was what it was."

Rex Cottle, the dean who followed Spruill, added, "We had to work through having a business school and an accounting school, but that really wasn't a problem; we just figured out a way to work together."

The two schools share students, resources, and space, as evidenced by the fundraising campaign for Holman Hall. The introductory letter was signed jointly by Dean James Davis and Dean Randy Boxx.

Dean Cyree corroborated the wonderful relationship between the two schools. "We get along grandly," he said. "We share students and space. We don't tend to fret on it much. Yes, it's unusual, but it is what it is."

Flesher went on to explain why the structure — from the accounting perspective — is so practical for Ole Miss.

"Almost all of our graduates (about 96%) go into public accounting," he said, "In other words, they are going to be auditors for CPA firms. They don't go into business upon graduation. Since auditors are expected to be independent of their clients, we feel that it is important for them to be independent of business students even while they are in college. That independence carries over into the accounting students' professional lives.

"Also, accountancy is a separate profession (with stringent admission standards) governed by codes of ethics and federal laws. In many respects, we are closer to the law school than the business school. In fact, we have several courses that are cross-listed with the law school."

• • •

The University of Mississippi School of Accountancy is the only separate school of accountancy at a major university in the United States.

In 1979, the Ole Miss annual listed two separate deans for the school of accountancy and business.

A number of major universities had separate accounting schools during the 1970s and 1980s; however, since that time all have been re-joined under a single organizational structure except Ole Miss.
The University of Mississippi School of Accountancy is the last vestige of a trend started nearly 35 years ago.

# Academic Deans

## Accountancy

**Dr. Edward Milam**

Approved by the Board of Trustees of State Institutions of Higher Learning in June 1978, the School of Accountancy became one of the first separate schools of accountancy in the United States. The program commenced in the 1979 fall semester with 320 students studying for careers in the areas of public, industrial, and governmental accounting. The curriculum of study is designed to provide students with both a broad background of general education and an in-depth understanding of the multiple facets of professional accounting. The school, located in Connor Hall and under the direction of Dr. Edward Milam, offers a five year program which leads to a Master's of Accountancy.

## Business

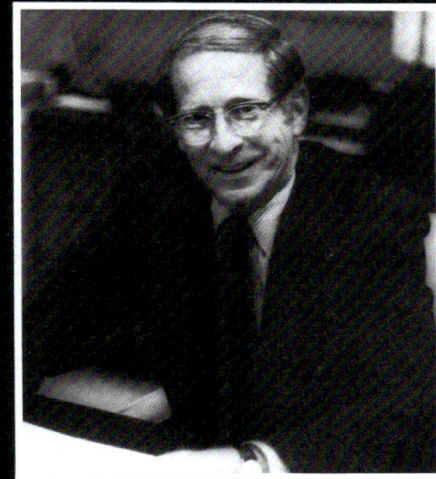

**Dean Carl Nabors**

As the problems of business have grown increasingly complex and increasingly related to social and economic movements, the need for persons especially educated to understand and to cope with these problems has grown. Since its establishment in 1917, the School of Business Administration has devised its courses and its curricula to be of use to the graduate who plans to find his place in a position of responsibility at the administrative level in private business, or at a similar level in government.

With an enrollment of 2507 students, the School of Business Administration under Acting Dean Carl Nabors teaches students the basic knowledge they will need for an administrative career in business or government and promotes the development of proficiency in practical application.

singing 'The Only Home I Know.' Neither the song nor the Summer Showcase production of 'Shenandoah' was that unusual. It was just that the athletic young tenor is the new dean of the School of Business Administration."

"The last performance I did was in *Annie*," Spruill said. "My daughter performed, too, as one of the orphans."

Spruill said he was "blessed as a child" with a squeaky, high voice. "So I got to sing a lot of first tenor parts," Spruill explained. "I sang Nanki-Poo in *The Mikado* and Frederick in the *Pirates of Penzance*."

**An Opportunity and a Last Straw**

Dean Spruill and his family loved living in Oxford. In fact, his favorite spots on Saturday mornings were Richard Howorth's Square Books (when it was still located on the second floor of a building next to Neilson's Department Store) and Smitty's restaurant.

"Heavens to Betsy!" Spruill exclaimed, "They would make butter and molasses biscuits for me: I loved it. There are so many wonderful memories from our time in Oxford."

Because of Spruill's success at Ole Miss — and because of his experience in administration, fundraising, *and* athletics — he was highly sought after by other universities, but he was reluctant to leave Ole Miss. Then, as with so many other deans in the business school, politics entered the picture.

In 1983, a survey was initiated by the Institute of Higher Learning about the quality of the engineering school at Ole Miss, as well as the quality of the engineering school at Mississippi State. Spruill received one of the surveys.

Dean Spruill with Dennis Tosh (center) and Chancellor Fortune (second from right)

The cover letter was standard for blind surveys, including the disclaimer *this is absolutely anonymous, tell us what you think.*

"I was naïve," Spruill said. "I believed them. So I told them what I thought and I was blunt. I wrote something to the effect of 'you can take everything at both of these schools, put them together and do the best you could with them, and they would probably not be as good as the ones at North Carolina State, or at Florida, or any of the major institutions that put money into quality programs, and I went on to list why I thought that was so."

Then, Spruill returned the survey and assumed that was the end of it.

The next week, Spruill was called to an administrator's office in the Lyceum, then to the chancellor's office, and finally to a meeting with a member of the IHL board.

"I was told *I was in trouble*, that *people weren't happy with me*, and that *I was not being a team player*. I thought to myself, *You've got to be kidding me? They have violated every rule of social survey research and I'm the one in trouble?*

The following week, Spruill met with John Palmer and explained the situation. Considering the lucrative offers that were waiting, along with Spruill's disdain for this sort of behavior, he told Palmer he was leaving.

"That was the genesis of my departure," Spruill said.

• • •

In the spring of 1985, Dean Spruill moved to Oregon, where he accepted the positions of dean of the business school and, later, vice president of university relations at Oregon State University.

# REX COTTLE
## DEAN 1985-1991

"Rex was big on research."

Keith Womer, *Chair of Economics and Finance and Interim Dean, 1999-2001*

On January 3, 1985, Dr. Rex Cottle became the seventh dean of the Ole Miss School of Business Administration. Cottle received his Ph.D. from Texas A&M University and had served as chair of the economics department at Clemson University for seven years.

Upon arrival, Cottle made his goal clear: to improve the scholarship pedigree of faculty, to recruit better-quality students, and to have the business school play a more visible role in the Small Business Development Center.

Cottle also stated publicly that "the business school is going to be managed like a business." His greatest challenge would prove to be the lack of institutional funds.

"We were experiencing very tight budgets when I took over," Cottle said. "That was the case during my entire tenure at Ole Miss, but that just provided an opportunity to do other things."

"We spent a lot of time on fundraising," Cottle said. Then, he clarified, "Really we were raising friends — going out and building friendships."

The university was going through great change during that period. Gerald Turner had been hired as chancellor in 1984. "I was

Rex Cottle was appointed dean in 1985. He came to Ole Miss from Clemson.

the first dean Turner hired from the outside," Cottle said.

The first notable administrator Turner hired was Robert Khayat, who served in the position of vice chancellor for university relations.

"It was an exciting time with a wonderful administration," Cottle said. "Robert Khayat was in development. It gave us an opportunity to really go out and devote time in the business community and learn more about the business community. With Gerald and Robert, it was kind of a family affair in terms of working together and pulling together to overcome some of the budget problems we were experiencing."

### A $1 Million Check

In 1986, John Palmer, then chairman of Mobile Communications Corporation of America, said, "We had a nice windfall profit. I had been working with Lynn Spruill and Rex Cottle and understood the struggles of the business school. So I wanted to help."

Robert Khayat remembered the day Palmer's check arrived.

"Gerald Turner, Don Fruge, and I inherited the major gifts

# AN ECONOMIC DEVELOPMENT JUGGERNAUT
## MISSISSIPPI SMALL BUSINESS DEVELOPMENT CENTER

The Mississippi Small Business Development Center (MSBDC) was founded in January 1981 by the U.S. Small Business Administration in partnership with state and local governments. The primary center is located in Oxford, Mississippi, though an additional seven centers are located throughout the state, along with seventeen additional counseling sites.

The MSBDC's primary function is to provide business management and technical assistance, training, and research to small business owners to improve their profitability and stimulate growth. This can include helping entrepreneurs to develop business plans, create marketing strategies, identify and access sources of capital, improve managerial skills, analyze financial records, and refine other business services as required. Research, both basic and applied, is available, giving the small businessperson more relevant data from which to draw upon for making decisions. The MSBDC offers small business owners loan packaging assistance; assistance to minorities, women, veterans, the handicapped, exporters, and inventors; and an interaction program between Mississippi educational institutions, businesses, and government.

The MSBDC also acts as a clearing house by referring clients to other existing business programs, such as those sponsored by the U.S. Small Business Administration, the Chamber of Commerce, and many education institutions.

Doug Gurley, state director of the Mississippi Small Business Development Center

Doug Gurley, state director of the MSBDC, said, "We were created because businesses were going bankrupt. So we were designed to work with existing businesses to keep them from going bankrupt. We kind of got stuck labeled a start-up group, but the majority of our time is really spent with existing businesses." Gurley added, "We also work with pre-ventures."

The MSBDC has helped more than 100,000 businesses since its inception.

"What has made us so successful," Gurley said, "is that we embrace change. It's based on needs assessment, always assessing the needs of your clients, your staff, and your stakeholders. That's a continuous task — asking what they need."

Gurley explained that his stakeholders include the U.S. Congress that supplies federal dollars, the SBA which those dollars flow through, host institutions that put in cash as well as indirect, in-kind investments, and the state of Mississippi.

"They all put money in, so we constantly have to ask them what they need. . .and then provide it."

The MSBDC also offers seventeen different workshops conducted throughout the state. These workshops address topics important to running and maintaining a small business profitably. Workshops topics include starting a small business, tax planning, record keeping, doing business with the government, financial management, and other special topics.

Gurley gave an example of the MSBDC's flexibility and responsiveness. "When Katrina hit, I brought in over seven out-of-state counselors, and we set up twenty-eight locations working with George Schloegel at Hancock Bank on the Coast. I brought food every day from Hattiesburg and took it out to all the locations. We were bringing counselors in for two weeks. They came from other states, and those states even paid for the counselors to come and help us. We put them in tents; we put them in churches; we put them anywhere that we could find a place to house them."

The MSBDC began expanding its programs in 1989 with the opening of a Jackson State SBDC. In 1990, they opened an additional eight centers, including one in Meridian, and in 1994, they opened another six, including one at East Central Community College. By 1995, there were nineteen SBDC centers spread across the state. A Rankin center was opened in February 2006, and Millsaps opened a center in 2011. Also in 2011, the MSBCD celebrated the opening of a new primary branch building on the campus of the University of Mississippi in Oxford, Mississippi. As of 2017, there were twenty-two centers throughout Mississippi.

campaign that was initiated by Porter Fortune," Khayat said. "We'd been receiving $50, $100, $500, and the occasional $1,000 gift. We received a check from John Palmer in 1986," Khayat said. "We had no warning it was coming. It arrived in a small envelope with no note, just a check. It was hand written on one of those small checks — the kind people use for personal accounts.

"The three of us stood in Chancellor Turner's office staring at this $1,000,000 check," Khayat said. "We nearly fainted."

Palmer's $1 million dollar gift, in 1986, was the largest private gift in the history of higher education in Mississippi.

Palmer said he was particularly proud of the immediate impact of the gift. "The first year after we started offering fellowships," he said, "the average GPA of MBA students jumped an entire grade point."

John Palmer and Chancellor Gerald Turner at the unveiling of the plaque to commemorate Palmer's $1 million gift.

tablished to attract a distinguished scholar in entrepreneurial studies.

The Sam and Mary Carter Lecture Series in Finance and Banking was also established to bring leading financiers from both the academic and business worlds to campus.

The first annual "Business Week" was jointly sponsored by the school, the Business Administration Alumni Association, and the Office of Career Services. The week included a job fair, a cookout for students, and three Otho Smith lecturers.

The Otho Smith Fellow Program brought to campus Allen Morgan, chairman of Morgan Keegan & Company; John Ferris, vice president of finance for Super Valu Food Stores; William Emerson, senior vice president of Merrill Lynch; and Jerry St. Pe', president of Ingalls Shipbuilding Corporation.

The Business Advisory Council laid the groundwork for a new business course, discussed plans to renovate some rooms in Conner Hall, and developed plans to assist in fundraising.

The Small Business Development Center established a Contract Procurement Center in Gulfport, Mississippi, to assist businesses in acquiring contracts with the federal government. In its first year, the center helped procure contracts exceeding $23,000,000.

## Early Accomplishments of the Cottle Administration

The new Management Information Systems program received excellent reviews from external consultants and was approved by the IHL for implementation.

Student credit hours increased seven percent during Cottle's first year as dean.

The faculty received three research grants, won a handful of research awards, and the School of Business Administration faculty taught 180 percent above the average faculty member on the Ole Miss campus.

The Michael Starnes Lectureship in entrepreneurship was es-

## A New York Jets Connection

Robert M. Hearin of Jackson attended the University of Alabama. However in the 1960s, as part of the Mississippi Banker's

Association, Hearin was actively involved in creating a Chair of Banking at Ole Miss. With the urging of Dean Ben McNew, Hearin became involved in the affairs of the Ole Miss business school (see photo on page 97).

In the 1960s, Hearin, the major stockholder in First National Bank (later renamed Trustmark National Bank) invested in and was named as a board member of Hess Oil and Chemical Company of New Jersey. Hearin and Leon Hess, president of Hess Oil, began a long and prosperous friendship.

In 1963, Hess led a consortium of investors to purchase the American Football League New York Jets. Hearin was one of those investors.

The two men later launched Yazoo Manufacturing, a company that sold lawn mowers, and in 1984 formed a holding company, Yazoo Investments, that purchased the stock of Mississippi Valley Gas for $45 million.

In 1987, Robert Hearin and Leon Hess gave $2 million to Ole Miss to establish three programs at the business school, including ten scholarships for ten years for outstanding students attending the School of Business Administration.

Dean Cottle called it "one of the most important gifts ever given to the business school." He added "the programs will help us achieve our goal of being a premier business school."

In a private conversation between Hearin and Dean Cottle, Hearin told him, "We'll see how you do. Then we'll see if we're going to give you any more."

"Which, of course, they did," Cottle added.

## Supportive Board and Alumni

During Cottle's tenure as dean, members of the Business Ad-

Leon Hess (right), the owner of the New York Jets, donated millions of dollars (along with his business partner Robert M. Hearin) to the school of business. He is pictured with Coach Bill Parcells.

visory Council included Jim Barksdale, COO of Federal Express Corporation; Charles Beall, Jr., chairman of Texas Commerce Bank; Louis Brandt, Jr., Brandt/TRW of Houston, Texas; and Howard McMillan, president of Deposit Guaranty National Bank; among others.

In addition, business school alum Sherman Muths (B.B.A., Business Administration, 1954) served as president of the Ole Miss Alumni Association from 1986-1989.

"Private support became a piece of our budget," Cottle said. "It wasn't just the icing on the cake; it was the whole top layer of the cake!"

Cottle said alumni support made it possible to attract quality students and quality faculty.

## Cleaning House

Dr. Keith Womer, who was hired by Dean Cottle in 1986 to run the economics and finance department, said, "Rex pretty much cleaned house . . . which caused some turmoil."

According to Womer, there was a group of professors in the marketing department who felt like they were an elite group ("and acted like it," Wormer noted). "There was a general impression," Womer explained, "that those folks should be listened to in all decision making."

Dean Cottle didn't think the "elite group's" academic credentials were particularly stellar, according to Womer. "Rex made it clear that there was only going to be one dean in the school, and that they had better get with the program."

"It was a bit of a turbulent time, but it all worked out as we replaced faculty — and in some instances expanded the business school," Womer said.

In a speech on October 10, 1988, Dean Cottle told the Rotary Club of Greenwood, Mississippi, that "in the four years since I've been at Ole Miss, we've replaced 55 percent of the faculty due mainly to increased scholarship requirements."

Cottle went on to say, "Every eight years, knowledge in the business world doubles. If your faculty does not continue to do research and learn, they won't be current."

"Rex was big on research," Womer said.

Despite the faculty being relatively young, Cottle noted that they were "quickly establishing a national reputation as scholars, publishing over ninety nationally refereed journal articles."

Dean Cottle (right) with Ole Miss Alumni Association President (and business school alum) Sherman Muths and his wife, Celia.

### Accreditation

As the school was facing reaccreditation, the AACSB noted several violations at the Ole Miss School of Business Administration. The most crucial of those was faculty to student ratio.

In the 1987 annual report to the chancellor and the IHL, Cottle wrote, "There are two options . . . available to the school in order to retain AACSB accreditation. First, the school could restrict enrollment by raising admission standards and reducing admission into business classes by non-business majors."

Cottle wrote that he thought limiting enrollment would have a profound negative impact on university enrollment and would prevent many Mississippi students from receiving a quality business education in the state.

"Second," Cottle wrote, "more faculty could be hired."

At the end of the report, Cottle pled for relief. "To compound these difficulties, the school's operating budget has been steadily declining while the student enrollment and the number of faculty conducting scholarly research has been increasing. Departmental operating budgets desperately need to be increased.

"The current situation is unstable. Now is the time to act. New faculty must be hired now for them to count in the AACSB reports which will be due in 1989-1990. The state of Mississippi needs a quality business school to promote economic development. The Ole Miss School of Business stands ready for the challenge."

### Peace with Accountancy and with Budgets

"We had to work through having a business school *and* an accounting school," Cottle said. "But that really wasn't a problem: we just figured out a way to work together."

The organizational structure of having the accounting school outside of business happened before I got there so I simply accepted it and moved on. We never really had any problems with each other. Our kids took accounting classes, and their kids took some of ours. When I look back over what we did, we laid the foundation for continued growth and development of the business school."

Although the budgets were always very tight and limiting, no one complained about it, according to Cottle. "We didn't have any money; we just worked around it.

"One time, the legislature talked about only having one business school in the state, rather than having all of these business schools and only having one engineering program. Ole Miss was going to have the business school and engineering was going to be at Mississippi State. I kept telling the legislators, 'Our best students are those guys who drop out of engineering, so we'd really like to keep our engineering school!'"

Cottle said the primary focus of the school was always on trying to make sure students competed when they graduated. "That's one thing that we really took pride in. We were able to position our people. We viewed students kind of as a product, so we continually tried to promote them, and that was one thing that we were so proud of — our graduates."

Cottle said they found innovative ways to enhance education without huge expenses. "We asked a lot of business executives to come talk to our students," he said.

Cottle created a course in executive decision making where student conducted case studies about businesses. Those business leaders would come talk to students about the problems that they'd encountered.

"We brought in the business leaders to present their findings," Cottle said. "Here's what I did; it may have failed, but here's why it failed, or it may have succeeded, and here's why it succeeded."

"We tried to create an environment where the business community could provide input to us to make sure our graduates were state of the art," Cottle said. "Really, it was trying to seek out our customers, if you will, that were going to be buying our students."

## Firing Line

On September 13, 1989, William F. Buckley brought his wildly popular "Firing Line" to the Ole Miss campus. The topic for the debate was "Resolved: The free market is the way to go."

Panelists included former Presidential candidates George McGovern, Gary Hart, and Jack Kemp; U.S. Representatives Newt Gingrich and Patricia Schroeder; economists John Kenneth Galbraith and Paul W. Warburg.

"To get the quality of these speakers to debate this topic is really something great," Cottle told the *Clarion-Ledger*. "It's an

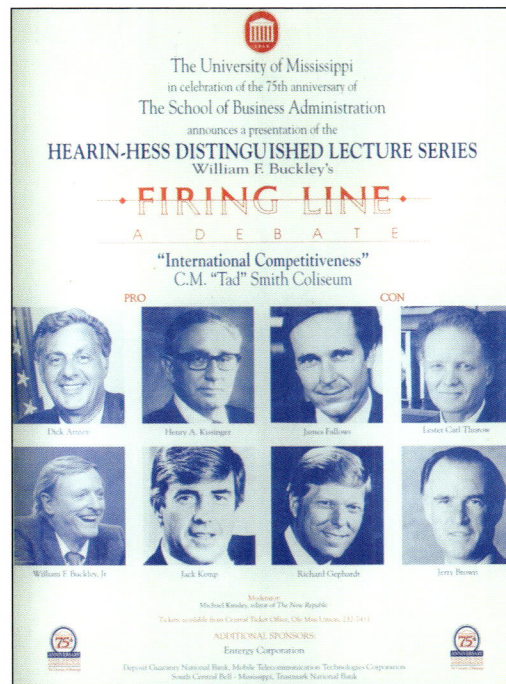

The original promotion poster for William F. Buckley's "Firing Line." On September 13, 1989, a group of notable economists and politicians gathered in Tad Smith Coliseum to debate the free market.

honor for them to be coming to the state of Mississippi, but then to have them at Ole Miss is really something."

## New Hires and Growth

New faculty hires in 1989 and 1990 included Robert Dorsey and William Rayburn, respectively.

From the time Cottle took the helm at the School of Business Adminstration, enrollment grew over ten percent. The Business Advisory Council developed plans to refurbish Conner Hall Room 100.

One of the members of the Business Advisory Council, Henry Holman, would play a huge role in the future of the business school facilities.

Cottle said, "Henry Holman was on my advisory council and was a great supporter of ours. He was a strong friend to the university," Cottle added, "That's true for so many people."

## Fond Memories

"I remember my wife and I coming to meet Gerald Turner for the interview. We walked onto the campus, and we said to one another, 'This is what a college campus should look like.' It was magnificent. Beautiful architecture, fine old buildings."

Cottle left Ole Miss to become provost at Wichita State. He was later selected as President of Lamar University.

"Looking back on a twenty-five-year career, I can tell you that Ole Miss and the experiences that we had there were second to none in academia."

Cottle is now the director of economic forecasting and labor relations Trinity Industries in Dallas.

# DONALD B. BEDELL

1990 • BBA BUSINESS ADMINISTRATION • SIKESTON, MISSOURI

Brad Bedell has served as president of Health Facilities Management Corporation of Sikeston, Missouri, which provides consulting services to thirty nursing homes in Missouri and Arizona, as well as to outpatient rehabilitation centers and pharmacies.

He was a fraternity officer while doing undergraduate work at Ole Miss and an officer in Phi Delta Phi legal fraternity while in law school. Following graduation, he joined the Lamar Order of the Ole Miss Alumni Association.

Bedell has been a member of various civic organizations and on the boards of the YMCA of Southeast Missouri, Quail Unlimited, and Ducks Unlimited. He has also devoted time to the Missouri Health Care Association. He is a former MHCA president and was its 2001 Member of the Year. He also has been a board member and a Regional PAC Chairman for the American Health Care Association.

In 2002, Bedell was appointed by Missouri Governor Bob Holden to a six-year term as a regent for Southeast Missouri State University in Cape Giradeau. He has been a member of the SMSU Foundation Board of Directors and, in 1998, established the Don C. Bedell Excellence Award through the Foundation to assist business majors. The scholarship honors his father, Don C. Bedell.

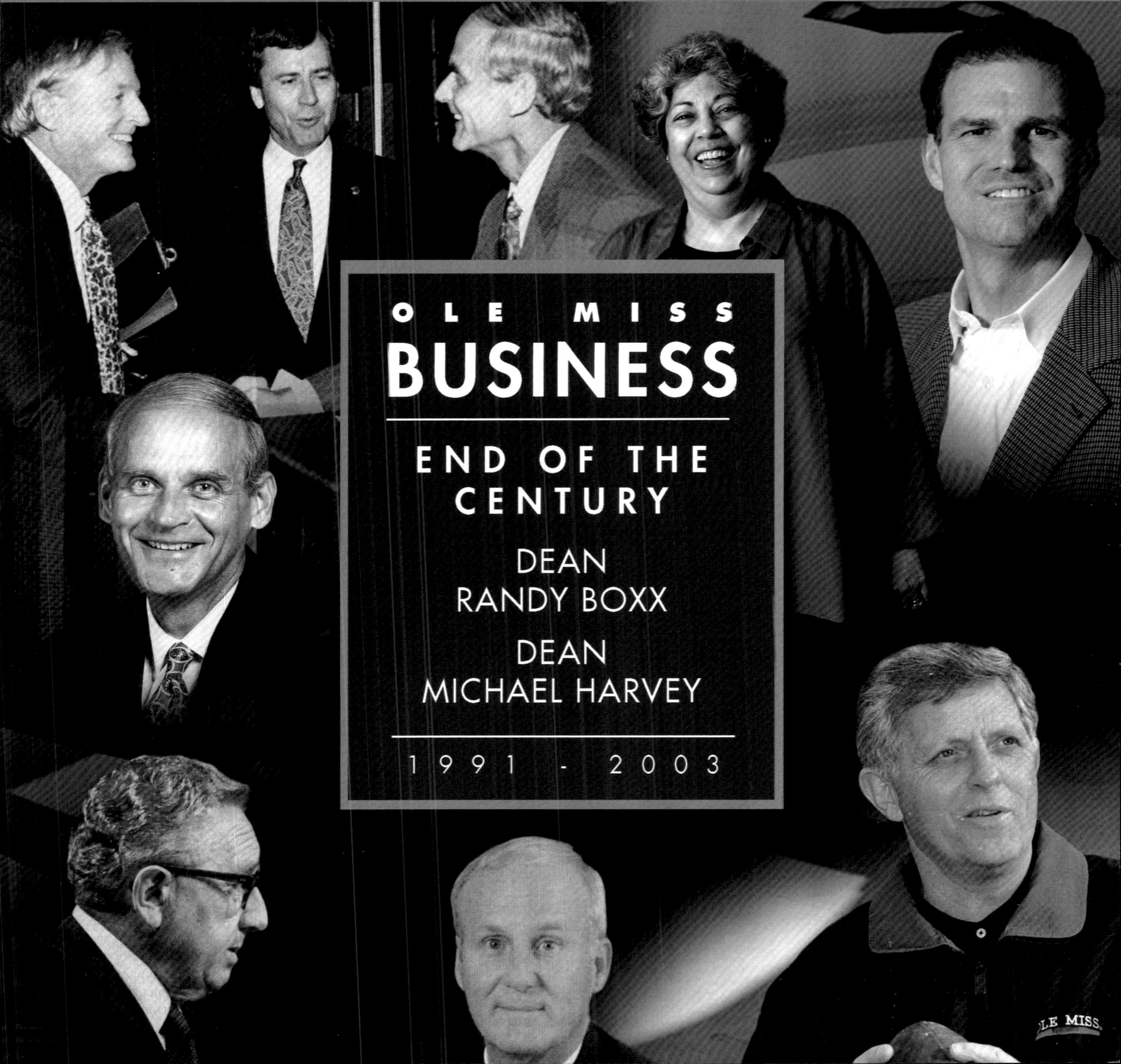

# OLE MISS BUSINESS

## END OF THE CENTURY

DEAN
RANDY BOXX

DEAN
MICHAEL HARVEY

1991 - 2003

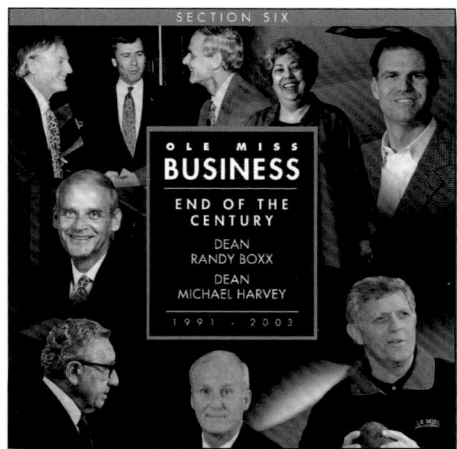

Clockwise from top left: *Firing Line* host William F. Buckley with Chancellor Gerald Turner and Dean Randy Boxx, Provost Carolyn Ellis Staton, Hank Holman, Chancellor Robert Khayat, Dean Michael Harvey, Henry Kissinger, Dean Randy Boxx.

# RANDY BOXX
## DEAN 1991-1999

"There wasn't a more honest, fair person around than Randy Boxx."

Del Hawley, *associate dean, School of Business Administration*

In 1991, when Rex Cottle left for Wichita State University, Chancellor Turner appointed Randy Boxx as acting dean. Boxx had been with the business school since 1972 and had accumulated seventeen years of experience as associate dean.

Since budgets were tight, the administration delayed a search. Boxx held the position of acting dean until 1993.

William F. Buckley, host of "Firing Line," is greeted by Chancellor Gerald Turner and Dean Randy Boxx.

### Firing Line, Again

In September, a special edition of the nationally-acclaimed PBS production "Firing Line" was taped at Ole Miss and hosted by the school of business. The event kicked off the 75th anniversary celebration of the School of Business Administration.

The panel of guests included William F. Buckley, Jr., William Kinsley, Henry Kissinger, Arianna Huffington, Jack Kemp, Richard Gephart, Richard Armey, Jerry Brown, and several others. The panel debated issues of international trade to an on-site au-

dience of more than 7,000 people.

The event was part of the Hearin-Hess Distinguished Lecture Series. The debate topic was: "Resolved: U.S. industry does not need protection."

The event exposed students to international business issues. Dean Boxx said, "We are preparing our students to work in a global economy and to succeed in a business environment that is becoming increasingly globalized." He added, "Most of our graduates today will pursue a career at some point that will deal with an aspect of international business."

### 75th Anniversary

The 75th Anniversary celebration culminated with a three-day series of events in April 1993. Included in these events was the semi-annual meeting of the Business Advisory Council (BAC), a group of thirty-two business executives from many major companies who provide extremely valuable support and advice to the

School of Business. Also included in these events were guest lectures and seminars by Edith Kelly, vice president of audit and quality at Federal Express; Larry L. Johnson, assistant vice president of South Central Bell; Larry Martindale, vice chairman of the Ritz-Carlton Hotel Company; and Pat Mene, corporate director of quality management at Ritz-Carlton. The celebration's grande finale was an awards banquet honoring many current and former Ole Miss business students and faculty members.

During the year, several special lectures were also presented as part of the Otho Smith Lecture Series. In addition to Edith Kelly and Larry Johnson, mentioned above, the business school hosted Lee Walker, former president of Dell Computers, and Dr. John Neeter, professor emeritus of management science and statistics at the University of Georgia.

To top off the 75th anniversary celebration, the school received

Henry Kissinger addresses the panelists of "Firing Line," as well as students at Ole Miss as part of the 75th anniversary celebration of the school of business.

notification of reaccreditation for all its programs for ten more years by the prestigious American Assembly of Collegiate Schools of Business (Ole Miss was a founding member of the AACSB).

Ole Miss was one of only 268 colleges and universities to be accredited out of 1,200 offering undergraduate degrees. The MBA program was one of 268 out of 600.

## A New Building and a Leap in Technology

Work began in the 1993 for the design and construction of a new business school building.

The annual report to the chancellor and IHL read, "This project, which is designated as the Conner Project, will consist of the complete renovation of the existing Conner Hall and the construction of a major addition to the current building. Several faculty committees were formed to participate in the programming phase, and the architectural firm of Jim Eley and Associates, Jackson, Mississippi, was retained. By the end of the 1992-93 academic year, the project had progressed to the point that drafts of the program and suggested floor plans had been completed."

Students returning to classes in January 1993 were greeted with a very special addition to the School of Business: the Advanced Electronic Classroom in Room 220 Conner Hall.

Dean Boxx wrote, "This classroom is the largest and most complex facility of its kind in the United States and possibly in the

The new Advanced Electronic Classroom (located in room 220 Connor Hall) housed fifty-five fully-networked computers in 1993.

entire world. It houses fifty-five fully networked microcomputers and a BARCO multimedia presentation system to produce a learning environment that is truly amazing. The Advanced Electronic Classroom is one of the most heavily-used facilities in Conner Hall. It is a showpiece of how technology can be applied to education to produce a practical and innovative learning environment in a broad spectrum of classroom activities. It was designed by a team of School of Business faculty members and funded totally from contributions from outside supporters. As a collateral project to the construction of the Advanced Electronic Classroom, a fiber-optic network was installed this year in Conner Hall, serving the school of business faculty and staff in the building. This network installation was supported in part by a grant from AT&T. It allows faculty and staff to communicate with each other through direct connections, receive and give assignments electronically, share a variety of software packages efficiently, and connect with a vast array of resources around the campus and the entire world."

## Strengthening the School

Associate Dean Del Hawley recalled, "We went through some bad budget years in the early years when Randy was dean, but he was a very effective leader. There wasn't a more honest, fair person around." Hawley added, "Which sometimes was a problem — he was a little too honest."

Hawley emphasized that Dean Boxx had a vision for the business school. Boxx wanted to build the school into something better than it was. Hawley said Boxx's motto was "business at the

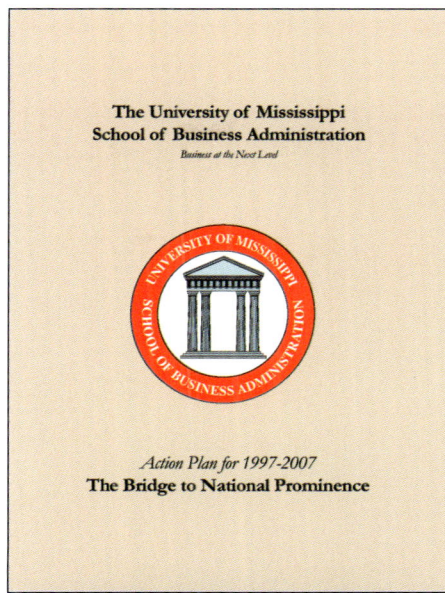

**The University of Mississippi
School of Business Administration**
*Business at the Next Level*

*Action Plan for 1997-2007*
**The Bridge to National Prominence**

Randy Boxx's "Action Plan" for the ten-year period 1997-2007 carried an annual funding figure of $4.3 million.

next level."

Boxx shepherded the School of Business Administration through a time when the new building was being planned. He also participated heavily in the fundraising.

All the while, according to Hawley, Boxx successfully recruited new faculty and students. By 1994, ninety-eight percent of the full-time faculty held doctoral degrees from a wide range of prestigious institutions.

"I always respected Randy," Hawley said, "and enjoyed working with him."

## An Action Plan

In the mid-1990s, Dean Boxx spearheaded a ten-year action plan entitled "The Bridge to National Prominence."

The action plan for 1997-2007 included four sections with goals for students, faculty, organizational structure and facilities, and Community.

For students, the actions included:
■ Raise median GMAT scores of MBA student to 600 or higher
■ Establish a Graduate Scholar Endowment Fund
■ Establish the MBA Office of Career Planning and Advising
■ Establish the Office of Mississippi Business
■ Establish the Undergraduate Curriculum Evaluation Process
For Faculty, the actions included:
■ Implement the Faculty Evaluation and Reward System
■ Establish the Faculty Development Fund
■ Establish Mississippi Educational Associates, Inc.
■ Establish Centers for Academic Excellence
■ Establish the Education Enhancement Fund
■ Further develop relations with regional and national businesses

For organizational structure and facilities, the actions included:

■ Create and fill the position of Assistant to the Dean for External Affairs

■ Create and fill the position of Director of Communications and Alumni Relations

■ Ensure well-qualified staff support

■ Establish the Technology Enhancement Fund

■ Ensure an organizational structure that is consistent with the School's objectives

For community, the action included: ensure growth of management and executive development programs.

The annual funding requirements for the action plan were $4,391,000. The endowment funding requirement was $34,000,000.

The action plan was bold and visionary, but it wouldn't be enough to keep Boxx in the top spot at the School of Business Administration.

### A $5 Million Gift

In 1997, the Robert M. Hearin Support Foundation announced a $5 million grant over four years to assist the University of Mississippi School of Business Administration in its march toward national prominence.

The Hearin Foundation grant was designed to underwrite the business school's long-term strategic plan by providing funds for retention and recruitment of nationally-prominent faculty members and for expansion of infrastructure services.

About the late businessman and philanthropist Robert M. Hearin of Jackson, Robert Khayat said, "Robert Hearin is clearly recognized as one of the most remarkable Mississippians of the 20th century." Khayat added, "His legacy lives on through the Robert M. Hearin Support Foundation, and we are extremely grateful for funds that provide the margin of excellence. We will carefully utilize this gift to implement critical elements of a strategic plan designed to gain national recognition for our School of Business Administration."

The $5 million gift brought the total donated by Hearin to $7.7 million.

"The Hearin Foundation grant crowns a semester of exciting events," said Dean Boxx. As part of the business school's 80th anniversary and the university's sesquicentennial, the Robert M. Hearin/Leon Hess Lecture Series at Ole Miss sponsored a third production of the PBS show "Firing Line," hosted by William F. Buckley Jr.

"The Hearin Support Foundation grant will enable us to continue strengthening our academic programs," Boxx said. "Mr. Hearin was a long-time friend of education. He saw investing in the business school as a means of promoting economic development in Mississippi, and we deeply appreciate the Hearin Support Foundation's grant."

The $5 million grant created seven Robert M. Hearin Chairs in Business Administration, as well as provided resources for general faculty development and infrastructure services. The grant also provided seed money for the Hearin Center for Enterprise Science, headed by Keith Womer, which brought in several million dollars of additional funding from Department of Defense grants over four years.

**Nobel Laureate Speaks During Sesquicentennial Celebration**

Dr. Gary Becker, the 1992 Nobel Laureate in Economic Sciences, delivered the inaugural Hearin Foundation Lecture Oct. 30 as part of The University of Mississippi's Sesquicentennial activities. Sponsored by the Ole Miss School of Business Administration, the lecture "Education, Human Capital and Economic Growth" was held in Fulton Chapel on the Oxford campus. The Hearin Lecture Series in the business school is made possible through a $5 million grant from the Robert

As part of the sesquicentennial celebration (and funded by the Robert M. Hearin Support Foundation) the business school hosted Nobel Laureate Gary Becker. Pictured with Becker (center) are Dean Randy Boxx (L) and Associate Dean Keith Womer (R)

## Holman Hall Completed

The new $22.6 million business and accountancy complex completed in 1997 was named Holman Hall. The state of Mississippi contributed $14.7 million; the remainder came from private funds, including a large portion from members of the Holman family (see profile on page 156).

The four-story, 55,000-square-foot building provided administrative and faculty offices for the School of Business Administra-

Holman Hall was completed in 1997 at a cost of $22.6 million. A major portion of the cost was underwritten by the founders of Jitney Jungle. See profile on page 156.

tion. Holman Hall has large classrooms with retractable screens and multimedia computer projection systems, group study rooms, study alcoves, seminar rooms, conference rooms, and extensive connections to the campus network, providing a technologically advanced learning environment.

"The North Hall" provided a structural connection between Conner Hall and Holman Hall, as well as administrative offices, faculty offices, and computer labs.

## Consultants, Again

In an effort to assist the School of Business Administration in reaching its goal of national prominence, the Ole Miss administration (through a grant from the Hearin Support Foundation) funded another series of evaluations by consultants.

In one of the reports, the consultants were critical of Dean Randy Boxx. They stated that the school needed new leadership in order to achieve its goals.

"Of course," Del Hawley said, "that was ridiculous. Randy was perfectly capable of leading us to those higher realms."

When Boxx realized he did not have the full support of the administration, he sought other opportunities and accepted the dean position at Millsaps College in the Else School of Management.

In the annual report to the chancellor and the IHL, Del Hawley, associate dean of School of Business Administration, wrote the following tribute to Dean Randy Boxx:

"Of course, the most critical change in the school's structure came with the retirement of Dean W. Randy Boxx in May. After almost thirty years of serving the University of Mississippi and the School of Business Administration, with seven of those years as dean and seventeen years as associate dean, Dr. Boxx left a lasting mark on the school that few will soon forget. His motto during his administration was Business at the Next Level, and he orchestrated the most momentous changes in the School's eighty-year history to take us to the next level of excellence in business education. For anyone who saw this school at the beginning and the end of his time as dean, it is hard to imagine a person who would not agree that the improvements he achieved were spectacular. Whether one considers the reputations of our faculty, the level of research productivity, the caliber of our degree programs, the success of our graduates, the level of our funding, or the quality of our physical facilities, the 'before' and 'after' conditions stand in stark contrast to each other. We all owe Randy Boxx a tremendous debt of gratitude for his outstanding contributions to our school and to the University of Mississippi."

During Boxx's last year, he eliminated overhead by more efficiently organizing the structure of the school. His faculty members also led the way to significant grant income, including:

■ A $238,000 grant from the Office of Naval Research to purchase computer and network equipment for the Center for Computational Economics;

■ A $298,000 grant from the Office of Naval Research to acquire computer and network equipment primarily associated with the Hearin Center for Applied Enterprise Science, and

■ A $418,000 for Dr. Keith Womer to develop a DEA model to give decision makers a tool for evaluating alternative policies and projects that connects constituencies with decision makers.

### Boxx to Millsaps

In a September 1998 interview with the *Mississippi Business Journal*, Boxx said,

"The faculty and I have built an extremely strong foundation for someone else to build upon. But there's always an emotional attachment to what you have set for yourself in terms of goals. And certainly there is also the emotional attachment after putting in roughly seventy hours a week to push those goals. From that energy and effort, though, comes a great deal of satisfaction that we did do what we wanted to do."

Boxx was hired in 1999 by Millsaps as dean of the Else School of Management. Later, he served as dean of Shenandoah University's Harry F. Byrd, Jr. School of Business.

Dean Randy Boxx served the business school for nearly thirty years — seven years as dean; seventeen as associate dean.

## Ex-business dean at Ole Miss takes new Millsaps post

■ Randy Boxx named dean of Else School of Management

**By Andy Kanengiser**
**Clarion-Ledger Staff Writer**

Millsaps College's new leader of the Else School of Management will be veteran University of Mississippi business dean Randy Boxx, officials said Thursday.

"Randy has an excellent track record as a teacher, administrator and fundraiser," said Millsaps President George Harmon. "His business skills, in particular, will lend a dynamic dimension to the School of Management."

The new post offers "a tremendous opportunity to create a truly unique world

elor's and master's degrees in business at the University of Southern Mississippi and doctorate at the University of Arkansas. He joined Ole Miss 28 years ago as a business professor.

Boxx received a salary of $120,350 as head of the 2,123-student School of Business Administration at Ole Miss. His salary at Millsaps, a private liberal arts college, was not available. He was among 80 to 90 candidates for the Millsaps post.

"Randy brings to the col-

# BRIAN WALKER SANDERSON

Brian Sanderson was the 2008 president of the Gulf Coast Business Council, a private, nonprofit corporation of more than 200 of the top business leaders on the Mississippi Gulf Coast. The Business Council focuses on issues of public policy that are important to the economic vitality and quality of life on the Gulf Coast.

Previously Sanderson served as deputy director of Governor Haley Barbour's Office of Recovery and Renewal, where he offered policy advice and formulation to Barbour, his staff, and state agencies, and worked closely with local governments and community organizations. Before working with the governor's office, he served as general counsel to the Governor's Commission on Recovery, Rebuilding, and Renewal and practiced law with the firm of Butler, Snow, O'Mara, Stevens & Cannada, PLLC, for six years.

Sanderson is a member of the Mississippi Bar and served as president of the state's Young Lawyers Division through July 2008. He served as second vice president and was a member of the Board of Bar Commissioners. He is a past president of the Federal Bar Association, Mississippi Chapter.

Sanderson is a past president of the board of directors of Boys and Girls Club of the Gulf Coast, was named the statewide New Board Member of the Year in 2004, and received the Kerly Award for outstanding service in 2006. He is past president of the Gulf Coast Ole Miss Club and was on the board of directors for the UM Law Alumni Chapter. He has served as a Big Brothers Big Sisters mentor. In 2005, he was selected as one of the Top 10 Business Leaders Under 40 in South Mississippi. Sanderson is a parishioner of St. Alphonsus Catholic Church in Ocean Springs and is married to Marie Thomas Sanderson of Jackson. Sanderson was selected as the Ole Miss Alumni Association Outstanding Young Alumnus in 2008.

# HOLMAN HALL
## THE HOUSE THAT JITNEY JUNGLE BUILT

Three cousins of the Holman and McCarty families from rural Carroll County, Mississippi, founded Jitney-Jungle in 1919. William Bonner McCarty served as the company's first president; Judson McCarty Holman served as president of McCarty-Holman, the company's wholesale operation, and William Henry Holman, Sr. served as president of the retail operation.

Jitney Jungle actually emerged from an earlier grocery business, the Jackson Mercantile Co., owned by William McCarty's father, William Henry McCarty. Before he died in 1910, the senior McCarty had hired Jud Holman as his bookkeeper. Jud and his brother William bought the business from the McCarty estate, enabling Will McCarty to go to law school. They operated branch stores in Jackson, which, by the end of World War I, they began

The first Jitney Jungle Store
East Capitol Street, Jackson, Mississippi 1919

converting to self-service, cash-and-carry operations after one of their charge-and-delivery stores ran into financial problems because of a railway workers' strike.

On April 19, 1919, under the new partnership arrangements, and guided by the principle that they would save their customers "a nickel on a quarter," the cousins opened their first Jitney Jungle store as a cash-and-carry grocery. It was located in downtown Jackson, on East Capitol Street. The name came from a slang term for a nickel and a play on the word "jingling" in the popular catch phrase "jingling your jitneys in your pockets." Within a year

William Henry
Holman, Jr.

the new store had made more money than all the other McCarty-Holman stores combined, which were soon either converted to Jitney Jungles or phased out.

The company grew at an unprecedented rate, even during World War II in the midst of food rationing.

In 1962, after William Henry Holman, Sr.'s death, his son William, then executive vice president of McCarty-Holman Co., began a five-year term as the presiding officer of the board. In 1967 he was elected president and served as CEO until 1998. In that period, Jitney continued its ambitious expansion, growing from a chain of 32 stores, all located in Mississippi, to a chain of almost 200 stores operating in Mississippi and five other Southeastern states.

Under the leadership of William Henry "Hank" Holman, Jr., Jitney Jungle was the first privately-held business in Mississippi to exceed $1 billion in sales.

Although Hank, Jr. was a Georgia Tech graduate, his children, Holly and Hank, were both Ole Miss graduates. When it was time to build a new business complex, Hank, Jr. stood ready to give back to the flagship business school in his home state.

In 1998, the new $22 million building was christened Holman Hall.

Over the years, saving "a nickel on a quarter" really added up.

William Henry
"Hank"Holman, III,
a 1986 business
school grad

# MIKE HARVEY
## DEAN 2001-2003

"He was tall, athletic, and full of charisma and energy."

Robert Khayat, *chancellor emeritus*

In, 1999, Dean Randy Boxx left the School of Business Administration to take the position as Dean of the Else School of Management at Millsaps. Keith Womer took over as interim dean while a committee searched for a permanent replacement.

The Hearin Foundation — the same group that funded "An Assessment of the School of Business Administration" — funded a professional headhunting team to put together a pool of candidates.

Chancellor Emeritus Robert Khayat recalled, "In 1999, I flew to Dallas twice to meet with our consultant, W.G. Ouchi. We met in the American Airlines lounge to discuss the best candidates for the deanship." He added, "I was deeply invested in getting the best candidate."

The search committee brought five candidates to campus for interviews, including Keith Womer (the internal candidate) and Michael Harvey (from the University of Oklahoma), but no single candidate stood out. It ended in a failed search.

Michael Harvey had already caused a ruckus during his interview

Mike Harvey came to Ole Miss from the Oklahoma University. He was hired to take the business school to the next level.

when he stated in no uncertain terms that he would make two things happen if he were hired as dean: first, he would move the economics department out of the business school and into liberal arts; second, he would make accountancy a part of the business school again.

One faculty member recalled Provost Carolyn Ellis Staton saying about Mike Harvey, "I just can't work with that man."

### Desperate to Fill a Void

During its history, the School of Business Administration had gone long periods with acting deans. Ben McNew served as acting dean for four years before his position was made permanent in 1969. Randy Boxx also served as acting dean for a number of years before Chancellor Turner appointed him as a full dean in 1994.

However, in both those instances, the school wasn't facing accreditation.

"As reaccreditation got closer," an economics faculty member said, "it looked like they kind of started to panic, because the administration didn't have anybody they knew they could bring in at the last minute. They brought Harvey back, made him a very good offer, and the business school went into the reaccreditation process with a full-time dean."

Khayat said, "Mike was highly recommended by the consultants, and I liked him. He was tall, athletic, and full of charisma and energy."

Khayat wasn't the only one excited about Harvey's hire. Gwin Scott, a business school alumnus who was serving as chair of the Business Advisory Board, said, "Mike was progressive, innovative, charismatic, and straightforward, and I was excited. He was what I would call — in the Ole Miss world — a non-traditional hire. He was heavy in business and not fully academic. We all liked that."

Harvey, in addition to his academic duties at Oklahoma, had started and/or managed manufacturing operations with revenues in excess of $70 million.

The annual report to the chancellor and the IHL in 2001 touted, "From 1987 to 1994, Dr. Harvey was a partner in Phillips and Harvey, Inc., a private company involved in the acquisition and development of business firms. Private businesses for which he has performed consulting or training services include Rockwell International, Xerox, Bell Helicopter, State Farm Insurance Co., International, and Conoco, Inc."

The report also touted Harvey's academic credentials: "Dr. Harvey holds the Ph.D. and M.S. in marketing from the University of Arizona and the M.B.A. and B.B.A. from Southern Methodist University. He was a faculty member at SMU from 1971 to 1988. His teaching and research focus on management, with an emphasis on international issues, and in 2000 he was recognized as Researcher of the Year at Oklahoma."

Khayat's goal, during his chancellorship, was to make Ole Miss a great American university. And hopes were high that Harvey would lead the business school to a loftier status and higher rankings.

## A Rocky Start

Harvey arrived full of vigor and enthusiasm. His first order of business was to oversee the reaccreditation process, which he did without any unforeseen issues. His second was to remove the economics department from the School of Business Administration.

Harvey made it clear to the economics faculty that he did not want them in the business school. They fought back. A few economics professors questioned Harvey's qualifications as a scholar. One referred to him as a "research fraud."

Harvey's proposal, however, appeared concise and rational:

The purpose of this document is to provide a rationale for the transfer of the Economics Area from the School of Business Administration (SBA) to the College of Lib-

The Daily Mississippian headline when Harvey announced he would move the economics department to the College of Liberal Arts.

eral Arts (CLA). The proposal is to transfer the entire faculty of economics, with associated support, from the SBA to the CLA. The initial motivation for the transfer of economics was to resolve the imbalance between the number of economics faculty and the extremely limited number of economics majors in the undergraduate SB program.

From the University's perspective, the rationale for transferring the faculty in economics to the CLA reflects a potential synergy of efforts; where, a very well respected faculty can make a contribution to the teaching and research missions of the University by capitalizing on natural linkages to a broad group of disciplines in the CLA. It is envisioned that the economics faculty could effectively interface with political science, history, engineering, the Croft Center for International Studies and the Lott Leadership Institute to name a few. With economics faculty located in CLA, a natural bridge can be maintained to business while, at the same time, the economics faculty could be affiliated with a college that is consistent with the educational direction of the economics faculty.

The climate within the SBA has been fragmented for many years. The imbalance of resources provided to economics, the size of the economics faculty in comparison to major, and basic orientation of economics faculty in contrast to the of SBA faculty have created a division that defines the SBA environment to date. The move of economics faculty to CLA has a potential for allowing both groups to move toward higher goals more in line with a professional working climate.

Harvey ended the proposal with —

Whereas the economics faculty would be transferred with an equitable share of operating funds, full salaries, Hearin Chair support, and other amenities; and

Whereas the economics faculty would still provide support for SBA required courses; and,

Whereas the move of economics to the CLA would allow both faculty groups to pursue mutually beneficial but separate destinies; then,

Therefore, as Dean of the SBA, I am proposing to relocate the economics faculty from the SBA to the CLA as soon as possible.

Though the proposal was professional, Harvey's reaction to individual economics faculty member seemed more personal.

At one point, Harvey told an economics professor that he planned to sequester the economics faculty to one end of the top floor of Holman Hall — and then build a concrete wall to keep them separate from the business school faculty.

Jon Moen, an economics faculty member who later became chair of the department, said, "I joked that we should spray paint on the wall, 'Dr. Harvey, Tear Down This Wall.'"

Moen continued, "There was also this bizarre vote that was taken with the entire faculty present. Two votes were taken with regard to moving the department. One with us (the economics department) voting, and one without us."

Provost Carolyn Ellis Staton struggled with Harvey's desire to separate the departments. Although she ultimately agreed to sign-off on the move, she said on more than one occasion, "My blood was spilled" over that decision.

**Progress in Year One**

Harvey's accomplishments in year one were well documented in his first annual report to the chancellor and the IHL.

An excerpt from the list included:

■ A 10-year AACSB reaccreditation was awarded
■ The school completed a comprehensive update of its strategic plan, which sets out specific goals and strategies to address the stated conditions.
■ The Robert M. Hearin Support Foundation provided a five-year extension of its original four-year grant to the School of Business Administration, providing $7.3 million of financial support over the five years of the grant. Much of this support is targeted specifically toward implementing changes and

improvements to allow the school to meet the stated conditions.

■ A comprehensive review and revision of the business doctoral program is underway and will be completed in the fall of 2002. The revised program will improve the efficiency and effectiveness of doctoral education while emphasizing the importance of teaching and research expertise that is contemporary, relevant, and marketable.

■ Three clinical faculty members were added this year, and one more will be for the 2002-03 academic year. These are non-tenure-track teaching positions funded by the Hearin grant. Clinical faculty are professionally qualified, and therefore bring a wealth of practical experience to the classroom. Since there is no research requirement for the faculty, they are assigned heavier class loads than other faculty, which helps to reduce the gap between student demand for courses and available sections in required courses.

■ The undergraduate advising office was enhanced through the addition of one full-time advisor and one full-time staff assistant. In addition, the renewal and expansion of the Hearin grant provided substantial funding for additional enhancements that will be put in place in the next academic year.

■ The fundraising function in the School of Business will be greatly expanded in FY03 thanks to funding from the Hearin grant to add staff and operating support in this essential area.

Efficiency didn't seem to be Harvey's problem. His problems stemmed more from personality issues, or, perhaps, he was simply misunderstood.

Gwin Scott agreed. "Mike was very good at external relations — board management, alumni relationships, selling the business school." Scott continued, "But I know internally, dealing with faculty members, the management side, was a little bit more challenging for him."

Perhaps Harvey's biggest misstep was circumventing Carolyn Ellis Staton's authority. Since Chancellor Khayat had been instru-

mental in hiring Harvey, he took advantage of direct communication with the chancellor (even though Harvey was directed to report to the provost).

In short order, the personality conflict between Dean Harvey and Provost Staton reached a boiling point.

On May 24, 2003, Staton called Harvey to her office. According to a memo drafted by Harvey and distributed to the entire business school faculty and the Business Advisory Board, Provost Staton said the following about Harvey's performance:

"You do not have internal or external support as the Dean of the School of Business Administration.

I cannot figure out what you do, you don't appear to do anything.

There is no direction or strategy in the school.

Good faculty are leaving.

The school is not making progress towards its goals, and

We have made a mistake and it is time to correct it."

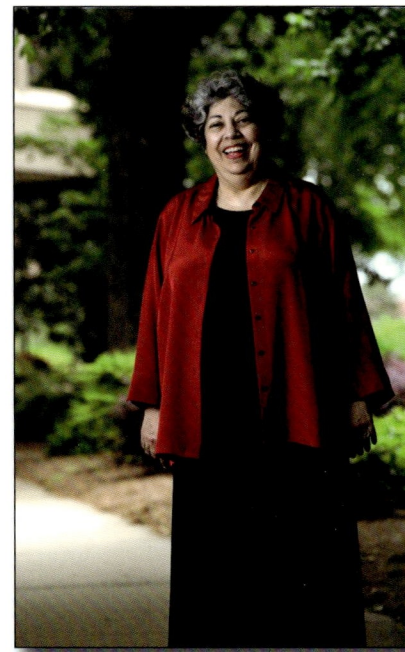

Provost Carolyn Ellis Staton and Dean Mike Harvey didn't see eye to eye.

Harvey's four-page memo in response (dated May 25, 2003) built a case that Provost Staton had no objective data to support her statements. He pointed out that all his initiatives had been passed by ninety percent plus of the faculty. He felt the Business Advisory Board would be unanimous in the their support for the direction of the school. He claimed to work seven days a week at the school dealing with faculty, staff, students, and alumni ("I can only assume that your information is secondary, perhaps collected through a selection bias from a handful of unsupportive faculty," Harvey wrote). He demonstrated progress toward goals set out in the strategic plan. Harvey admitted that faculty did leave for better-paying jobs and higher-ranking positions at his urging since he nurtured and developed faculty into better teachers and leaders.

Harvey ended the memo with, "I understand that it is your prerogative to make a change in administrators; we serve at your will. But I cannot accept what appear to be the fabricated reasons for my dismissal.

"I therefore have decided that I will not resign unless my resignation is supported by a comprehensive, fair, and constituency-wide evaluation of my past performance. A blank resignation could only be construed as not supporting those faculty and BAB members that have helped me point the SBA in the right direction. The stigma that might be attached to me for being fired is one that I can live with given that, 'people are known by their friends, as well as by their enemies.' Let's see what a 'show of hands' looks like and protect my successor and the SBA constituents from any possibilities of future impressionistic performance evaluations.

"Specifically, I request that you take a vote of confidence of the faculty, staff, and the Business Advisory Board. At the same time, I would like to have job-specific reasons for my termination given, in that I have never had a formal evaluation of performance and any suggestions for improvement in the twenty months since I have been at the university. Thank you for consideration of my request."

No vote was taken.

Gwin Scott said the members of the Business Advisory Board wrote a letter to Provost Staton and Chancellor Khayat.

"I wrote the letter," Scott said, "and it basically said 'Hey, we like him; we like what he's doing, we think he's doing a good job. The board unanimously and collectively embraces his continuing to be the dean."

Scott explained that the board had no official authority. Members were champions of the university and the business school, advocates, funders, mentors, and sounding boards for the dean.

"But we were sold on Harvey. Despite our feelings, the chancellor and provost moved ahead with removing him," Scott said. "That created a lot of debates; it created a lot of consternation internally. We had board members who resigned because they liked Mike so much."

In reflecting on the Harvey tenure, Scott admitted, "Harvey was a disruptive figure If you don't have diplomacy in that sort of environment, it's going to be your demise."

Chancellor Emeritus Robert Khayat expressed sadness over the twenty-month tenure. "What started out as such a promising era for the business school ended on such a sorrowful note."

Harvey remained on the faculty at Ole Miss until 2012. He taught in Arizona from 2012-2016. He had been offered a position at West Virginia for the fall of 2016, but Harvey died unexpectedly before the semester started.

• • •

Randy Boxx quietly led the School of Business Administration through extraordinary growth, increased national exposure, and the completion of a new $22 million home in the 1990s.

At the turn of the century, highly-touted Mike Harvey was hired to transform the school. Though he never built his concrete wall to sequester the economics faculty, he ran into another one of his own making.

As the school — though battered — entered the new millennium, it would turn once again to an internal candidate to relieve the wounds left from years of contention.

# LTC SHELDON ALLEN MORRIS

2000 • BBA • JACKSONVILLE, FLORIDA

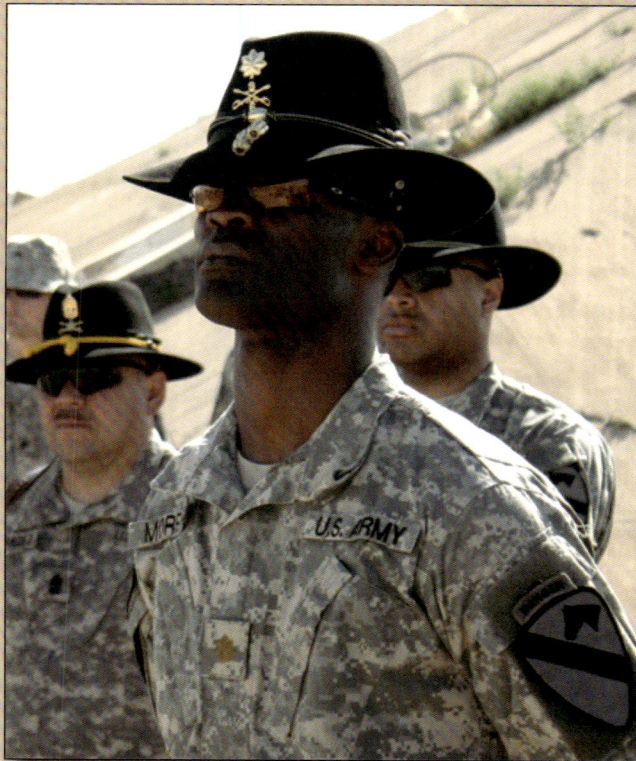

Maj. Sheldon A. Morris served as the assistant operations officer for the 3rd Heavy Brigade Combat Team, 1st Cavalry Division.

A native of Jacksonville, Florida, Morris played three years of football as a wide receiver while at Ole Miss. For two years, he was on ROTC scholarship, and during his senior year, he earned a football scholarship. Morris also was a member of Phi Beta Sigma fraternity.

In May 2000, Morris was commissioned as a second lieutenant in the infantry. He moved to Fort Benning, Georgia, that same year and attended the Infantry Officer Basic Course, Airborne School, Bradley Leaders Course, and Ranger School. After graduating Ranger School in 2001, Morris moved to Fort Hood, Texas, and was assigned to the 3rd Heavy Brigade Combat Team, 1st Cavalry Division. Morris served as a rifle platoon leader, scout platoon leader, and company executive officer before deploying to Iraq in support of Operation Iraqi Freedom II. After returning from Iraq in 2005, Morris attended the Infantry Company Command Course at Fort Benning before another stint at Fort Hood. He deployed to Iraq for his second tour in 2006 to Baqubah, Iraq, as the assistant operations officer and company commander of Alpha Company 1-12 Cavalry.

Morris returned to Fort Hood in 2007, but he deployed for a third tour in December 2008 to Tal Afar, Iraq, in Nineveh Province, commanding the Headquarters and Headquarters Troop 6-9 Cavalry. After his promotion to the rank of major in April 2009, Morris assumed the duties of the 3rd Heavy Brigade Combat Team liaison officer to 25th Infantry Division before redeploying to Fort Hood, Texas. Morris was stationed at Fort Leavenworth, Kansas, for schooling.

Morris's awards and decorations include the Bronze Star Medal with four oak leaf clusters, Meritorious Service Medal, Army Commendation Medal with three oak leaf clusters, Army Commendation Medal with "V" device, Army Achievement Medal with three oak leaf clusters, Valorous Unit Award, Meritorious Unit Citation, Combat Infantry Badge, Expert Infantry Badge, Parachutist Badge, and Ranger Tab.

Morris was given the Ole Miss Alumni Association Outstanding Young Alumni Award in 2010. He is married to the former Chelsea D. Carter of Bryan, Texas, and they have one daughter, Lauren.

# THOMAS PATRICK KRUTZ

2001 • BBA, BUSINESS ADMINISTRATION • JACKSON, MISSISSIPPI

Patrick Krutz, a 2001 graduate from the University of Mississippi, is the founder and co-owner of Krutz Family Cellars, a company producing award-winning wines in Sonoma County, California. After graduating from Ole Miss, Krutz, a native of Jackson, Mississippi, intended to pursue a graduate degree or even follow in his father's footsteps and get a law degree. Meanwhile, he decided to take some time off to see the world. During summer 2002, Krutz decided to see what the wine business would be like. Upon returning to Mississippi, he packed his car and headed to California. Patrick moved to Carmel, California, where he first worked at The Cheese Shop, which has sold wine, cheese, and gourmet foods since 1973. There he met people who mentored him in the art of winemaking.

Krutz Family Cellars was founded in summer of 2003 in Monterey County when Patrick Krutz produced sixty cases of wine. The idea was to purchase a ton of grapes a year in order to produce a small amount of wine for family and friends. However, demand soon changed that plan, and Krutz Family Cellars continues to grow in an effort to supply that demand. Krutz now produces about 2,000 cases per year.

While Patrick enjoys roaming California's idyllic vineyards searching for the perfect grapes for his wines, he hasn't forgotten his Mississippi roots.

The K-squared bottle and his business card feature original art that is reminiscent of the Delta. A small magnolia blossom graces the other side of the business card. Patrick catches early morning Ole Miss games on satellite TV at a Santa Rosa sports bar where the bartender calls him "Mississippi." He tries to attend as many Ole Miss baseball and basketball games as he can and even attends at least two football games a year during the busy harvest and crush season.

"I still have Mississippi plates, Ole Miss to be exact," he says.

Krutz Family Cellars has won multiple awards in the San Francisco Chronicle Wine Competition, including a double gold medal for their 2011 Chardonnay Martinelli Vineyard Russian River, a gold medal for their 2010 Magnolia Series Cabernet Sauvignon Napa Valley, silver medals for their 2011 Pinot Noir Soberanes Vineyard Santa Lucia and their 2012 Zinfandel Napa Valley, and bronze medals for their 2011 Pinot Noir Akins Vineyard Anderson Valley and their 2009 Cabernet Sauvignon 'Stagecoach Vineyard' Napa Valley.

Krutz and his wife, the former Rebecca Kuchar, have two children, Patrick Jr. and Ellie Jayne.

# BRIAN REITHEL
## QUIETLY PREPARING FOR THE DEANSHIP

During the tenure of Deans Randy Boxx and Mike Harvey, one faculty member of the School of Business Administration — Brian Reithel — dedicated much of his time to projects in the university's central administration.

### A Planning Initiative

In 1994, the University of Mississippi began an institution-wide planning initiative to prepare the university for the 21st Century. In Robert Khayat's book, *The Education of a Lifetime*, he wrote: "We asked Brian Reithel to organize the planning effort."

When the complete list was presented, it contained more than 4,000 ideas. Eventually, the group whittled that list down to 967."

Gloria Kellum said, "As a part of that strategic planning, Dr. Reithel provided excellent faculty leadership to the overall planning process for faculty, staff, student, and alumni participation."

### Computers and Trash

One of the projects that emerged from the planning sessions was the "computer on every desk" project. The intention was to provide faculty and staff with personal computers. Within a year, Dr. Reithel (along with three other faculty members) were managing a university-wide million-dollar personal computer distribution, first to faculty and then to staff.

"The computer on every desk initiative forever changed the technological focus of our faculty," Kellum said, "which evolved into a very sophisticated and integrated teaching system for all

Brian Reithel served as an associate vice chancellor for university Affairs before he was appointed as dean of the business school.

the faculty."

"We installed network connections in every faculty office, every dorm room, and classroom — everywhere, all over campus," Reithel said. "Over the space of about a 26-month period we literally went from being very backwards, in terms of technology, to being listed by *Yahoo* as one of the top 100 most wired campuses in America."

Kellum noted, "Brian's amazing understanding of technology and its application to institutions and humans was an important skill he brought at a much-needed time in the life of Ole Miss."

In terms of the university's overall strategic planning effort, "We grouped all 4,000 of these ideas into clusters. Then we put out a document that was called *A Call for Champions*," Reithel said. "We asked members of the university community to volunteer to the part of a particular area of endeavor and to get together and come up with specific proposals that we could then seek funding for to advance and improve the university."

Some of the proposals were not funding centric. One cluster of concepts was to enhance the teaching and learning environment on campus. A big part of that initiative involved simply picking up trash.

"Before Robert became chancellor, people used to dump trash in the parking lots," Reithel said, "there was trash all over the place. We literally had groups of people volunteer to *police* — for lack of a better word — their zone on campus to pick up trash.

We started cleaning up the campus by hand! Later, we talked to the people at Disney about how they managed the appearance of their properties (they'd done extensive studies on how far somebody is willing to walk with a piece of trash in their hand) and we learned that you needed to have trashcans all over the place. So part of what we did was just buy attractive trashcans and put them all over campus and it radically changed the look of Ole Miss."

## A Sesquicentennial Celebration (and Campaign)

Based on Reithel's leadership on the Sesquicentennial planning process in 1995, Chancellor Khayat asked Reithel to co-chair the Sesquicentennial Celebration and Capital Campaign.

"The Sesquicentennial," Reithel said, "was really three things: first, it was a strategic planning effort for the university; second, it was a public relations campaign that lasted four-and-a-half years; and third, it was the quiet phase of the university's Commitment to Excellence Campaign.

By the summer of 1995, the Sesquicentennial planning had mapped out the direction for Ole Miss for the 21st Century.

In addition to his duties in the central administration, in 1998, Dean Boxx asked Reithel to be the department chair for the MIS Department in the business school.

When the sesquicentennial ended in 1998, Reithel was appointed co-Director of the Commitment to Excellence Campaign.

"I continued in that role through the end of the fundraising campaign in December of 2000, when my title was changed to associate vice-chancellor for university relations."

Kellum said, "Reithel worked tirelessly on the Commitment to Excellence Campaign that raised over $525 million and provided funding for student scholarships, faculty/staff support, and new academic programs such as the Honors College."

## Back to Business

"I'd been intimately involved in fundraising and strategic planning for the university since 1995," Reithel said, "so I continued in the administrative role until 2002. Then, Mike Harvey asked me to come back to the business school and be the MIS Department chair full-time, to help him, to help the business school. We had accomplished all the goals that Robert and Gloria and I set out to accomplish back in 1995, so I felt like it was a good time. I came back to the business school on a full-time basis."

In reflecting on Reithel's tenure as a leader in university relations, Kellum said, "Brian Reithel's sense of humor, caring attitude, and commitment to Ole Miss were wonderful and made him a very important part of the renaissance at Ole Miss."

Reithel co-directed the sesquicentennial committee, co-directed the Campaign for Excellence (which raised $525 million), resurrected the Ole Miss forensics squad, and managed the opening of the Gertrude C. Ford Center.

The University of Mississippi has given birth to many dreams, including those of FNC co-founders Robert Dorsey, John Johnson, William Rayburn, and Dennis Tosh. During a lunch meeting at a local sandwich shop famous for its sweet tea, these four men sketched big plans on a little paper napkin.

The meeting took place in the mid-1990s, when residential mortgage lenders were struggling with archaic systems to assess the true value of a property. "What if," asked Rayburn, "we could automate the way appraisals are processed? What if we could convert paper to data to knowledge that mortgage lenders could use to make better loans faster? That would be fantastic!"

With combined expertise in accounting, business, finance, technology, and real estate, a dream team was formed.

Lawrence Farrington recalled a reception that was held after a Business Advisory Board meeting in the early 1990s. "I remember it clear as a bell," Farrington said, "Dennis Tosh was representing the other three partners at

## Oxford software firm sells for $475M

### FNC to keep operations in city, double workforce

ASSOCIATED PRESS

OXFORD, Miss. - Real estate information provider CoreLogic is buying Oxford-based FNC Inc. for $475 million.

CoreLogic, based in Irvine, California, announced the purchase Thursday, saying it wants to integrate FNC's real estate appraisal software into its products.

"We expect property valuation to be an area of significant future domestic and international growth," CoreLogic CEO Anand Nallathambi said in a statement.

FNC Marketing Director Jon Fisher told The Oxford Eagle that FNC will maintain its operations in Oxford, where the company is building a $20 million corporate headquarters, promising to more than double its workforce to 600.

"CoreLogic is investing in FNC because they believe in our strong industry position and our potential for growth and is committed to helping us grow and suc-

that time, and he walked up to me and said, 'We have been working on this project for a while, and we are ready to go with it. We just need funding.' And I said, 'Well, what are you looking for?' and he gave me an amount that I said, 'Dennis, I don't have that change in my pocket! Good gosh!' He was talking about a bunch. I just couldn't do it. So Dennis said, 'Well, we'll go out and we'll find somebody.' He came back with the same story. And maybe I'd had a little sip of wine, and I said, 'Dennis, could you use half of it and maybe we can launch this thing and get it started, and I'll see if I can get two or three other partners (hoping that Jan would be one).

"That's exactly what we did," Farrington said, "We all met over at the business school, and we worked out a deal."

Jan Farrington, who *did* eventually opt to invest, said, "The light went off when we met with them. We were trying to decide if that was something that we really should do, and the four of them started explaining what the company would do, and the potential. I could see that the potential was there, but the truly remarkable thing was that we saw *in them* the reason they could be successful — because of who they were. Bill was such a salesman. He's got a PhD in finance, but you know he could sell anything to anybody. John Johnson, who was the PhD in economics, he was a visionary in the computer world. Then, of course, Bob Dorsey had all of this technology and brain and information — and PhD in physics. He filled another gap. And Dennis was such a businessman. He was like the glue that held them all together in a way. We said, 'These guys have got a perfect formula here.'

"They didn't get in each others' way," Farrington said. "They just all worked together."

With the help of the Farringtons, these four pioneers secured funding, crafted a never-before-seen solution for standardizing collateral valuation, sought the technological expertise of Ole

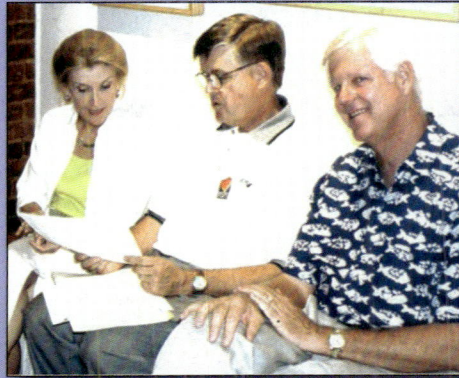

"We said, 'These guys have got a perfect formula here.'"

**Jan Farrington**

# Industry Innovators

FNC, a $475 million company built by UM professors, began with a napkin and some 'street cred'

*By Michael Newsom*

Bob Dorsey (left), John Johnson, Dennis Tosh and Bill Rayburn

*Uncredited photos courtesy of CoreLogic/FNC*

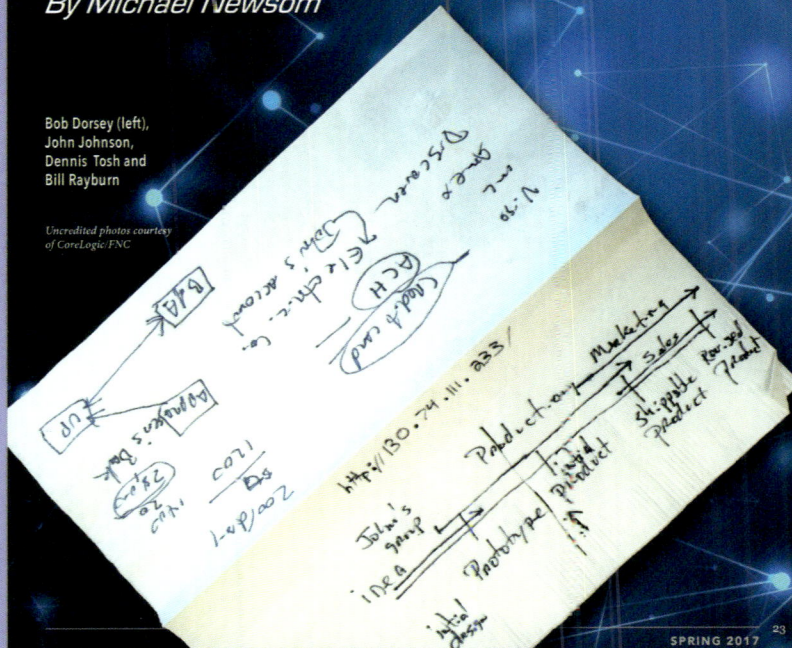

SPRING 2017  23

Miss graduate student Duncan Chen, and landed their first major client. For nearly two decades, the nation's largest residential mortgage lenders and servicers depended on FNC's Collateral Management System for compliance and efficiency; and the company was recognized as one of the most rapidly growing tech companies in America.

With their roots stemming from a laid-back college atmosphere, Dorsey, Johnson, Rayburn, and Tosh all remained forward-thinking in their management styles. The company grew to employ more than 250 professionals in Mississippi, California, and in client offices nationwide. They built a new Oxford headquarters and they lent support to countless philanthropic projects across the state.

In 2016, the four founders sold FNC to Corelogic for $475 million. As a result of the sale, more than forty FNC investors, founders, and long-time employees became instant millionaires. All thanks to a paper napkin and an Ole Miss professor who dared to ask, "What if?"

Opposite page: The *Clarion-Ledger* headline when FNC sold to Corelogic. Top, Jan and Lawrence Farrington with Tommy Tosh. Above, a page from the *Ole Miss Alumni Review* featuring FNC. Right, the four professors who founded FNC.

# DR. JILLIAN JAMES FOSTER

## 2008 • MBA

Jillian Foster is director of pharmacy at Baptist Memorial Hospital-North Mississippi in Oxford. She is a student preceptor and leads a team of thirty-eight employees in maintaining quality care for patients. She received one of sixteen national grants to establish a pharmacy residency training program.

Foster graduated from the UM School of Pharmacy with a Doctor of Pharmacy in 2004 and completed Ole Miss' MBA program in 2008.

She completed a health policy fellowship with Sen. Thad Cochran in 2004-05. She also completed a pharmacy practice residency and specialty residency with an emphasis in pharmacy management and administration at North Mississippi Medical Center in Tupelo. She worked as the pharmacy benefits manager at NMMC, where she managed the employee pharmacy.

Foster served as chair of the American Society of Health Systems Pharmacists Council on Public Policy in September 2009. She was president of the Mississippi Society of Health System Pharmacists in 2007-08 and has been on the Mississippi Pharmacists Association executive committee.

She has been named both MSHP's and MPhA's Outstanding Young Pharmacist of the Year and has published several columns in the *American Journal of Health-System Pharmacy*. She was awarded the Ole Miss Alumni Association's Outstanding Young Alumni Award in 2012. She has served as president of the Ole Miss Pharmacy Alumni Chapter, and has been a member of the Oxford Rotary Club and the Delta Gamma Alumnae Chapter, and a volunteer at the Oxford Medical Ministries Clinic.

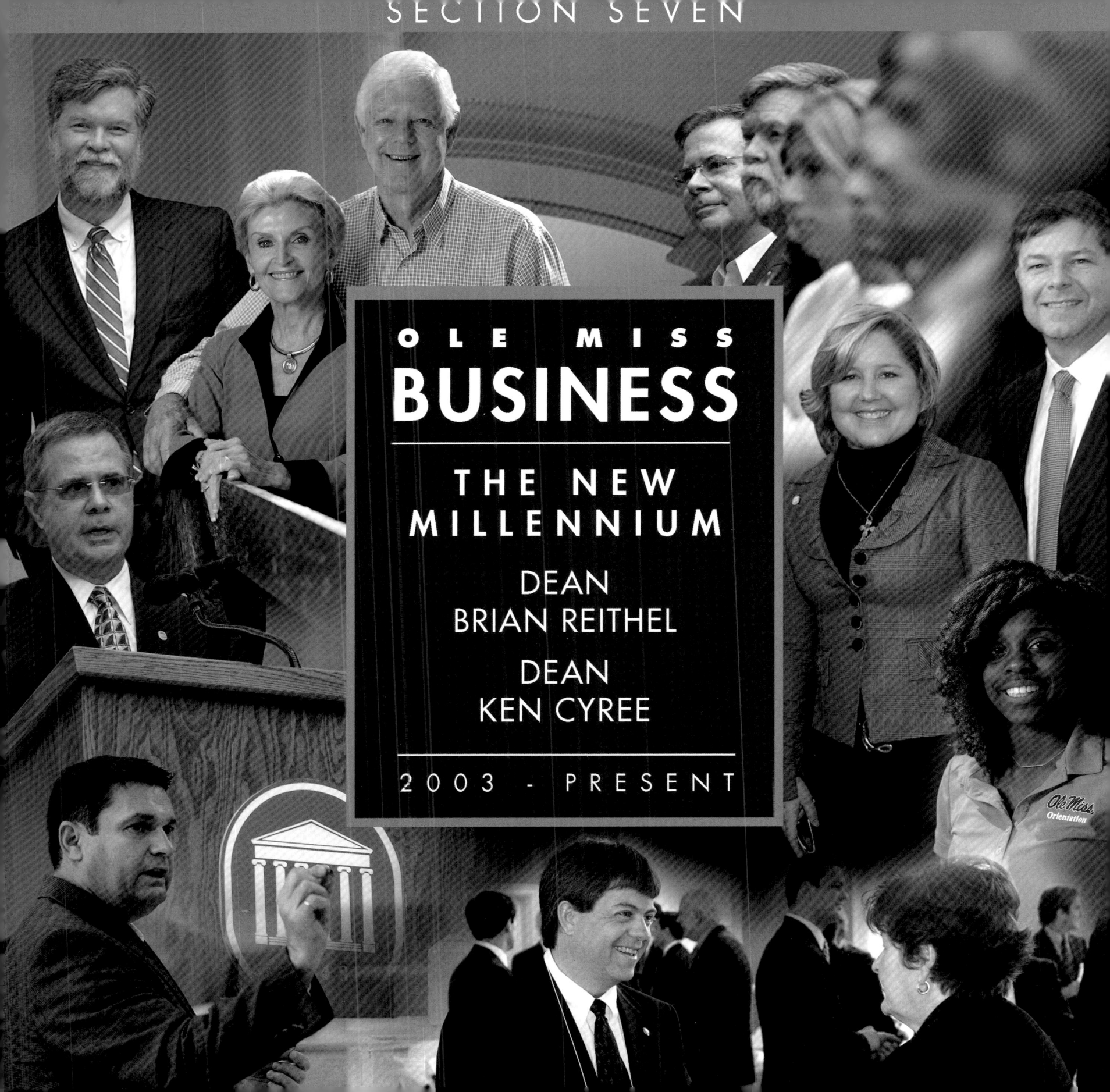

# OLE MISS
# BUSINESS

## THE NEW MILLENNIUM

DEAN
BRIAN REITHEL

DEAN
KEN CYREE

2003 - PRESENT

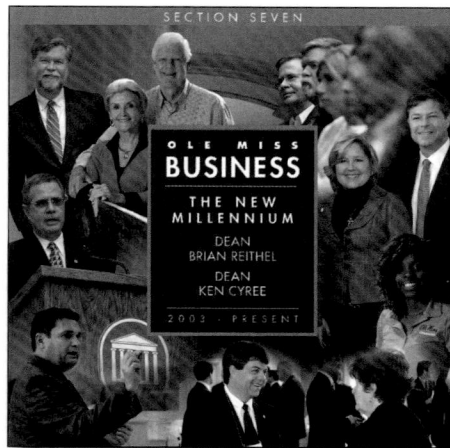

SECTION SEVEN

OLE MISS
BUSINESS

THE NEW
MILLENNIUM

DEAN
BRIAN REITHEL

DEAN
KEN CYREE

2003 · PRESENT

Clockwise from top left: Dean Ken Cyree, Jan and Lawrence Farrington, Chancellor Jeff Vitter and Dean Cyree viewing a panel discussion at the Center for Innovation and Entrepreneurship, Karen and Bruce Moore, Shamessia Lee, Dean Brian Reithel at a conference, Tony Ammeter, Chancellor Vitter at the 100th anniversary celebration in September 2017.

# BRIAN REITHEL
## 2003-2007

"Brian will bring the kind of harmony they need to have."

Provost Carolyn Ellis Staton

After Mike Harvey stepped down as dean, Carolyn Ellis Staton believed the School of Business Administration needed some strong, yet gentle, leadership. Based on his past performance with the university, she tapped Brian Reithel to step in as acting dean.

According to the June 17, 2003, edition of *The Daily Mississippian*, Staton said, "We want to let everyone settle in and get to work for a while. I think what they need most is some stability and peacefulness. Brian Reithel will bring the kind of harmony they need to have."

Brian Reithel took the reins as dean in 2003.

### A Positive Outlook

From the very beginning, Reithel saw a silver lining.

"On the positive side," he said, "we had enjoyed some growth in enrollment over the years and had some very dedicated, talented people on the faculty. We had a great team, a wonderful building. All of the pieces were there — and were substantial — in order for us to come together and push ahead into the next chapter of the business school's life."

Reithel admitted there was a lingering note of disharmony over the economics department being moved out of the school of business, as well as the difficulty of the spat between Dean Harvey and Provost Staton. But he was quick to point out, "We had people who were doing an excellent job in the classroom, as well as some super research going on."

Reithel had some looming funding issues to face. The school had two different non-sustainable sources of funding that the three previous deans had arranged. This included some funding from the Robert M. Hearin Foundation, as well as some federal funding from the Office of Naval Research, both of which were about to come to an end.

The substantial infusion of one-time money was supposed to catapult the business school into national greatness. Reithel questioned whether it would work in the long run (at least in alignment with the intent of the funding) because of the temporary nature of the grants.

"When I became dean," Reithel said, "we had some limited-duration, discretionary money, along with some limited-duration large financial commitments that had been made to faculty members, and we needed to figure out a way to have more sustainable funding over time."

Reithel, in his previous positions on campus, had several years of strategic planning/fundraising experience and he had dealt with university alumni, foundations, corporations, the federal government — virtually all of the constituencies necessary to put together a plan for more permanent funding.

## Biggest Challenges

In addition to facing the end of one-time monies, the biggest challenge Reithel faced was the continuing growth in enrollment combined with flat funding from the university.

"It was clear that what we needed to do," Reithel said, "was to develop some more sustainable sources of funding and develop some strategies for dealing with the enrollment growth."

The university viewed the business school as an area that should have open admission — that any student at Ole Miss could enter the business school. This open-admission policy was part of a multi-pronged strategy that the university had employed in the past to address higher education accessibility in the state of Mississippi.

"That's a nice view of things," Reithel said, "but when our student body keeps growing and our faculty doesn't, it's a problem."

While Reithel was dean, he was able to convince the administration to add several new faculty lines (especially since the school was open to *all* students). They also approved funds to replace the lost one-time money.

## Accreditation Changes and a Pre-Professional Program

The School of Business Administration also had to address the new accreditation regime that AACSB had implemented. The organization radically changed the accreditation standards in the early 2000s. The school of business had some work to do in order to come into alignment with where the accrediting body saw collegiate schools of business going. But that also fit perfectly with some of Dean Reithel's vision for the school.

Reithel explained that he wanted to put *some* kind of admission standards in place for the business school.

"We began the process of working with the provost's office to establish a reasonable GPA requirement to move into upper division classes (basically to be admitted to a specific major in the business school)."

Reithel hoped, over time, the higher standard would enhance the quality and competitiveness of the undergraduate student body.

"We could raise the admissions bar gradually over time, taking advantage of the natural growth we were having anyway, and try to improve the overall reputation of the business school," Reithel explained.

By revising the undergraduate core curriculum, along with the movement toward improving the undergraduate student experience, the school managed to get (and could justify) some course fees attached to core classes — a new and sustainable source of funding for the business school.

"We used those course fees to help us establish the Business Pre-Professional Program," Reithel said.

It provided all business majors with a subscription to *Business Week* magazine and other significant professional development benefits.

"Every week, students would have news about the latest developments in business to weave together and discuss with their professors in class," Reithel added.

## Online MBA

It was evident to Reithel that there was going to be an opportunity, and a need for, an online master's program in business administration. There was a lot of hesitancy and resistance on the part of the faculty about the prospects of that program.

"Some people were enthusiastic," Reithel said, "but there were a lot of others who needed to learn more about online programs . . . to decide whether it would be right for us or not."

Reithel appointed groups of faculty members to go visit other leading business schools. "Reputable, serious business schools that had successful online MBA programs," he said.

"The intent was to learn from them what they were doing, why they were doing it, how they had arrived at that, and bring that knowledge back to share with other members of the MBA faculty."

The faculty teams visited other schools. Reithel was a part of the group that went to Indiana University. The delegations returned and shared what they learned with the MBA faculty, and Ole Miss developed the framework for what, at the time, was called the professional MBA.

"We called it the professional MBA because it was to be aimed at working professionals," Reithel said.

But it was also an Ole Miss MBA. "When someone earned their MBA from Ole Miss, we didn't want to make any distinction on their diploma about whether it was online or in person. It was an Ole Miss MBA."

Reithel and the school's leadership team developed a financial plan and worked with the provost and other offices on campus to find the seed funding to get the professional MBA started. They also developed a plan for how revenue would be shared.

"That was part of developing another sustainable stream of enhanced funding for the business school," Reithel said. "If we succeeded with the online MBA, it would create a new stream of cash flowing into the budget that was sustainable over time."

Ole Miss's online MBA is now ranked among the top 25 in the nation.

## Speaker's Edge

"When I became dean of the business school," Reithel explained, "I sat down with JoAnn Edwards (who had worked to with Reithel when he was the director of the Lott Leadership Institute) and said, 'JoAnn we really need to do something to help our MBA students have an edge in the marketplace presenting themselves.'

"I think one of the exceptional benefits of getting a degree from Ole Miss is that students obtain a level of social polish that is not available at most public universities. It is one of the great strengths of the university"

Edwards and Reithel came up with the concept for a new program called the "Speaker's Edge." It would be a professional development program conducted during the winter intersession.

The Speaker's Edge program gives Ole Miss MBA students an advantage when they enter the business world

Coaches and trainers would put the MBA students through an intense professional speaking education.

"I always thought back to how impressed I was every time I

went to a presentation with someone from IBM," Reithel said. "I was always so amazed by how polished they were and how professional they were. They had an edge over other vendors, and I wanted our students to be those kinds of presenters."

Reithel credits Edwards' energy, and industry, and creativity — along with her resources from the university's forensics (debate) team — in making the program a success.

"It has been a real gem in the business school's list of accomplishments," he added.

## Career Coaching

Reithel and his team also launched Career Coaching. The school paid retired business people, alumni, and other business-savvy Oxford residents to meet with every junior in the school each year. The school ultimately decided to make it a requirement for students who were enrolled in Marketing 351.

"Every junior business student had the opportunity to sit down one-on-one with someone who Ole Miss had hired and trained, who had good business experience, and who could talk to them one-on-one about their future," Reithel said. "They could say to the students, *What are you going to do?* and *How are you going to market yourself?* and *What kind of careers are you thinking about?* and *Have you started on a resume yet?* and *You need to get a resume going,* and *We want you to try to do internships.*"

The school encouraged students to participate in student internships between their junior and senior year.

"This was another way of enhancing the undergraduate educational experience at Ole Miss," Reithel said.

## Entrepreneurship

Next on Reithel's list was creating a culture of entrepreneurship in the business school. The Undergraduate Core Curriculum Committee discussed having an entrepreneurship class —something Ole Miss had not made available in the past.

"We needed to be willing to change — not just teach the same thing the same way forever and ever, but to adapt to the changing realities of the modern business environment and the global competitive reality that we all face," Reithel said. "I was excited that our faculty members were willing to consider and embrace changes that were good for the business school. It was courageous on their part to be willing to try to do something different, and to celebrate entrepreneurship, and that thread is now permanently woven into the fabric of the school.

"We obtained new funding from Provost Staton for the management department to hire two faculty members, one of whom would be an entrepreneurship faculty member," Reithel said.

The campus MBA program already had a course in which the students wrote business plans. Two of the MBA students, Matt Hedges and Andrew Jones, created a business plan for importing Argentinian wine into the U.S. as a table wine.

"Associate Dean Del Hawley told me they just did a great job in his class," Reithel said. "So I suggested we use some of our funding to send them to the Elevator Competition at Wake Forest University."

Ole Miss had never competed before.

The competition is an elevator pitch. The organizers put the students in the elevator with some noted alums from Wake Forest, and the students make their pitch. Hedges and his teammate won the contest.

Matt Hedges was featured in the *Ole Miss Alumni Review* for his venture that had its beginnings in a business school class.

The winners, if they agreed to locate the business near the Wake Forest campus, were offered assistance in funding the start up.

"Matt came back and told me about it. I said, 'Matt I've got my Business Advisory Board meeting coming up shortly. Will you make your elevator pitch in front of the Business Advisory Board?' He agreed. I said, 'At the end of it, I want you to say something like, *I'm Matt Hedges and I want to start this business here in Mississippi, and I'm looking for your help to raise a million dollars to start this business.'* And he asked, 'Should I really say that?' and I said, 'Yeah, just see what happens after the meeting.'"

Hedges made his pitch. After the meeting, a few members gathered around him to ask questions.

"We managed to pull together the funding to start Vino De Sol, which is up and running now, and their wines are available in all 50 states."

Hedges was featured on the cover of *BusinessFirst*, a magazine featuring Ole Miss School of Business Administration alumni, faculty, and students.

"I'm proud that we, collectively, started that culture of celebrating entrepreneurship," Reithel said.

## The Gillespie Business Plan Competition

"I came across an opportunity to work with Joe and Jean Gillespie and the Gillespie family, who had made a gift to the university," Reithel said.

Reithel worked with the Gillespie family to create the Gillespie Business Plan Competition. The competition is open to any student on campus.

"The competition is part of this powerful culture of entrepreneurship that we now have," Reithel said.

The Gillespie Business Plan Competition winners receive thousands of dollars. There is also a component that helps provide the winners with space and start-up assistance at Insight Park, the business incubator on campus.

The competition is held every spring.

## Katrina and the MSBDC

In 2005, when Hurricane Katrina hit Mississippi's Gulf Coast, Doug Gurley, state director of the Mississippi Small Business Development Center, and Dean Reithel were at a conference for the National Association of Small Business Development Centers.

Reithel and Gurley rallied support from the other states' Small Business Development Centers. They pledged to send people to the Gulf Coast to help small business owners get going again.

The volunteers assisted in applying for federal disaster loans, and they helped develop strategies to get businesses open again, and to get their paychecks flowing again.

"I literally went to Mike Ducker and Rose Flenorl at FedEx with a request for some one-time disaster relief money. Many others also rallied behind our efforts with financial support. We put campers on the Gulf Coast since there was no place for our counselors to stay. Everything was gone. We hired people to manage the camps, and we brought in our own direc-

When Dean Reithel arrived at the Long Beach office of the MSBDC, nothing but a slab remained.

tors from all over the state, as well as directors from other states."

Over the course of several months, volunteers counseled more than 1,400 small business owners whose buildings had been lost, whose customer base had been wiped out, whose records were

# SPEAKER'S EDGE
## OLE MISS MBA STUDENTS LEAVE WITH AN "EDGE"

The Speaker's Edge competition is unlike any other speech event in the country. The program challenges Ole Miss MBA students to express ideas, knowledge, and understanding clearly and effectively.

Inspired by a discussion between Dean Brian Reithel and JoAnn Edwards, the Speaker's Edge competition brings industry professionals, retirees, working alumni, and students together, requiring competitors to adapt their message to different audiences and different situations.

Ole Miss MBA students spend a week and a half working with world-class communication coaches to discover the strengths and weaknesses of their own personal style. The program culminates in a two-day competition, where students give three different presentations.

The first of these three presentations is "The Marketplace."

The second presentation focuses on "Informative Communication." The final presentation centers on "Ethical Dilemmas." A Speaker's Edge champion is named for the student with the best performance in all three categories.

The spoken word remains a critical skill in any industry. Speaker's Edge has become a hallmark of the Ole Miss MBA Program.

The goals of Speaker's Edge are multifaceted. First and foremost, the program aims to provide an opportunity to nurture and grow a student body that understands the value of the spoken word — to graduate students who have the confidence and experience to enter into the global conversation. The competition also provides an opportunity for Ole Miss graduates/alumni to return home and give back by judging the competitors. Finally, Speaker's Edge provides a competitive speech component woven into the fabric of this university that is intense, productive, and well done. This is the university where "everybody speaks."

Speaker's Edge offers two different experiences — one for students and one for alumni.

For students, early preparation is offered in the fall semester. While Speaker's Edge is a competition, winning is not the final assessment of student growth and mastery of presentation concepts. A sense of accomplishment — the actual feedback from coaches, judges and peers — all factor into the assessment. Ultimately, win, lose, or draw, the student's overall experience is the real value of this program.

For alumni, the experience is more in giving back. In 2014, over sixty judges attended the two-day event. Typically, judges become invested in the students' growth. A reception that follows the competition allows for a more informal interaction.

![Trent Lott Leadership Institute logo]

# MEMO

Hello, all.

I send you greetings and deepest thanks from the lovely University of Mississippi campus. Your presence, flexibility, hard work and positive spirit made for an enjoyable and challenging two days.

Here are some numbers which indicate the magnitude of your work:

118 MBA and Accountancy student participants

1,062 preliminary round ballots written - providing critical feedback

76 Judges from all across the country writing those ballots

14 coaches from every corner of the united states preparing these students

$1,000 check from Katherine Anderson presented to the Champion by Printz Bolin in her absence.

20 classrooms used every hour and fifteen minutes in our new location at Lamar Hall, along with the Alumni Center and Yerby Conference Center.

Below are the finalist and winners for those who could not attend or had to leave early. Finals were presented in the lovely Overby Center Auditorium.

Save the date for next year! January 11-12 2018.

Many thanks and I hope to see you next year,

*Edwards*

JoAnn Edwards, Director of Special Projects at The Trent Lott Leadership Institute

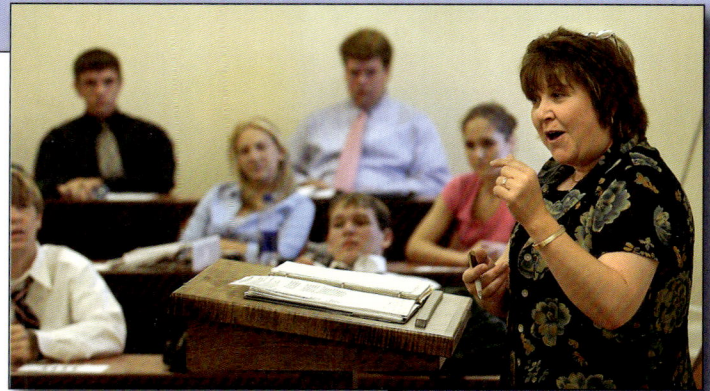

Above: JoAnn Edwards talks with students about public speaking and presentations.

Right: A memo from Edwards touting the success of the 2017 Speaker's Edge competition.

gone, and whose employees only wanted to get back to work.

"We even worked with the IRS to get the tax transcripts business owners needed to apply for the federal disaster loans," Reithel said.

"Del Hawley and I went down to survey the devastation. Doug Gurley and his staff did some incredible, incredible work," Reithel said. "Hurricane Katrina is a big deal in the history of the state of Mississippi. Now, it's a big deal in the history of the business school, because we were there responding just a handful of days after the hurricane hit, helping small business owners get their businesses going again.

"Aside from the Katrina disaster," Reithel said, praising the MSBDC, "if you look at the number of jobs created, the number of Mississippians touched by their work, it's staggering. The MSBDC doesn't get celebrated enough."

Dean Reithel said, "The faculty had to be the ones, ultimately, to make all of this happen."

business faculty. According to Reithel, "The long-term impact of these documents on faculty performance expectations and faculty culture is tremendous."

## Tenure and Promotion

Reithel and Mike Harvey (when Harvey was dean) had started a dialogue about changing the tenure and promotion document for the business school.

"The official document that was still on file with the university was literally decades old," Reithel said.

Under Reithel's deanship, the school gained approval from the university for a new set of tenure and promotion standards. The standards guide faculty culture; they guide what faculty members focus on, and they articulate expectations of members of the

## A Team Effort

Reithel credited the faculty, staff, and alumni for the strides made during his tenure. "A lot of people worked on these initiatives, he said. "I'm fortunate that I was dean and I got to be the encourager and the cajoler and the person who said, 'Well, it would be nice if we could do this or if we could do that,' and people bought into it.

"The faculty had to be the ones, ultimately, to make all of this happen."

# KEN CYREE
## 2008-PRESENT

"Dean Cyree is, first and foremost, a good man. I also appreciate that he is excellent with numbers and with people."

Danielle Beu Ammeter, Ph.D.
*Assistant Dean for Undergraduate Programs and Instructional Assistant Professor of Management*

In 2007, Dr. Ken Cyree was named Outstanding Teacher of the Year in the School of Business Administration. The following year he was named interim dean. After a nationwide search in 2008, Cyree was named the eleventh dean in the history of the school.

Cyree wasted no time in setting goals. In his initial vision statement, Cyree set the following goals:

1. Continuing to add value to our students through a deep understanding of business fundamentals.

2. Augmenting these fundamentals with specific knowledge in certain areas, such as finance, marketing, and management.

3. Attracting and retaining the best faculty in order to accomplish one and two.

In 2009, Dean Cyree established a list of concrete goals. Some of those milestones have been met. Others are close to being realized.

**Those met include:**

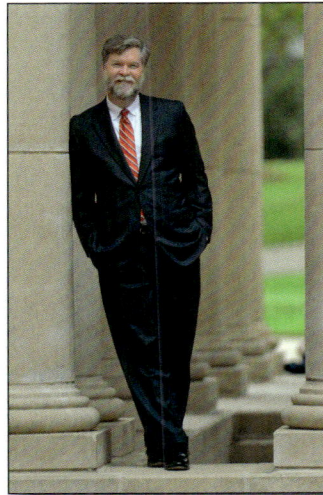

Ken Cyree has served as dean since 2008.

■ Our MBA program is the flagship program in the state, but our goal is to be ranked at 70 or better in the country.

■ To add a leadership class in the MBA program to help our MBA students learn to be better leaders.

■ To create an Entrepreneurship Center to provide more expertise and to interface with business more effectively.

■ Longer term, we hope to start a type of venture capital fund to finance Ole Miss student ideas that emerge from our entrepreneurship program and other areas, such as the Gillespie Business Plan Competition. Finance and other students can also benefit by helping manage the financial aspects of the fund to gain experience in start-up financing.

■ We plan to add a career placement specialist to help students find jobs and hone their job-seeking skills.

■ We recently started an entrepreneurship major to provide in-depth study for our students wishing to start a new business or to innovate within existing businesses.

**The milestones that are still within reach include:**

■ Our five-year goal is for the business school undergraduate program to be ranked at 75 or better.

■ We are also pursuing a supply chain management minor, which is a natural fit since we are close to Memphis and have good contacts at Fed Ex, AutoZone, UPS, and other firms who specialize and utilize supply chains to compete.

■ To partner with the Center for Manufacturing Excellence

■ We hope to partner with the law school to provide a joint JD/MBA program

## Budget Constraints

Much like the ten deans before him, Dean Cyree has faced budget constraints that prevent him from hiring more faculty and staff to meet the demands of increased enrollment.

Total enrollment in 2009 (graduate and undergraduate) was 2,903. In the fall of 2017, enrollment was 3,888.

"The large growth in student enrollment during my time as dean has been a challenge as well," Cyree said.

Growth in student enrollment is important for Ole Miss' ability to withstand cuts in state budget appropriations, but without growth in the number of faculty, enrollment growth presents serious challenges, especially when it comes to offering enough classes to meet the demands of the students.

"We have handled some of the growth using technology to create online classes, and this has been a good way to address our classroom and faculty constraints," Cyree said. "We have found that students like the online experience as much as (or sometimes more than) the in-person class format for some of the classes.

"Tight budgets have forced us to get very good at doing a lot with a little," Cyree said. "We are very efficient in terms of staff, administrators, and infrastructure, and we have managed to produce results in research, teaching productivity, and program quality that exceed other schools of business with budgets, staff, and faculty that are several times larger than ours. A key element of this ability to do a lot with a little is that we focus on teamwork and mutual respect. We couldn't do what we do unless many people were willing to work together and work hard to make this business school as good as it can be."

Tony Ammeter, Ph.D., associate provost for outreach and continuing Studies and dean of general studies, pointed out that Dean Cyree's enthusiasm and energy go a long way toward overcoming budget challenges.

"When Ken walks by my office," Ammeter said, "he always cheers: 'Go, Tony, go!' It is incredibly motivating, especially when you are working on a problem with that seems insurmountable. His sincere enthusiasm and optimism communicates that he appreciates you being there and trying."

Dean Cyree with Jimmy Fried, the school's first MBA graduate.

## Alumni Support

Dean Cyree emphasizes the importance of alumni support in the environment of state budget cuts and reduced funding for higher education.

"We are fortunate that we have had generous alumni and friends donate more than 80 endowed gifts that support faculty, scholarships, and academic programs," Cyree said.

Many Ole Miss alumni provide their time and expertise. Cyree points to the active boards operating within the school. In addition to the Business Advisory Board, the school has supportive boards in the areas of insurance, real estate, banking, entrepreneurship, and the MBA program.

"Alumni visit classes and speak to students on up-to-date issues in their industry," Cyree said. "And, we have alumni who help recruit students to come to the Ole Miss business school." Alumni and friends of the business school also serve as mentors and judges for student competitions.

Cyree insists that alumni involvement is key in helping the school to achieve its mission. And alums have reciprocal feelings about the business school.

Melanie Dowell (BBA 1980), executive director/corporate client group director of Morgan Stanley and president of the Business Advisory Board, said, "The students who graduate from the Ole Miss School of Business take more than a diploma with them when they graduate. Our students are infused with the spirit of the people who are Ole Miss. A business degree from Ole Miss is like no other in that you are not only academically ready for the world that awaits you but you are also ready to skillfully and respectfully interact with people of all descriptions."

Karen and Bruce Moore (1982, finance and accounting) agreed. "Due to the leadership of Dean Ken Cyree," Bruce said, "this program has opened doors for many students to achieve distinguished professional careers. As the business school continues to expand and attract stellar students from a diverse geographic area, Dean Cyree has capitalized on the reputation of the school."

Although there are far too many support alumni to name, Cyree points to some of the more successful as inspiration to students — Jim Barksdale, Lawrence Farrington, John Palmer, William Yates, III.

"Many generous alumni and friends have made large endowed gifts that help us perform our mission," Cyree said.

Some of those include Frank R. Day, Bruce Moore, John Palmer, Jack "Bouncer" Robertson, Christine and Clarence Day, Bert and Dot Allen, Dixie Carter, Maurice Colly, Terry Crawford, Alfred Dantzler, Yvonne and Clyde Edwards, C.C. Eason, Mac Elliott, Bill Bryson, Tom Quaka, Walton and Tom Gresham, Eddie Gatlin, Phil Hardin, Maureen Liberto, Julius "Judy" King,

Dean Cyree with (L to R) Jan Farrington, William Yates, 2017 winner of the Farrington Distinguished Entrepreneur of the Year Award, and Lawrence Farrington.

Forrest Mobley, James Sterling Reckling, Peyton Self, W. Clif Shirley, Tom Scott, Mike Starnes, Mr. and Mrs. James E. King, Denny and Faye King, Charles White, Randy Long, Johnny and Sharon Maloney, Anne and Cecil Fox, Bobby Dunlap, Donna Ruth Roberts, Lib Quirk, J. Ed Turner, Tommy and Susan Thames, Edwin Gillespie, Bo Tigue, Mike and Jane Strojny, Steve Rowell, Thomas Murphree, Chip Crunk, Wert Yerger III, Charlie

Porter, Scott Wegmann, and David R. White.

## Rankings

Dean Cyree pointed to the double-edged sword of rankings. "All deans hate rankings when they work against you," he said. "However, if they are favorable, every dean would use them and publish them to make the school look good."

Rankings, though flawed like any rating process, do provide some value to consumers.

"We have been very fortunate that we have moved up the rankings since I have been dean," Cyree said.

The Ole Miss School of Business Administration's undergraduate program was ranked in the top 100 in the latest *US News* ranking. The MBA program has the highest ranking ever in *BusinessWeek*, at 68 overall and 36 for public institutions.

"A good part or our ranking success is due to the publishing and research of the faculty," Cyree noted, "and I am happy to have helped contribute to that in my time as dean."

The Risk Management and Insurance program at Ole Miss is consistently ranked in the top ten largest in the nation. Last year, the RMI program was one of only 12 in the United States to be designated as a Global Center of Insurance Excellence by the International Insurance Society's forum in London.

## Rigor and Competitions

"Much of our efforts in recent years have been aimed at handling the growth in enrollment while still maintaining academic rigor," Cyree said.

In addition to high classroom standards, the school participates in a number of competitions, including:

- Bloomberg Trading Challenge
- Annual Tennessee Valley Authority Investment Challenge
- Gillespie Business Plan Competition
- Innovation Boot Camp
- Annual SEC MBA Case Competition
- Speaker's Edge
- Collegiate DECA — state and national levels
- Alpha Kappa Psi — regional and national competitions
- Association of Information Technology Professionals — AITP — annual regional and national levels

## A Different Challenge

Many of the deans who preceded Cyree dealt with political pressures from legislators and governors and the IHL board of trustees members over what classes should be taught, who should be hired, and what political stances/propaganda should be promoted or admonished.

In a reflection of cultural mores, Cyree has encountered a different kind of strong-arming.

"I've received no pressure about the curriculum," Cyree said. "The only pressure I've had is from parents. They are typically trying to get their child in a closed section, which is *possibly* not the fault of the child, but most likely is because they procrastinated." He continued, "Some parents are adamant about wanting their child to skip pre-requisites (which we do not do) or have their son or daughter re-admitted when they are dismissed."

Cyree said he occasionally gets pressure from an alumnus to admit a student to the MBA program who does not make a sufficient test score. "But we do not do that either unless their GPA offsets some of the lower test scores," he said.

"I have had some calls from chancellors, governors' offices, athletics departments, and other important leaders who put in a good word for either a job candidate or MBA applicant, although none of them has ever done anything inappropriate."

## Student Behavior and Technology

Cyree said he has noticed a change in student behavior because of the impact of technology. The change is both negative and positive.

"On the negative side," Cyree said, "students are much more likely to look at texts in class or pull up Facebook on their laptops. Not paying attention in class for any reason impacts, at least, their learning, and in the case of looking at Facebook, their neighbor who is also looking at the screen."

"On a positive note," he said, "the internet has allowed for faster research on topics and a large amount of information literally at the students' fingertips. It is important to learn about trends and the latest business developments, but not everything you see is true or correct, so students have to learn to be discerning. You can also look up topics in class in real time, such as an exchange rate or the price of a stock, where we had no ability to do that in years past."

Cyree points out that the good students also seem to be more serious than ever before — and that they work hard and want to learn as much as possible.

## A Culture of Entrepreneurship

Dean Cyree brought a spirit of entrepreneurship to the business school. In fact, he started the Center for Innovation and Entrepreneurship.

Rich Gentry, assistant professor of strategy and entrepreneurship said, "Ken let us focus on improving student entrepreneurship and took responsibility for evangelizing our efforts and attracting more people (like our entrepreneur in residence) into the school."

Clay Dibrell, the William G. Gresham entrepreneurial lecturer and co-director of the Center for Innovation and Entrepreneurship, added, "Ken was instrumental in hiring Dr. Rich Gentry and myself to enhance entrepreneurship offerings throughout the university. This was quite an achievement, as I understood that we

were the only two new faculty lines during those lean years. During my job interview with Ken, he told me how important entrepreneurship is to the state of Mississippi and wanted entrepreneurship to be embedded in our culture. Because he is a man of his word and through his leadership, entrepreneurship has exponentially increased across campus with new student competitions, the creation of a major and a minor in entrepreneurship,

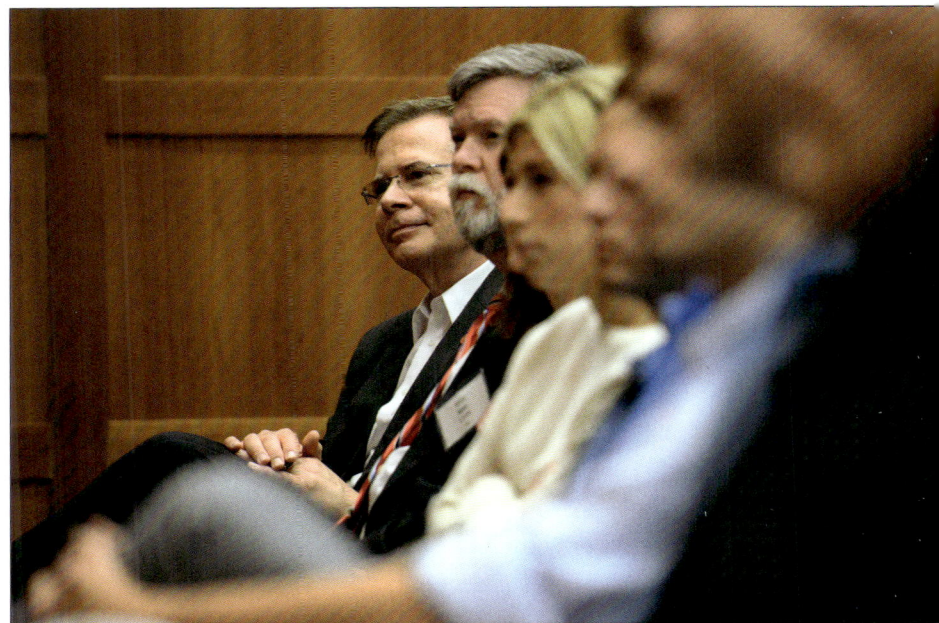

Chancellor Jeff Vitter and Dean Ken Cyree listen to a 2016 panel discussion at the Center for Innovation and Entrepreneurship.

and the founding of the Center for Innovation and Entrepreneurship. All of these initiatives have flourished at Ole Miss during his tenure as dean."

Jan and Lawrence Farrington (1958 BBA), Ole Miss alums who have been supportive of the entrepreneurship program, said, "We are so grateful that Dean Cyree took the lead in enhancing the entrepreneurial program. His leadership has been invaluable — he understands fully how important it is for our university and our state."

# DR. DEL HAWLEY
## A GUIDING FORCE FOR FIVE DEANS

Dr. Del Hawley has served the School of Business Administration for 31 years. He is not only senior associate dean and associate professor of finance at the School of Business Administration, but he also serves as the school's CFO, COO, and CIO. In addition to those roles, Dr. Hawley teaches an online course on financial modeling using Microsoft Excel that he designed.

Dr. Hawley has served alongside five different deans during his tenure.

Brian Reithel, who served as dean of the school from 2003-2007 said, "I do not think there has ever been an associate dean like Del in the past — and I doubt that we'll ever have another one in the future.

"My firmly held opinion is that Del has had a tremendous impact on the overall life and trajectory of the school, ranging from his herculean efforts on the Holman and Conner Halls construction/renovation projects, through his steady stewardship of the school's day-to-day financial operations and budgetary processes, and to serving as a trusted confidant to several deans and as a member of the school's leadership team."

To many, Dr. Hawley is the holder of much of the school's institutional history.

Dean Ken Cyree said, "Del Hawley has been an instrumental figure in the success of the Business School. He is one of the best administrators I have ever been around. He makes logical and rational decisions, and understands the constraints and environment in which we operate.

"He has been a constant and vigilant proponent of the Business School for decades and has worked for five deans in this time."

Cyree added, "Del knows more about the inner workings of Ole Miss than almost anyone on campus and is well respected by others in his abilities and dedication."

Dean Cyree wants to cultivate innovative, impactful leaders.

### Looking Back, Looking Forward

When Cyree was asked to look back on his tenure and his accomplishments, he said, "I think the beginning of the Center for Innovation and Entrepreneurship (see profile on page 186), along with the Rebel Venture Capital Fund (RVCF) are some of the best moments in my tenure as dean.

"I am also proud of the publishing success the faculty have had, some of which goes to hiring good faculty, and some which is attributed to rewarding those that publish in highly-ranked journals."

In addition, adding a career preparation team to help students learn job skills for the rest of their careers is a highlight. Another historic accomplishment is in moving to online classes for many of the undergraduate classes. Also, starting the general business major with the core classes being online or live as students' desire.

As for his vision for the future of the school, Cyree said, "Our vision is for the Ole Miss Business School to create innovative, impactful leaders with strong work ethic, who are valuable team members and problem solvers, to improve Mississippi, the region, and the world."

# MS. CANDIE SIMMONS

2002 • BBA; 2008, MBA • OCEAN SPRINGS, MISSISSIPPI

Candie Simmons is a senior vice president and regional marketing director for Regions Financial Corporation in Jackson, Mississippi. In this position, she provides marketing and advertising support for the bank and its lines of business throughout the state. Additionally, she develops relationships with media and purchases advertising in these markets, and serves as the community and public relations representative for this region.

A native of Ocean Springs, Mississippi, Candie in 2002 received her bachelor of business administration degree in marketing from the University of Mississippi. She also earned her master of business administration degree from the University of Mississippi. While in college, she received the Excellence in Mississippi Scholarship and was a member of the Chancellor's Honor Roll and National Society of Collegiate Scholars. She was also a member of Alpha Kappa Alpha Sorority, Inc., and was selected as a Leadership Fellow based on her academic achievements, leadership skills, and community service.

After graduating, Simmons began her career working with UM in the Admissions Office as admissions counselor for Northwest Mississippi, Jackson Public Schools, and Georgia. After this, her career branched to UM's Alumni Affairs office and then, eventually, to Regions Bank in 2006. Through her hard work, she gained the title of southwest regional marketing director.

Candie was selected as a 2013 Top 50 Leading Business Woman, and she is active with Alpha Kappa Alpha Sorority, Inc., where she is serving her second term as treasurer for her local chapter and was voted 2013 Soror of the Year. She is also an active volunteer with the Diabetes Foundation of Mississippi and serves as a Board Member for the Cure Sickle Cell Foundation and Make-A-Wish Mississippi. She is also the current treasurer for the Community Foundation of Greater Jackson. Candie completed a three-year term on the national board of the Ole Miss Alumni Association, then later served as a member of the organization's executive committee. She is currently serving another three-year term on the national board of the Ole Miss Alumni Association and she previously served as chair of Jackson State University's Entrepreneurship Advisory Council. She can often be seen working with the American Heart Association, The Catch 22 Foundation, Bethlehem Center, and has served on the planning committee for the Economic Smart Fair. Outside of work, Simmons enjoys traveling, spending time with friends, and being outside.

# THE CENTER FOR INNOVATION AND ENTREPRENEURSHIP
## SUPPORTING AND RECOGNIZING ENTERPRENEURS

The Center for Innovation and Entrepreneurship (CIE) was established in 2013 as part of the business school's ongoing effort to evolve along with the rapidly-changing business world. The center aims to increase the passion of students and mold them into the entrepreneurial leaders of the future. That goal is achieved through a multi-pronged approach. CIE facilitates multiple organizations including a student entrepreneurship club; sponsors events such as elevator pitch competitions, idea development workshops, and a business plan competition; and maintains support initiatives including a mentoring system, a student-led consulting program, international trips, and start-up weekends.

Just two years into its operation, the center's forward-looking approach and dynamic offerings were recognized when it won the 2015 Award for Emerging Entrepreneurship Center from the Global Consortium of Entrepreneurship Centers.

The CIE gives students the chance to take fledgling ideas and turn them into real businesses. Various competitions put students on the fast track to refining their business plans and models. The Gillespie Business Plan Competition, held each spring, is the marquee event of the year. Students submit their plans, and those that judges deem most feasible are entered into a final round, receiving coaching from mentors to prepare for the competition.

A dress rental business, Curtsy, won the Gillespie business plan competition in 2016.

Winners of the Gillespie Competition receive funds so that they can take their business plans and turn them into actual businesses, so the exercise is not only theoretical—for some students, it can be the beginning of an entrepreneurial career that starts even before graduation. The funds come from an endowment honoring Edwin C. Gillespie, a 1943 business administration graduate, established by his family in 2006.

The center sponsors various other pitch competitions, including the Fall Business Model Competition, in which participants can choose either a traditional, for-profit track or try their hand at the emerging world of social entrepreneurship, building businesses that are engineered to solve social problems.

The CIE is just as much about collaboration and cooperation as it is about competition, however. Through receptions, speakers, workshops, and the school's network of graduates and regional businesspeople, the center connects students with each other and with the people they will need to know once they graduate.

Speakers have included men and women from a wide variety of industries, including tech, finance, hospitality, and healthcare, to name only a few. Mentorship cuts both ways. Students learn from the faculty and from visiting entrepreneurs and, once they get their feet on solid ground, put their own knowledge to work by consulting with local businesses. The CIE also sponsors programs to help students start real businesses in Oxford by offering coaching, legal advice, financial assistance, and manufacturing.

The CIE's faculty are drawn from the school of management and all hold Ph.D. or MBA degrees. Each member of the faculty brings unique areas of specialization to the table and many have spent time in industry in addition to their academic pursuits, so they are well-positioned to mentor students.

The center's mission is extremely student centered, but ultimately, its goals go far beyond the university's walls. As part of the dedication to improving Mississippi's economy, a commitment that dates back to the business school's founding, the CIE wants to build up students that will start and improve businesses in the state. The impact that thoughtful, dedicated entrepreneurs can have, especially in an economically-challenged place, are tremendous.

As the CIE's reputation continues to build and successes pile up, the center will only continue to improve, and with that improvement will come even greater innovation and a brighter economic future for Mississippi.

## Farrington Distinguished Entrepreneur of the Year Award

Every year the business school selects one business or entrepreneur to recognize as the Ole Miss Entrepreneur of the Year. The winners are nominated by the community and selected by the Dean of the School of Business Administration. The past winners are:

**Jan & Lawrence Farrington**
(2010)
**Drs. Robert Dorsey**
**John Johnson**
**Bill Rayburn**
**Dennis Tosh**
(2011)
**Stephen Johnston**
(2012)
**Matt Hedges**
(2013)
**Dr. Henry Jones, II**
(2014)
**Clark Love**
(2015)
**William Yates**
(2016)

APPENDIX

# THE DEANS
# 1917-PRESENT

James Warsaw Bell
1917-1941

Ben B. McNew
1966-1979

Michael Harvey
2001-2003

Horace B. Brown
1941-1949

M. Lynn Spruill
1980-1984

Brian J. Reithel
2003-2007

McDonald K. Horne
1949-1950

Rex L. Cottle
1985-1991

Ken Cyree
2008-present

Carl Nabors
*Acting Dean 1979-1980*

• • •

Keith Womer
*Acting Dean 1999-2001*

Clive F. Dunham
1950-1965

W. Randy Boxx
1992-1999

# MEMBERS OF THE BUSINESS ORDER

William R. Aikins
R. Julian Allen lll
Nicholas J. Angelozzi Jr.
Louise M. Avent
Robert W. Bailey
Diane D. Barrentine
Donald B. Bedell
Ronnie L. Bethay
C. Marion Black
M. Guion Bond Jr.
Barry G. Bouchillon
W. Randy Boxx
Louis K. Brandt Jr.
William A. Brown
Perrin L. Caldwell
John M. Christian
Jack Cooke Jr.
Mr. & Mrs. Rex L. Cottle
David W. Cowart
Terry Crawford
Frank R. Day
Melanie W. Dowell
Micheal E. Dowell
Robert Holmes Dunlap
Johnny H. Dykes
Jimmy Edwards
Michelle E. Edwards
W. Mac Elliott
Micheal E. Ellis
Mike Ely
S.L. Farrington
Roger M. Flynt Jr.
Edward O. Fritts
William N. Fry Jr.
O.T. Gaines lll
Ralph M. Garrard
Charles G. Gates
H. William Gates lll
John A. Gilliland
Kenneth B. Glenn
T. Michael Glenn
William Gottshall Jr.
Richard M. Green
Walter D. Gurley Jr.
Lyttleton T. Harris IV
Hap Hederman
Van E. Hedges
Matthew A. Hedges
Charles R. Herron lll
Dewey C. Hickman
R. L. Holley
Mr. & Mrs. W. Henry Holman Jr.

Daniel Clyde Hughes Jr.
Charles V. Imbler
Larry L. Johnson
Stephen Johnston
David Baxter Jones
Mark B. Jordan
William H. Keener
Julius W. King
Steven W. Laird
Morris Lewis lll
Ronald N. Magruder
Edward Maloney
J. Lamar Maxwell Jr.
Howard L. McMillan Jr.
Paul Wilson McMullan
Patrick E. McNarny
Theodore J. Millette
Thomas D. Moore
Johnny Morgan
William H. Morris Jr.
Willard Ross Neely ll
William Neville lll
Mr. & Mrs. William Richard Newman lll
Joe W. Overstreet Jr.
John Norris Palmer
Henry Paris
Gail J. Pittman
Charles F. Porter
Martis D. Ramage Jr.
Jon Reeves
Donna Ruth Roberts
Jeffrey B. Rogers
J. Richard Schwalje
Gwin C. Scott Jr.
Robert E. Seibels lll
Susan A. Simmons
Michael S. Starnes
Matthew A. Thornton
George W. Tomlinson
Charles E. Vianey
R. Preston Wailes
Robert E. Warren
William P. Wells
J. Dan White
H.A. Whittington Jr.
Charles D. Wilson
James B. Wolf
Norman Keith Womer
Ronald A. Yancis
Jack B. Yates
Wirt A. Yerger Jr.

# 2017 BUSINESS ADVISORY BOARD MEMBERS

William Alias
Bill Andrews
Alon Bee
Jill Beneke
Dottie Berry
John Cassimus
Jeffery Conley
Terry Crawford
Chip Crunk
**Melanie Dowell (Chair)**
Stephen Ethridge
Gus Ezcurra
William Fry
Bill Gates
Dan Hughes
Ben James
Bob Jacobs
Randy Leister
Johnny Maloney
Michael Mitchell
Nash Neyland
Chris Posey
Ella Jane Putnam
Elizabeth Randall
Jeff Rogers
Steve Rowell
Tim Rutledge
Gwin Scott
Preston Thomas
Matt Thornton
Wanda Truxillo
Bill Turner
Stan Viner
Brian Wikle
Adams Withers

# THE SCHOOL OF BUSINESS ADMINISTRATION FACULTY 2017-2018

| NAME | DEPARTMENT | TITLE |
|------|-----------|-------|
| Dr. Milam Aiken | MIS | Chair of the Department of MIS and Professor of Management of Information Systems |
| Mr. Owens Alexander | Management | Instructor of Management and Entrepreneurship<br>Entrepreneur-in-Residence for the Center for Innovation and Entrepreneurship |
| Dr. Bahram Alidaee | Marketing | Interim Chair for Department of Marketing<br>Professor of Production Operations Management and Pharmacy Administration |
| Dr. Tony Ammeter | MIS/Management | Associate Provost of Outreach<br>Dean of General Studies; Associate Professor of MIS & Management |
| Dr. Danielle Ammeter | Management | Assistant Dean for Undergraduate Programs<br>Instructional Assistant Professor of Management |
| Ms. Meg Barnes | Management | Instructor of Management and Director of Undergrad Career Preparation |
| Dr. John P. Berns | Management | Assistant Professor of Management |
| Dr. Travis Box | Finance | Assistant Professor of Finance |
| Dr. Victoria Bush | Marketing | Professor of Marketing; Donna Ruth Roberts Business Women's Lecturer |
| Dr. Seong Byun | Finance | Assistant Professor of Finance |
| Dr. Melissa Cinelli | Marketing | Assistant Professor of Marketing |
| Dr. Sumali Conlon | MIS | Associate Professor of MIS |
| Dr. Sam Cousley | Marketing | Instructional Associate Professor of Marketing |
| Dr. Aleta Crawford | Management | Instructional Assistant Professor of Management |
| Dr. Ken Cyree | Finance | Dean of the School of Business Administration<br>Frank R. Day/Mississippi Bankers Association Chair of Banking; Professor of Finance |
| Dr. Walter Davis | Management | Associate Professor of Management |
| Ms. Violetta Davyenko | Finance | Instructional Assistant Professor of Finance |
| Dr. Clay Dibrell | Management | Professor of Management; William W. Gresham Jr. Entrepreneurial Lecturer;<br>Co-Director of the Center for Innovation and Entrepreneurship |
| Dr. Cong Feng | Marketing | Assistant Professor of Marketing |
| Dr. Stephen Fier | Finance | Holder of the Liberto/King Professorship of Insurance; Associate Professor of Finance |
| Dr. Dwight Frink | Management | Holder of the PMB Self Chair of Free Enterprise; Professor of Management |
| Dr. Kathleen P. Fuller | Finance | Associate Professor of Finance; Tom B. Scott Jr. Chair of Financial Institutions |
| Dr. Bart Garner | MIS | Instructional Assistant Professor of MIS; Director of IT Services |
| Dr. Richard J. Gentry | Management | Associate Professor of Management<br>Co-Director of the Center for Innovation and Entrepreneurship |
| Dr. David Gligor | Marketing | Assistant Professor of Marketing |
| Dr. Maria Gondo | Management | Associate Professor of Management |

# THE SCHOOL OF BUSINESS ADMINISTRATION FACULTY 2017-2018

| NAME | DEPARTMENT | TITLE |
| --- | --- | --- |
| Dr. Bud Hamilton | Management | Instructional Associate Professor of Management |
| Dr. Del Hawley | Finance | Senior Associate Dean; Associate Professor of Finance |
| Dr. Paul Johnson | Management | Assistant Professor of Management |
| Dr. Saim Kashmiri | Marketing | Assistant Professor of Marketing |
| Dr. Lynn Kugele | Finance | Instructional Assistant Professor of Finance |
| Dr. Andre Liebenberg | Finance | Gwenette P. and Jack W. Robertson Chair of Insurance; Associate Professor of Finance |
| Dr. Ivonne Liebenberg | Finance | Instructional Assistant Professor of Finance |
| Dr. Andrew Lynch | Finance | Assistant Professor of Finance |
| Dr. Frank Markham | Management | Instructional Associate Professor of Management |
| Dr. Christopher Newman | Marketing | Assistant Professor of Marketing |
| Dr. Milorad Novicevic | Management | Associate Professor of Management |
| Dr. Scott O'Brien | Finance | Instructional Assistant Professor of Finance |
| Dr. Jamison Posey | MIS | Instructional Assistant Professor of Management Information Systems |
| Dr. Cesar Rego | Marketing | Professor of Production Operations Management |
| Dr. Brian Reithel | MIS | Professor of Management Information Systems |
| Dr. Robert Robinson | Management | Chair of the Department of Management; Michael Starnes Professor of Management |
| Mr. Stuart Schafer | Management | Instructor in Management |
| Dr. Jeremy Schoen | Management | Assistant Professor of Management |
| Dr. Matthew Shaner | Marketing | Assistant Professor of Marketing |
| Dr. Hugh Sloan III | Marketing | Associate Professor of Marketing |
| Dr. Rachel Smith | Marketing | Visiting Assistant Professor of Marketing |
| Dr. Neil Southern | Marketing | Instructional Assistant Professor of Marketing |
| Dr. Bonnie Van Ness | Finance | Chair and Professor of Finance, Holder of the Otho Smith Professorship |
| Dr. Robert Van Ness | Finance | Director of Doctoral Programs; Professor of Finance; Bruce Moore Scholar of Finance |
| Dr. Scott Vitell | Marketing | Professor of Marketing; Holder of the Phil B. Hardin Chair in Marketing |
| Dr. Douglas Vorhies | Marketing | Professor of Marketing; Holder of the Morris Lewis Lectureship |
| Dr. Kathleen Wachter | Marketing | Associate Professor of Marketing |
| Dr. Lloyd "Chip" Wade | Finance | Assistant Professor of Finance |
| Dr. Mark Walker | Finance | Associate Professor of Finance |
| Dr. Allyn White | Marketing | Assistant Professor of Marketing |
| Dr. Hyun-Soo Woo | Management | Assistant Professor of Management |

# TAYLOR MEDALISTS

Mr. William H. Bailey
Mr. Henry R. Wagner
Mr. Roy E. Cox
Mr. Gordon H. Meador
Mr. J. M. Fried, Jr.
Mrs. Willye Dotson Holder
Mr. Finley E. Belcher
Dr. Ned Williams
Mr. Thomas O. Metcalfe Jr.
Mr. Robert L. Alexander
Mrs. Hazel Irene Garrett McLain
    Myers
Mrs. Betty Adams Cunningham
Mr. Owen K. Williamson
Mr. John H. White Jr.
Capt. John E. Arnold
Mrs. Wanda Goodman McCharen
Mr. Richard H. Montgomery
Mr. Miles M. Shatzer
Mrs. Weida Goodman Walker
Mr. William C. Smallwood, Jr.
Dr. William Hall Wallace
Mr. John W. Barksdale III
Mrs. Kathryn Frierson Bendall
Mr. William D. Windham, Jr.
Mr. Edward P. Connell Sr.
Mrs. Claire Joanne Marlar
Mr. Eldon Franklin Nauman
Mr. Richard E. Van Houten
Mr. Loy G. Martin
Dr. Sarah L. Flowers Boling
Mr. Nick A. Mavar Jr.
Mr. James L. Barksdale
Mr. Raymond Carl Hill
Mr. Miller P. Holmes Jr.
Mr. Franklin T. Lambert
Mr. Fred E. Bourn Jr.
Mrs. Lu Alice Hill Harding
Mr. William P. Johnson
Mr. Albert Simmons
Mr. Jesse B. Tutor Jr.
Mr. Gary W. Patterson
Mrs. Mary Lamar Poovey Chustz
Mr. G. F. Woodliff III
Fr. Troy W. Mashburn, Jr.
Mr. Richard B. Roper
Mrs. Martha Hamberlin Thomas

Ms. Carolyn Beth Mitchell
Mr. Don H. Littleton
Mr. John P. Nail
Ms. Donna Dukes Wade
Mr. Don B. Cannada
Mr. T. David Cowart
Mrs. Laurie Newton Howorth
Mr. Max L. Waldrop Jr.
Ms. Margaret A. Wilson
Mrs. Beatriz Luisa Alonso
Mr. Stevens M. Bailey, Sr.
Ms. Martha L. Brosius
Ms. Rebecca Flemmons Herren
Mr. Jimmy C. Smith
Mrs. Helen Haffey Brock
Mrs. Lori Purcell Burwell
Mrs. Bridget Schmitz Crawford
Mr. John L. Lucas
Mrs. Martha Stephens Cranford
Mr. W. A. Lemly
Ms. Rosemary Johanna Steinbeck
Mrs. Carolyn Ray Wakefield
Mrs. Reatha Huey Clark
Mr. Richard M. Outzen Jr.
Mr. Jimmy R. Sledge Jr.
Mr. Bill H. Benson
Mrs. Lee Porter Beyer
Mrs. Sue Ellen Smith Miller
Mr. Irby Turner III
Mrs. Nell King Bieger
Mr. Jack B. Pearson Jr.
Mr. Roland O. Burns Jr.
Mrs. Rebecca Annette House Dewan
Mrs. Susan Hall Peterson
Mrs. Judy Waller Shannon
Mr. M. B. Williams
Mr. Bob Fugate
Ms. Cheri D. Green
Mrs. Carolyn McKay Taylor
Mrs. Randy Ratcliff Winford
Mrs. Judy Moore Allison
Mrs. Vivian Spear Farris
Mr. David A. Frederick
Mrs. Tracey Moore Hall
Mr. Kenney M. Hanks
Mr. Lantz E. Harvey
Mr. Jeffrey M. Johnson

Mr. James E. Knight Jr.
Mr. R. Scott Russell
Ms. Patsy A. Thomason
Ms. Virginia L. Walker
Mrs. Phyllis Ray Davis
Mrs. Mary Lisa Browning Delashmet
Mrs. Stacey Tyner Earnest
Mrs. Donna Brown Jacobs
Ms. Margaret Ann Cotros Varnell
Mr. Eng C. Wang
Mrs. Rhonda Franks Wilbanks
Mrs. Angela Dawn Barber
Mr. Eric A. Cimon
Mr. Curtis J. Gabardi
Lt. Cmdr. Paul Karlsson, USN
Mr. Cal Mayo, Jr.
Ms. Joy Tutor Pitts
Mr. Robert H. Rhea
Mrs. Jo Wong VanMeter
Mrs. Angela Dawn Young Williams
Mr. Wayne J. Alliston
Ms. Cecilia Klotz Bacon
Mr. Jason V. Calvasina
Ms. Patricia L. Hobbs
Mr. Andrew A. Sippel
Mr. Samuel L. Whitt Jr.
Mrs. Stephanie McGee Rippee
Mr. Michael J. Scribner
Mrs. Maelyse McElwain Webb
Mrs. Kay Summers Williams
Ms. Sook P. Woo
Mrs. Linda Devault Booker
Mrs. Mary Howell McIntosh Gann
Mr. Gerald D. Garner
Mr. Guy C. Hannibal
Mrs. Kelly McLaughlin Holtz
Mrs. Kristina Crosswell Johnson
Mrs. Marsha Burks Kennedy
Mr. Say J. Wong
Mr. H. M. Caldwell
Mr. John W. Daughdrill Jr.
Mrs. Mary Patton Goerke
Mrs. Roane Rayner Grantham
Mr. Steven G. Holley
Mr. Scott A. Johnson
Ms. Linda L. Neyman
Ms. Marion Elizabeth Noblin

Mr. William S. Rhea
Mrs. Sherry Wallace Holmes
Ms. Rita J. Rhea Hutcheson
Mr. John R. Kinsey
Mr. John P. LaCour
Mr. Charles E. Malouf
Mrs. Christine Brewer McLeod
Mr. Gerald G. Monroe
Ms. Susan J. Norris Robinson
Mrs. Christine Barrett Vanelli
Mrs. Shannan E. Reed Adkins
Mr. William Thomas Barry, Jr.
Ms. Nichole L. Bassett
Mrs. Amy Williams Chatham
Mrs. Emily C. Smith Fish
Mrs. Tina File Floyd
Ms. Charlotte G. Glidewell
Ms. Jennifer A. Hufford
Mr. Thomas E. McFadin
Mr. Brian K. Roberson
Mrs. Mary Mathews Sliman
Mr. Oscar L. Thomas Jr.
Mrs. Mandy Martin White
Mr. Cory T. Wilson
Mr. Derek A. Berry
Mrs. Leslie Michelle Comer Coughlin
Mrs. Wendy Miller Cromwell
Mr. Brad Gray
Mr. Liang Soon Koh
Mr. James A. Nail Jr.
Mrs. Eleanor Leigh McKnight Tannehill
Mr. William G. Yates III
Mr. Daniel C. Zebrowski
Mr. Christopher M. Adair
Mr. Michael Allen Carraway, Jr.
Ms. Cay Clark
Mrs. Valerie Nichols Comer
Mr. Harry H. Eielson
Mr. Adam Benjamin Farlow
Mrs. Cathryn Ledbetter Hull
Mr. Scott W. Pedigo
Mrs. Michelle Miller Smith
Mrs. Amy Bland Arrington
Mr. Dodds M. Dehmer
Mr. Richard M. Dye
Mrs. Nora C. Stephens Gooch
Mr. William B. Hicks

# TAYLOR MEDALISTS

Mr. Jason L. Honeycutt
Mrs. Stephanie J. Wilson McDonald
Mrs. Gina Tompkins Merritt
Ms. Leslie E. Price
Ms. Allison S. Williams
Mr. Roy E. Alexander, Jr.
Mr. Anthony J. Baker
Mr. Michael A. Dunavant
Mrs. Casey Turner Etheridge
Mr. Mark H. Payne
Mr. John R. Pittman, Jr.
Mr. Robert E. Seibels IV
Ms. Valerie Sprenger
Mrs. Tina Marie Wood White
Mrs. Joy Ann Warr Wiginton
Mrs. Ashley Jolliff Ayres
Mrs. Laura Koon Barbour
Mrs. Lisa Williams Bush
Ms. Lesley G. Casto
Mr. John D. Jones
Ms. Medita V. Karam-Laville
Mrs. Sara Whelan Randall Morgan
Mrs. Amy S. Hadank Reeves
Ms. Penny R. Wood
Mr. Starling B. Cousley
Mrs. Christina Goodman Jenkins
Mr. Jay Knighton
Mr. Brian A. Metzger
Mr. Nikola Vujic
Mrs. Julie Rogers Walker
Mrs. Macey Fisher Young
Mr. Hunter Carpenter
Mrs. Anna Gambrell Chambers
Mrs. Brooks Burnette Elfert
Mr. Richard C. James
Mr. Richard O. Lautenschleger II
Mrs. Leigh McLaurin Lowery
Mr. Joshua C. McCrory
Ms. Jacqueline R. Mills
Ms. Sarah B. Young
Mrs. Amy Andrews Behroozi
Mr. David B. Blackburn
Ms. Brooke J. Boral
Mrs. Pamela Jill Perry Carter
Ms. Jill L. Case
Mr. Stephen C. King
Mr. Dan K. Lomax
Mr. Brian D. Marble

Mrs. Dorothy Horn Nash
Mrs. Alison Dickey Schmelzer
Mrs. Irena Mihailova Snider
Mr. Christopher A. Childers
Mr. Breck R. Hines
Mr. Timothy E. Hotard
Mrs. Amanda Robins Poe
Mrs. Sara Schauberger Robertson
Mr. Andrew Paxton Scott
Mr. David L. Splaingard
Mr. William K. Stubbs
Mr. Micajah P. Sturdivant, IV
Ms. Amanda K. Fong
Ms. Dana L. Gillespie Houpt
Mrs. Amanda Moore Kellum
Mrs. Ellie Griffith LaPorte
Mr. Pavel V. Lazaridi
Ms. Mary Beth Mayer
Mr. Asylbek A. Osmonov
Mr. Matthew Adam Parker
Mr. John H. Summerford
Ms. Laura Ann Thompson
Mr. Morrow Bailey
Mr. Nicholas Scott Brown
Mrs. Rachel Byrd Brownlee
Mr. Bradley Webster Crawford
Mrs. Sarah Stevens Easterling
Mrs. Beth Shepard Hunt
Mr. Russell Ellis Pennington
Ms. Eugenia Marie Powers
Ms. Stephanie Suzanne Ray
Mr. Drew Landon Snyder
Dr. Meredith Gore Warf
Ms. Tyndale Brickey Bloom
Mrs. Amy Thompson Cole
Ms. Jennifer Diane Glass
Mrs. Andrea Lenee Goodman
Mr. Adam Joseph King
Mr. William Scott Kitchens
Mrs. Catherine Parnell Matthews
Mr. Jeremy Michael McKnight
Mrs. Carol Anne Marion Miconi
Mrs. Shea Sides Rea
Mr. Charles Matthew Barrett
Mrs. Kera Massey Cooper
Mr. Joshua Nathaniel Debold
Ms. Kristin Clay Dunavant
Mrs. Alley Neveleff Farrell

Mr. William Brett Galloway
Mrs. Emily Evans Holly
Mr. Jeremy David Jones
Ms. Jennifer Leah Jordan
Mrs. Ashley Hooper Katsuyama
Mr. Brent Michael Kitchens
Ms. Olena Olexandrivna Kulikova
Mr. Steven Ray Mathis
Mr. Joseph Nabil Shayeb
Ms. Kaleena Lashae Wortham
Mrs. Johanna Faulk Bullard
Mrs Catherine Brewer Cannada
Mrs. Eleanor Marie Hightower James
Mrs. Kelley James Jenkins
Dr. Mark Gill Kosko
Mr. Philip Grayson Metcalf
Mr. Clark Ryan Mills
Mrs. Caroline Murphree Roberson
Mrs. Caroline Dye Walker
Ms. Whitney Marie Farrell
Ms. Kathleen Louise Finnegan
Ms. Carolyn Eley Golding
Ms. Scarlet Amber Jones
Ms. Shannon Rae Keys
Mr. William Scott Moseley
Mr. Steven Clarke Nix
Mrs. Cassi Thrash Franks
Mrs. Amy Gregory Hill
Ms. Amanda Michelle Holsworth
Mr. Bryan Allen Jones
Mr. Kemp Mosley
Mr. Warren Hays Pate
Mr. Hal Scot Spragins, Jr.
Mr. Scott Andrew Stewart
Mr. Wei Wei
Mr. Robert Preston Derivaux, Jr.
Mr. Robert Pratt Dunlap
Mrs. Anna Ruth Jones Ford
Mr. Maximilian Graupner
Mr. Clayton Gregory Jarrell
Ms. Lindsay Nicole Presley
Mr. Martin Triplett Richardson
Mrs. Martha Campbell Robertson
Ms. Caryn Watson
Mrs. Katherine Cliburn Widdows
Mr. Ronald Tyler Wilson
Mr. Winsor Yu-Liang Yuan
Ms. Jane-Claire Marietta Baker

Mrs. Margaret Grace Joyner Barefoot
Ms. Hannah Sayle Flint
Ms. Claire Elizabeth Graves
Mr. John Samuel Holt Irving
Mrs. Blair Harden Jussely
Ms. Christine Marie Sims
Ms. Lauren Elizabeth Williams
Ms. Mallory Alyse Britt
Ms. Lauren Childers
Ms. Karessa Lynne Duran
Ms. Cynthia Ann Fry
Ms. Emily Jane Laird
Ms. Barrett Brown Lingle
Mr. Christopher Allan Mattox
Mr. Daniel Safley Reynolds
Mr. Igor Shkilko
Ms. Emilee Christine Young
Mr. Matthew Collins Garber
Ms. Sara Stevens Hazard
Ms. Ellen Marie Karp
Ms. Mary Margaret Myers
Mr. David Ford Thompson
Mr. Derek Anthony Vandunse
Mr. Patrick Kin-Wing Lo
Mr. Walker Semmes Dowell
Ms. Chelsea Janelle Harris
Ms. Katrina Briscoe Hart
Ms. Sofia Emma Hellberg Jonsen
Ms. Ann Marie Mercier
Mrs. Bramlett McLaurin Myers
Ms. Caroline Diane Purcell
Ms. Caroline Murer Rohde-Moe
Mr. Richard Tyler Tutor
Mr. Johan Carl Albert Backstrom
Ms. Orrin Marie Emanoil
Mr. James Wesley Howell
Ms. Kristin Nicole Leaptrott
Ms. Xinyi Long
Ms. Betsy Kate Nicholas
Ms. Anna Claire Wammack
Mr. Paul Jackson Gunn
Mr. Nathan Cole McCall
Ms. Sierra Danielle Little

# THE SCHOOL OF BUSINESS ADMINISTRATION STAFF
## 2017-2018

| NAME | TITLE |
| --- | --- |
| Hussein "Sam" Hammoud | Manager of IT Services |
| Beth Whittington | Assistant to the Dean for Undergraduate Student Services |
| Stella Connell | Communications Specialist |
| Ashley Jones | Director of MBA Administration |
| Stephanie Crosbie | Senior Academic Counselor |
| Melanie Hall | Senior Academic Counselor |
| Jasmine Phillips | Career Planning Specialist |
| Kimberly Phillips | Academic Counselor |
| John Forester, Jr. | Academic Counselor |
| John Rogers | Project Manager |
| Kathryn Mikell | Senior Administrative Secretary |
| Rebekah Kesler | Administrative Coordinator |
| Kenya Thigpen | Program Assistant |
| Amy Johnson | Records Coordinator |
| Kathryn Shoalmire | Project Coordinator |
| Susie Potts | Senior Staff Assistant |
| Lila Neely | Senior Staff Assistant |
| Teresa Rowsey | Senior Administrative Secretary |
| Chad Hathcock | Multi-Media Specialist |
| Cynthia "Cobie" Watkins | Coordinator of Student/Alumni Programs |
| James Flanders | Program Coordinator for the General Business Program |
| Wesley Dickens | Coordinator of Career Preparation/Internships |
| Jasmine Phillips | Career Planning Specialist/Employer Relations |
| Walter "Doug" Gurley | State Director of Mississippi Small Business Development Center |